The Gift of Reading:
Part 1 – Reading the Bible in Submission to God

J. Alexander Rutherford

Unless otherwise indicated, all Scripture quotations are from The Holy Bible, English Standard Version® (ESV®), copyright © 2001 by Crossway Bibles, a publishing ministry of Good News Publishers. Used by permission. All rights reserved.

ISBN-13: 978-1-9990172-7-9

2nd Printing

Copyright © 2019, 2021 J. Alexander Rutherford
Teleioteti publishing, Airdrie AB
All rights reserved.

To contact Teleioteti publishing for information or to provide feedback, please visit us at **https://teleioteti.ca** or email us at **info@teleioteti.ca**.

DEDICATION

This book is dedicated to all the teachers who have taught me to read and love the Bible. To Noel Sterne, who was the first to teach me that reading the Bible takes hard work. To Kerry Pretty, who first introduced me to hermeneutics, thinking about how we come to understand and apply the text. To Brad Copp, whose passion for Scripture inspired me to read and love it more and whose careful attention to the text taught me many of the skills I use every day in devotions and study. To Fred Eaton, who helped me solidify the doubts I had about some approaches to biblical interpretation and helped me pursue a whole-Bible approach to interpretation. To Rikk Watts, who helped me to think through the issues concerning the New Testament's use of the Old. To Iain Provan, who showed me how to think carefully and critically about my own assumptions in reading the text. And to Phil Long, who showed me how to pay careful attention to the way the stories of the Bible are told and observe the details of the text.

CONTENTS

Dedication iii

Contents v

Analytical Outline vii

Acknowledgments xi

Series Introduction xiii

Introduction 1

Part 1 – We Need Eyes to See 7

   1. The Bible is the Document of God's Covenant 9

   2. The Bible's Worldview - Theology 27

   3. The Bible's Worldview - Story 45

   4. The People(s) of the Bible 61

Part 2 – We Need Ears to Hear 75

   5. Knowing When We Have Read Well 77

   6. Knowing How to Read Well 97

   7. Knowing the Styles of Biblical Writing 119

   8. Knowing Bible Translations 157

   9. Knowing Biblical Languages 171

   10. Knowing Tools for Reading Better 189

   11. Evaluating Exegesis and Application 203

Part 3 – We Need Hearts to Understand 209
   12. Beginning with Faith in God 211
   13. We Submit Ourselves before Him 217
   14. To Learn with Humility 221
   Conclusion 225
   Works Cited 229
   About Teleioteti 237

ANALYTICAL OUTLINE

I. INTRODUCTION
II. PART 1: WE NEED EYES TO SEE
    1. CHAPTER 1: THE BIBLE IS THE DOCUMENT OF GOD'S COVENANT
        A. The Bible is a Covenant Document
        B. The Nature of the Bible as a Covenant Document
            a. The Nature of the Bible
                i. Inerrancy
                ii. Authority
                iii. Sufficiency
                iv. Clarity
            b. The Structure of the Bible
        C. The Bible Guides Us in Fulfiling God's Purpose
    2. CHAPTER 2: THE BIBLE'S WORLDVIEW - THEOLOGY
        A. Yahweh: The God who Is
            a. Yahweh is Holy
            b. The Authority, Control, and Presence of Yahweh
        B. Man: Rebellious Kings
        C. Kingdom: The Rule of God
            a. God's Heavenly Reign
            b. God's Earthly Reign
            - Excursus: The Gospel and the Kingdom
            c. God's Eschatological Reign
    3. CHAPTER 3: THE BIBLE'S WORLDVIEW – STORY
        A. The Prologue: Creation and Fall
            a. Creation

- b. Fall
- B. Redemption Initiated – The Old Covenant(s)
  - a. God's Covenant with Noah
  - b. God's Covenant with Abraham
  - c. God's Covenant with Israel
  - d. God's Covenant with David
- C. Redemption Accomplished – The New Covenant
- D. Redemption Consummated – the New Creation
4. CHAPTER 4: THE PEOPLE(S) OF THE BIBLE
   - A. The Old Covenant People of God
     - a. The Establishment of Israel
     - b. The Commission of Israel
     - c. The Nature of Israel
   - B. The New Covenant People of God
     - a. The Establishment of the Church
     - b. The Commission of the Church
       - i. Internal Versus External Holiness
       - ii. Church Versus National Polity
       - iii. Exilic Versus Secure Existence
     - c. The Nature of the Church

III. PART 2: WE NEED EARS TO HEAR
1. CHAPTER 5: KNOWING WHEN WE HAVE READ WELL
   - A. Identifying the Right Responses to Scripture
     - a. Validity
     - b. Appropriateness
     - - Excursus: The Proverbs and Appropriate Application
     - c. Fittingness
     - - Excursus: Fittingness and Typology
     - d. Examples
2. CHAPTER 6: KNOWING HOW TO READ WELL
   - A. (1) Pray
   - B. (2) Identify the Passage for Study
   - C. (3) Identify the Contexts
   - D. (4) Identify the Translational Difficulties and Establish the Text
     - a. Translation Differences
     - b. Textual Differences
   - E. (5) Observe the Text

           a. Agassiz and the Fish
     F.   (6) Identify the Passage's Relation to the Surrounding Contexts
     G.   (7) Apply the Passage
     H.   (8) Check Your Understanding
     I.   Conclusion
3.   CHAPTER 7: KNOWING THE STYLES OF BIBLICAL WRITING
     A.   Narrative
           a. How Narratives Communicate: Plot and Scene Arrangement
           b. How Narratives Communicate: Description
           c. Study Strategy: Storyboarding
     B.   Poetry
           a. How Poetry Communicates: Terseness and Imagery
           b. How Poetry Communicates: Lines and Parallelism
           c. Study Strategy: Mapping Parallelism
     C.   Didactic Prose
           a. How Prose Communicates: Grammar and Logic
           b. How Prose Communicates: Indicative and Imperative
           c. Study Strategy: Arcing and Sentence Diagramming
           - Excursus: Review of English Grammar
     D.   Prophecy
           a. How Prophecy Communicates: Symbolic Imagery
           - Excursus: Apocalyptic and Prophecy
           b. Study Strategy: Intertextuality
4.   CHAPTER 8: KNOWING BIBLE TRANSLATIONS
     A.   Bible Translation
     B.   Translation Theories
     C.   Bible Translations
           a. ESV
           b. KJV
           c. NASB
           d. NET
           e. NIV
           f. NLT
           g. NRSV
           h. The Message
5.   CHAPTER 9: KNOWING BIBLICAL LANGUAGES

  A. The Importance of the Biblical Languages
  B. The Appropriate Use of the Biblical Languages
    a. Ground Rules for Language Study
    b. Word Studies
    c. Grammar Studies
6. CHAPTER 10: KNOWING TOOLS FOR READING BETTER
  A. Tools for Understanding Biblical Books and Passages
    a. Introductions to the Bible
      i. General
      ii. Historical
      iii. Theological
    b. Bible Dictionaries
    c. Commentaries
      i. Popular
      ii. Semi-Technical
      iii. Technical
  B. Tools for Grasping the Unity of Scripture
  C. Tools for Original Language Study
    a. Lexicons
    b. Bible Software
7. CHAPTER 11: EVALUATING EXEGESIS AND APPLICATION
  A. Is it Valid, Appropriate, and Fitting?
  B. Can it Be Argued from the Text?
  C. Does it Illegitimately Appeal to Extra-Biblical Data?
IV. PART 3: WE NEED HEARTS TO UNDERSTAND
  1. CHAPTER 12: BEGINNING WITH FAITH IN GOD
  2. CHAPTER 13: WE SUBMIT OURSELVES BEFORE HIM
  3. CHAPTER 14: TO LEARN WITH HUMILITY
V. CONCLUSION

ACKNOWLEDGMENTS

The completion of this project and the ideas found within owe themselves to a great many people. Above all, I am completely dependent upon the Spirit of God in all that I have done and do. Without his daily sustaining grace, I would not have pushed through the various trials that arose and continued throughout the writing process. Without his guidance, I know there would be nothing of profit found in this book. Without his action in my heart, I never would have turned to God and desired to rightly interpret his Word. For all of my life and work, I am indebted to the grace of God poured out by Christ Jesus through the Spirit.

God works through means, and there are many people he has placed in my life who have contributed to this volume. First, without the patience of my loving wife Nicole, I would not have had the time and space—literally, my desk and bookshelves take up a massive chunk of our small home—to finish this project. She has also shown great faith in allowing me to set aside one day a week to devote to ministry; I am thankful for her faith in this and God's continued provision. Second, without the many friends who have challenged me in my thinking and raised good questions over the years, I never would have been able to complete this work. Among others, this includes Jonathan Hawes, Raphael Haeuser, Daniel Supimpa, Brad Copp, Fred Eaton, Phil Long, Eliezer Arriola, Joel Nafziger, Andre Roberge, and surely many more. I am especially thankful for Brad, who looked at an early manuscript and offered feedback on the whole project and its details. I pray that this book will be of profit to all those who helped shape it and many more.

I am once again grateful for my dear friend Josh Arriola, who has crafted wonderful covers for all my books!

To God be the glory, to him alone. *Soli Deo Gloria.*

SERIES INTRODUCTION

> His divine power has granted to us all things that pertain to life and godliness, through the knowledge of him who called us to his own glory and excellence. – 1 Peter 3:3

God has not left his people without help in the day of trouble—or in the day of prosperity, for that matter. The Bible is God's gift to his people, revealing to them Jesus Christ and the salvation he has accomplished. But the gift of Scripture does not end in revealing our need for salvation and God's provision for it; Scripture is sufficient for the entire Christian life. In his first epistle, Peter tells us that God's divine power has given us everything for life and godliness (1 Pet 3:3, cf. 2 Tim 3:16-17).

In *God's Gifts for the Christian Life*, J. Alexander Rutherford unpacks how God through the Bible has given us what we need to live faithfully in his world. Each volume unpacks the Scriptural teaching against the background of contemporary culture and shows how the Bible provides a firm foundation for our lives. Each volume is intended to be short, around 110-150 pages, and accessible to the interested reader. The primary audience is theologically interested lay Christians (Christians who are not in paid ministry and have no formal theological training), students, and pastors. Several parts are planned, but only the first is in progress.

Part 1, the Christian mind, addresses some of the questions raised by philosophy, especially how humans know anything and gain knowledge. Of Part 1, Volume 1 addressed epistemology, particularly how God has equipped humans to know him and his world. This is Volume 2, Part 1: this volume considers how God's word functions authoritatively in our lives, namely the nature of reading and applying the Bible (hermeneutics). Volume

3, *The Gift of Seeing*, will present a biblical perspective on metaphysics (the limits and nature of knowledge).

INTRODUCTION

> For whatever was written in former days was written for our instruction, that through endurance and through the encouragement of the Scriptures we might have hope. – Romans 15:4

There is no question more important to the Christian than this, "Can I understand the Bible?" Those who answer "yes" to this question are among the precious few who have withstood the barrage of attacks levelled against God's Word and its clarity over the last several hundred years. This book and its second part are for those who need to hear that they can understand God's Word and who are ready to learn how they might do so better.

This is a book on exegesis, the practice of reading in order to understand, specifically biblical exegesis, the practice of reading the Bible. It is the first of two parts; together, parts 1 & 2 present a biblical hermeneutic, a theory of how to interpret the Bible that is rooted in the teaching of the Bible. I hope to show in the following pages that the Bible is accessible to contemporary Christians—whether they be new Christians, mature believers, pastors, or scholars—and how we can go about reading it. Here in Part 1 I hope to give a framework with which to begin reading the Bible. I intend only to give a framework, a basic outline. Several books could be—and have been—written on the subjects raised in this book. It is not my intention to replace every other biblical study resource with this volume. Instead, I hope to lay out a methodology for reading the Bible according to its own claims. By doing so, I hope to equip the reader with a foundation for reading the Bible, a foundation that can be built upon with the many other resources available. By laying exegesis on a biblical foundation, I do not intend to nullify all other contributions to the field of biblical studies but to give the reader a way to learn from the best biblical studies has to offer without being drawn away from the biblical text by the trends within interpretation that are not founded on the Bible's own teaching. This book will be most helpful when used in conjunction with regular reading of the Bible and with supplementary aid in building exegetical skills. This could mean reading the Bible with an experienced Christian or reading some of the other books or articles mentioned in the following pages. In a teaching setting, I envision a specific role for this book; it would lay out the presuppositions for interpreting the Bible and give a method to begin such study. Class work and teaching would then focus on learning the skills outlined in the second section of this book. The second part of my series *God's Gifts for the Christian Life* will also prove helpful in this regard. However, it will be many years before that project is completed.

In *The Gift of Reading – Part 2*, this books companion, I intend to lay out at greater depth the theory of interpretation that underlies this work. That work will provide an answer to the many challenges raised against biblical clarity today and prove helpful in a more advanced hermeneutics class or for the reader who has already learned biblical interpretation from a different perspective. Therefore, the reader who has some background in biblical interpretation may desire to begin there, with *Part 2*, lest the approach of this present book deceive the reader as to its sufficiency for the task it undertakes. Indeed, I hope that this volume will show that reading the Bible is in many ways simple—hard work, yes, but not impossible work reserved for scholars and specialists alone.

The intended audience for both parts is intentionally broad. I hope to write with enough lucidity that a pastor could give this book to an interested person in his congregation and have confidence that it will be understood. I also hope to go to sufficient depth that pastors, students, and even scholars will also profit from reading it.

Before we begin, let us consider the question above; can you and I understand the Bible? First, the Bible is a book like this one, so your ability to make it this far should encourage you that you can indeed read. Yet many of us learned in high school or university that texts cannot communicate, that my communication with you through these words is an illusion. The only meaning present, some would claim, is what you bring (this is part of a literary approach known as Deconstructionism).

Others of us were taught that a massive historical-cultural gap separates the biblical writers from us so that only the scholar with knowledge of the ancient world can actually know what it says. I suspect that many of us, even though taught these things, have the nagging feeling in the back of our minds that this cannot be true: we understand Jesus most—at least some—of the time, do we not? We know we must repent and believe the good news of Jesus Christ and that murder and adultery are wrong! For those of us who feel the tension between what we have been told and what we experience, the Bible brings us great comfort.

It tells us that we can understand it. For example, young people are expected to read and meditate on the Law in order to resist sin (Ps 119:9-14). All of us are called to teach others at some point in our lives, and we are to do so in light of an understanding of God's word (Deut 6:4-9, 20; Eph 6:4; Tit 2:1-10). It is clear that the Bible was not written for the scholar but for us that we might learn and grow (Ps 102:18; Rom 4:23, 15:4; 1 Cor 9:10), and Luke considers it a Christian virtue to measure what Paul preached by the word (Acts 17:11). During the Reformation, Martin Luther saw this truth in 2 Timothy 3:16-17, writing in *The Bondage of the Will*,

> In a word: if Scripture is obscure or equivocal, why need it have been brought down to us by act of God? Surely we have enough obscurity and uncertainty within ourselves, without our obscurity and uncertainty and darkness being augmented from heaven! And how then shall the apostle's word stand: "All Scripture is given by inspiration of God, and is profitable for doctrine, for reproof, for correction?" (2 Tim. 3:16).

It is true that the Bible does not ever say, "you who are reading this can understand it," yet it assumes this throughout. Therefore, our question cannot be "can we understand the Bible?" Instead, we must ask, "how has God made it possible for us to understand the Bible?" There are several different approaches to answering such a "how" question today. Though many philosophers are stuck on the "can" question, those who get to the "how" use intricate philosophical analysis to come to the answer. The problem with this, however, is that when they are done, reading looks nothing like our common experience of reading. Furthermore, the "meanings" they find seem to be (conveniently) the very things they have been saying the whole time. Others ask how texts were read in the past, following the church fathers and Greeks in allegorical reading (looking for a spiritual meaning behind the words) or maybe reading as the 1st century Jews did. Still others labour hard to recreate the world in which the biblical texts were written in order to understand what the biblical authors intended to say to their audiences.

I will argue in the second volume that all these approaches fall short in one way or another. I hope to offer an alternative that is based on reading the Bible according to what it is. The Bible is, above all, a piece of writing, so there is a sense in which we need to read it like any other written document. Yet, there is a difficulty here: we recognize that there are many sorts of written documents. We read resumes differently than we do blog posts, and blog posts differently than novels—and all these differ from dictionaries! So we need to use basic skills of reading, yet we need to know what the Bible actually is if we are to interpret it. To know what the Bible is, we need to pay attention to both what it says about itself and what it shows about itself.[1] The Bible is thus our source for the knowledge of how to read it. The Bible tells us what we need to know: it is the standard by which we judge what it is and is not.

Yet the Bible is huge, too big for anyone of us to comprehend entirely. Furthermore, I have some gifts, but you have others; reading the Bible in its entirety probably requires both of us—in fact, God says it does (1 Cor 12:12-31; Eph 4:11-16). Therefore, we turn to the Bible as our standard, yet we need to read it with the help of others. We need to read it in the **context** of community.[2]

---

[1] There is a circle here, yet such a circle is inevitable when we are dealing with ultimate authorities. However, this is not a vicious circle, a self-destructing argument. It is more like a spiral, we start with an understanding and continue to refine it in interaction with our authority, God's Word. For more on this, see my book, *The Gift of Knowing: A Biblical Perspective on Knowing and Truth*, God's Gifts for the Christian Life Part 1 - The Christian Mind I (Vancouver: Teleioteti, 2019).

[2] "Context" is a key word that will appear throughout this book. Essentially, "context" refers to the setting in which something is found, to the environment to which it relates. Above—in this context—I am using "context" to refer to the setting in which Christians must engage with Scripture. Christians must read scripture in interaction with, for the sake of, and with the help of Christian community. In the

This book is itself an act of reading the Bible in community. I am standing on the shoulders of many great men and women who have come before us and am attempting to lead you in reading the Word. To do this, to read the Bible, takes a lot of work—even with the help of community. Reading is itself a labour, but this is accompanied by the need to learn many new things and, as we read the Bible, the added burden of difficult truths with which we must wrestle.

These three aspects of or perspectives on our task—namely, the biblical text, Christian Community, and hard work—lay behind everything that follows. These three factors are essential at every step of interpreting Scripture.

Having addressed the necessary issues, we can begin to answer the question, "How has God made it possible for us to read the Bible?" Or rephrasing this, "what do we need to read the Bible as God intends us to?" We need three things to read the Bible: *eyes to see, ears to hear, and hearts to understand.*

First, we need eyes to see. We need to look at the Bible with the appropriate lens, with right eyes, to see it. We need to know *what the Bible is* and *what the Bible is about* in order to make sense of each of its parts. In the first section of this book, we will look at the nature of the Bible and how having the right eyes—the proper lens—lets us see correctly.

Second, we need ears to hear. The Bible is God's communication to us. Like any communication, having someone speak is not sufficient; someone needs to listen. To read the Bible, we need to know how to listen really well. Because the Bible is in some ways like every other book, everyone reading this book can, in theory, read the Bible. Yet things get complicated when we factor in bible translations, the original languages, and difficult passages. For this reason, in the second section of the book, we will look at what it means to read the Bible well and how we can do this.

Third, we need hearts to understand. The Bible is God's Word, yet humans are by nature in rebellion against God, so our default disposition is

---

study of literature, and so in reading the Bible, "context" refers to the words, sentences, paragraphs, chapters, books, and book in which a particular object of study (word, sentence, etc.) is embedded. It interacts with all these layers of the text, which form a literary context or setting. Context in this sense, the text in which words and sentences are embedded, is what gives parts of a text their meaning.

hostility toward God and his word: we do not want to understand it! All acts of reading, especially reading the Bible, are moral acts. We choose to love our neighbours by listening to them; we choose to love God by listening to him. We need submission to God to follow the text where it leads, to change our views and believe what at times seems unbelievable. This is my recipe for reading the Bible well: eyes to see, ears to hear, and hearts to understand. May the Lord grant us these things:

> Let not our eyes be blinded
> > by the lord of this world,
> Let not our ears be blocked
> > by the lies of sin,
> Let not our hearts be hardened
> > to despise your Word.
>
> Give us eyes to see
> > and understand what you say.
> Give us ears to listen carefully
> > and attentively to your voice.
> Give us hearts to humbly submit
> > and bow ourselves before you.
>
> Your word is a light unto our path;
> > let us see it.
> Your word is hope for those in need;
> > let us hear it.
> Your word is a foundation for our feet;
> > let us believe it.
>
> To you be all glory and honor and praise,
> > Today and for the rest of our days,
> > Amen.

—Part 1—

We Need Eyes to See

THE BIBLE IS THE DOCUMENT OF GOD'S COVENANT

> But their minds were hardened. For to this day, when they read the old covenant, that same veil remains unlifted, because only through Christ is it taken away. – 2 Corinthians 3:14

The first thing we need to read the Bible is eyes; we need to look at it in the right way. Would we not read a letter very differently if we knew it was from the government rather than a spouse or a reputable account of history differently than the Lord of the Rings? In the first case, we expect the letter to be impersonal and carry the authority of those ruling over us; in the second case, we trust the words of a reputable historian to accurately describe history. In contrast, we would not use the Lord of the Rings to write a history of the Middle Ages.

There is a sense in which we need to know what a book is before we can read it. To understand any one passage, a part, we need to know something about the book, the whole. When we are confused about a detail or a scene, we know to read on or quickly skim what we have already read. We know from practice that books are self-interpreting. The Bible is more complicated than a novel or a letter from the government, yet the principle remains the same. For centuries this principle has been captured in the phrase, "Scripture interprets Scripture" or "Scripture is its best interpreter." To understand the Bible, we need to look at individual passages in light of the whole Bible. This requires great familiarity on our part; we need to be voracious readers of Scripture.

Yet we are not alone in this; God's people have been reading the Scriptures for over 3000 years and have become very good at it. At the end of each chapter of this book, I will recommend resources that can help us grow in various skills and enrich our understanding of the Bible. In this first section, we will look at what the Bible is. In this chapter, we will consider the type of document the Bible is and its features. In the next two chapters, we will look at the **worldview** the Bible teaches;[1] that is, we will look at its teaching about the universe and our place in it. First, in Chapter 2, we will look broadly at the biblical teachings about God, man, and the Gospel. Second, in Chapter 3, we will look at the **metanarrative**, or universal story, that the Bible teaches.[2] In Chapter 4, we will consider the peoples of the Bible, the differences between God's Old Covenant and New Covenant People. For now, let us consider what exactly the Bible is.

If someone were to ask you what is the Bible, how would you respond? Eventually, after explaining that it is God's very words given to man, we would describe it as a "book." Yet, what kind of book is Scripture? It is clearly not a novel nor a dictionary; is it a theological textbook or a self-help book? Having heard the acronym BIBLE, maybe you will describe it as *Basic Instructions Before Leaving Earth*. Yet does that accurately describe the Scriptures?

This question matters: we have already seen that we read books according to what they are, so a misunderstanding of what the Bible is will lead us to misread it. As we will see in *The Gift of Reading – Part 2*, this is one reason people misread the Bible: they misunderstand for one reason or another what the Bible is. I will argue in this chapter that the Bible is a covenant document: it is a written testimony to God's relationship with his people designed to

---

[1] A worldview is essentially the interpretive framework, or the glasses, through which we view the world. That is, all of us look at the world with "rose-coloured glasses": none of us see it without interpreting it. This interpretation comes from our worldview: I recognize a tree as a God's handiwork and praise him because he created it. An atheist thinks it is a testimony to evolution and wonders at the marvellous fact that something so intricate happens to exist. We will talk more about what a worldview is in Chapter 2.

[2] A metanarrative can be described as the story of history, or an interpretation of all events that have happened and will happen. We will discuss metanarratives in Chapter 3.

guide them in their relationship with him so that his purpose in the covenant might be fulfilled.

A. The Bible is a Covenant Document

To begin with, the Bible is a *covenant* document. This assumes we know what a covenant is. A covenant refers to a formal relationship enacted between two parties. In our day, a (biblical) marriage is a covenant. I pledged to my wife that I would be her husband, performing all the obligations implicit in that role, and Nicole pledged to be my wife, performing all the obligations implicit in that role. We took an oath, our vows, confirming our commitment. The Bible is full of covenants, such as Abraham's covenant with Abimelech (Gen 21:25-34), yet six are especially important. We will consider all six in Chapter 3, but it should suffice for now to consider the two major covenants discussed in the New Testament.

First is the Old Covenant, made at Sinai between Yahweh—God—and Israel. This covenant legislated Israel as a holy nation, setting them apart from the rest of the nations by their devotion and service to Yahweh: they were to live solely for him and represent him by acting in specific ways. Their relationship was consistently endangered by their sin, so this covenant also included a sacrificial system designed to (temporarily) remove the consequences of sin (cf. Heb 10:4). According to Hebrews 8, this covenant is fading away; it has become obsolete. The reason for this is the arrival of the New Covenant in Christ Jesus. The New Covenant deals once for all with human sin and legislates the Kingdom of God, Jesus's universal reign in heaven as manifest on earth through the Church (e.g. Luke 20:14-19; Acts 28:31-Rom 1:6; Rom 3:31-26; 1 Cor 15:22-28; Heb 1:1-4).[3] The Bible is a covenant document; specifically, it is the legal document governing God's New Covenant made with all who believe in Jesus Christ. The Old Testament is the covenant document governing his Old Covenant people Israel, yet it is also the foundation for the New Testament. Both Testaments together form the Bible.

There are two ways we can show that the Bible is a covenant document. The first is what it tells us about itself. The New Testament never refers to

---

[3] These are only a few examples; we will look more at the kingdom of God in following chapters.

itself as a completed unit, though we can identify it as such by its own features (such as the way the Book of Revelation closes off both the Old and New Testaments). To learn about the nature of the New Testament, and so the Bible as a whole, we need to pay attention to what it says about the Old Testament.

The New Testament authors consider each other to be in the same position as the Old Testament authors and consider each other's work to have the same character as the Old Testament; it is Scripture (cf. 2 Pet 3:15-16; 1 Tim 5:18).[4] Therefore, to learn about the New Testament, and the whole Bible, we can consider what the New Testament says about the Old. It is a curious thing that the New Testament summarizes the Old Testament as "the Law" (Matt 5:18, Luke 16:17, John 10:34, John 15:25; 1 Cor 14:21). When we hear "Law," we think of rules and regulations that must be obeyed: this is not too far off, yet the Hebrew word *Torah* and the Greek word *Nomos* (both translated Law) are being used a little more specifically. The Law often refers specifically to the legislation surrounding God's covenant with Israel, legislation found in Genesis-Deuteronomy (*the Torah*). "Law" refers specifically to a covenant document. The New Testament extends this title to refer to the entire Old Testament. Specifically, in 2 Corinthians 3:14, Paul calls the Old Testament the Old Covenant. According to the New Testament, then, every book of the Old Testament is part of the Law, the document governing the Old Covenant. By extension, we can see how the New and Old Testaments together—with their shared similarities to the Old Testament—is the document governing the New Testament believers.[5]

We can confirm this observation by paying attention to what the Bible shows us about itself, to what we see when we pay careful attention to it. Both the Old and New Testaments are clear that the first five books of the Bible, the *Torah*, are a covenant document (e.g. Judges 8:31). If we begin here, we are able to identify three functions displayed by all the passages in this document. First, there are legal texts, texts intended to legislate certain behaviours within God's covenant people (e.g. Exod 20:1-17; Lev 1:1-7:38). These texts address how the people of God were to behave towards God and

---

[4] 2 Peter refers to Paul's letters as "Scripture" and Paul refers to Luke's Gospel here as "Scripture."

[5] The name "New and Old *Testament*" is actually derived from the Latin word for covenant, *testamentum* (cf. Luke 22:20, "new covenant" is *novum testamentum*).

towards each other (e.g. Exod 20:1-17). Second, these are accompanied by case laws, narratives or scenarios that illustrate the laws (e.g. Exod 21:23-22:15). Third, there are accounts of the behaviour of the parties in the covenant: Genesis 1 – Exodus 19 gives a history of God's creation of and interaction with the world, especially with the ancestors of Israel. On the other hand, Exodus 32:1-35 recounts Israel's failure with the golden calf, and Numbers 16:1-50 gives an account of the rebellion of a man named Korah and its results.[6] These accounts are found both in narrative and poetic form (e.g. Exod 15). Thus, we find in the *Torah* (Gen-Deut) the laws governing the covenant, examples of what it looks like to live the laws, and narratives about God the covenant maker and about Israel's successes and failures in the Covenant.[7] These features of the *Torah*, of the Law as a covenant document, are displayed throughout the rest of the Bible.

As we will see below, the Old Testament was historically divided into three sections (see Luke 24:44): the Law (*Torah*), the Prophets (*Nevi'im*), and the Writings (*Ketuvim*).[8] The Law most clearly displays the legislative aspect of the *Torah*; the Prophets most clearly display the historical aspect; and the Writings most clearly display the instructive aspect, showing what Covenant life looks life. We could summarize each of these sections respectively as *The Covenant, Covenant Life,* and *Covenant Living*.[9] Extending this analysis to the New Testament, Miles Van Pelt has observed that the New Testament displays the same pattern: the Gospels give an account of the covenant institution and legislation, Acts recounts the history of the New Covenant, and the Epistles give instruction in living out the Covenant. On this analysis,

---

[6] It is interesting to observe that this feature of the Torah is unique in ancient covenant documents; we have records of similar covenant documents from peoples around Israel, yet none of these have extensive narratives woven throughout the legal texts.

[7] It may interest the reader to observe that every text in the Torah, in fact in the Bible, has these three functions. Every text is normative, telling us what we ought or ought not believe/feel/do; every text is historical, it is an expression of God's past covenant interactions with his people (e.g. the Laws are embedded in discourse, accounts of God speaking to his people); and every text is instructive, showing us not only what but also how to live out this covenant.

[8] The books of the Old Testament are ordered differently on this division, a list is provided in the following section.

[9] These titles are those of Miles Van Pelt, whose work first helped me see the significance of these sections.

the entire Old Testament has the same function as Genesis in the Torah: it shows us who God is and gives a history of his actions that lay the foundation for the New Covenant. Thus, paying attention to the biblical texts themselves confirms what the New Testament says about the Old Testament and, by implication, itself. We see, then, that the Bible is a covenant document.

B. The Nature of the Bible as a Covenant Document

We have already seen that the nature of a document determines the way we read it. That the Bible is a covenant document informs our reading in two different ways; it tells us about the nature and purpose of what is written in it. First, as a covenant document, the Bible is a Word from our covenant Lord and has the same attributes ascribed to all his actions; it reflects and communicates his character. It is also an intentionally ordered document. That is, in some writings, the order of the contents does not affect our interpretation (such as a grocery list, anthology, or resume). However, when it comes to the Bible, the order has some significance. Consider with me the characteristics or attributes of the Bible and then the order of the Bible.

a. The Nature of the Bible

It is beyond the scope of this book to give a detailed account of the Bible's nature (I will recommend some resources at the end of the chapter for the interested reader and will take up this topic in the second part of *God's Gifts for the Christian Life*). But we can consider four significant features of the Bible that result from its nature as a covenant document given by Yahweh, our Covenant Lord. These are *inerrancy, authority, sufficiency,* and *clarity* (traditionally, *perspicuity*).

i. Inerrancy

As God's Word, the Bible carries his exhaustive knowledge and perfection; thus, it is inerrant. That is, as God knows all truth and cannot be wrong, so the Bible as his Word—an act of his speaking (2 Tim 3:16)—has the same attribute. Accuracy is essential for a covenant document, and perfect accuracy for a document legislating a covenant with God himself, for those in covenant relationship must trust their covenant Lord. When we say the Bible is *inerrant*, we are claiming that it accurately communicates the perfect knowledge of God in every area to which it speaks. Inerrancy is a necessary result of Scripture being the speech of an inerrant God; it is also the result of Scripture being a trustworthy guide in our covenant relationship with him. But, more importantly, it is the explicit claim of the Bible. Consider that Jesus identifies Scripture as truth itself (John 17:17, cf. Ps 119:43). Additionally, the Scriptures repeatedly claim that they are unbreakable and sure (e.g. Isa 40:5-8; Ps 119:83, 89, 96; John 10:35).

Practically, if the Bible is the speech of Yahweh, who is perfect and who created and exhaustively knows all things, there is nothing in all the creation that could say it is wrong: nothing and no one has the authority to correct God (consider Isa 40; Job 38:1-42:6). Inerrancy means that we can trust everything Scripture says; the implication for our interpretation is—among other things—that we can trust what it says about itself: no passage of Scripture is ever in error. The New Testament, therefore, can help us better understand the Old. (We will see, however, that there is danger in not paying careful attention to what exactly the New Testament authors are saying about the Old.)

ii. Authority

Following naturally from inerrancy is Scripture's authority. If Scripture cannot err, then we are obligated to believe everything it says: it has authority over all our thinking. More so, as the very words of God our creator, king, and covenant Lord, Scripture carries God's own authority. Yes, Scripture has the same authority that commanded light into being (Gen 1:3) and the dead to rise from the grave (John 12:43-44), which controlled the elements (e.g. Josh 10:11-14). God has the authority to command and correct our thoughts, actions, and emotions; his Word has this same authority. Though some today attempt to separate God's authority from his Word, with a moment's thought, the foolishness of such an attempt is evident. None of us would receive a legitimate letter from our president or prime minister—or the CRA (or IRS)—and ignore it because it was only a letter! We recognize that their authority is extended to their actions and the products of their actions, such as speeches, laws, and letters. Inerrancy means that it is ignorant for us, finite human beings, to disagree with Scripture. Authority means that it is foolish, dangerous, and morally disobedient to disagree with Scripture.

iii. Sufficiency

As God's Word, the Bible is sufficient to accomplish its purpose. As God is omnipotent, able to do anything that he desires, so his Word unfailing accomplishes his purposes:

> "For as the rain and the snow come down from heaven
>   and do not return there but water the earth,
> making it bring forth and sprout,
>   giving seed to the sower and bread to the eater,
> so shall my word be that goes out from my mouth;
>   it shall not return to me empty,
> but it shall accomplish that which I purpose,
>   and shall succeed in the thing for which I sent it. (Isa 55:10-11)

Sufficiency is essential to the Bible's covenantal nature. Scripture is intended to govern our relationship with God, show us how to live before him in this world. Sufficiency means that as the product of an omnipotent God, it succeeds in this. Paul says as much in 2 Timothy 3:16-17,

> All Scripture is breathed out by God and profitable for teaching, for reproof, for correction, and for training in righteousness, that the man of God may be complete, equipped for every good work.

Scripture may not tell us every detail we would love to know about Akkadian marriage ceremonies—that is, it does not tell us everything—but it is sufficient to guide us in faithfulness to God. This does not mean, as some have claimed, that Scripture only tells us about "faith and practice," as if Scripture is only trustworthy when it speaks of God and when it gives instructions on how to act. When we consider what Scripture actually teaches us (including the nature of truth, the creation of the world, etc.), we see that Scripture is sufficient to equip us with all that we need to interpret the world correctly so that we can act for God in it. In other words, Scripture gives us a complete worldview.[10]

iv. Clarity

---

[10] I argue this point as far as it concerns knowledge and truth in the first volume of this series, *The Gift of Knowing*.

As God's Word, the Bible is also clear. A covenant document is not complete if it is only a truthful account of the covenant lord's words providing sufficient detail to govern the relationship; it also needs to be clear. A covenant document needs to communicate if it is to fulfil its purpose. Thus, clarity is also an expression of God's omnipotence or control: if God intended Scripture to govern our lives and reveal himself, he is surely capable of ensuring it does so. We have discussed clarity already in the introduction to this book, yet its importance deserves reiteration. If Scripture is not clear, then we are hopeless. If Scripture is the source of our knowledge about God, essential to worshipping him (Ps 145:18; John 4:21-25; 1 John 3:18); about the Gospel, essential to our salvation (Rom 10:5-17); about God's will, essential to the purpose for which he created us (2 Tim 3:16-17); and if Scripture is our only testimony to the truth of the resurrection and its meaning and it does not communicate these things clearly, we are above all people lost fools (cf. 1 Cor 15:12-19).

What would it say about God if he intended to communicate with us yet failed? We have already seen that this is his intention, and the Bible is clear that he is perfectly capable of accomplishing all of his will; therefore, we can be confident that he has succeeded in his purpose. Scripture is, therefore, clear: it is sufficient to communicate everything we need to do the good works for which God created us (cf. Eph 2:10). As a covenant document given to us by Yahweh, our covenant Lord, Scripture is inerrant, authoritative, sufficient, and clear. I have also claimed above that Scripture is *ordered*, that it has an intentional structure.

b. The Structure of the Bible

There are many types of literature in every language; some of these are long enough to have not only paragraphs but also sections and chapters, and maybe even books. Of these larger pieces of literature, we could identify two broad categories: there are those in which order and structure are incidental or variable, unessential to their meaning, and there are others for which structure and order are vital to their meaning. There is also a significant middle area where the order is important, yet the loss of order is not catastrophic. For example, if you were to jumble the chapters of a novel, the result would be a confusing mess: reading the chapters in order is essential to reading the novel correctly. Yet, jumbling the articles of a dictionary would only make navigation difficult; the meaning would remain the same.[11] We have received the Bible in a specific order; our question should be, does this order matter?

Is the Bible a document like a dictionary where the order is inconsequential to interpretation, or like a novel, where the order is essential? We will see that it is somewhere in between: order matters, yet ignorance of the order is not catastrophic. The latter point should not be controversial: Scripture has been interpreted for thousands of years, and many interpreters have understood it well without (intentionally) paying close attention to its order. Yet, I contend that close attention given to the Bible shows that it is indeed ordered intentionally and that this order matters. We can see this by asking three questions: what is the order of the Bible, does this order demonstrate a structure, and is there significance to this ordered structure?

First, what is the order of the Bible? In answer, you might pull out your English Bible now and look up a table of contents or recall a list of books long ago memorized, yet things at this point get a little complicated. There is some debate over the order of the New Testament, but it is clear that the Old Testament originally had an order quite different from the present order of our English Bibles. The reasons why they differ are not malicious; they are simply products of history and translation. However, it is significant that the New Testament has something to say about the order of our Old Testament, and it affirms the historical Hebrew order.[12] We can arrive at this conclusion by looking at two key texts and the supporting evidence from the rest of the New Testament. Consider, first, Jesus's words in Luke 24:44,

---

[11] Analogously, it is annoying to find radically different organizations in different grocery stores, yet the differences in organization do not hinder us from getting the supplies we need. For the student of Hebrew, compare the organizational principles of BDB and HALOT: if we set aside the differences in data gathering and interpretation, the content is largely unaffected by BDB's choice to organize by root and HALOT's choice to organize by lexical form.

[12] There are minor variations among Hebrew orders of the books, primarily they differ on the location of Ruth and Isaiah. I believe a good argument can be made, however, for the order printed in contemporary Hebrew Bibles. This order is based on the Masoretic Text, a very well-preserved tradition of copying the Hebrew Bible. However, the order of the specific books is not as important as recognizing the groups according to which the Bible is organized, so we do not need certainty on the placement of Ruth and Isaiah to affirm the argument above.

> **44**Then he said to them, "These are my words that I spoke to you while I was still with you, that everything written about me in the Law of Moses and the Prophets and the Psalms must be fulfilled."

Why does Jesus summarize the Old Testament as *Moses, the Prophets*, and *the Psalms*? In fact, the Old Testament is regularly summarized as *the Law*, or *the Law* and *the Prophets* (e.g. Luke 24:17, Acts 13:15, Rom. 3:21). Why these titles? What may not be readily apparent to us is that the Old Testament has historically been summarized with the acronym TaNaKh, the Torah (*Law*), Nevi'im (*Prophets*), and Ketuvim (the *Writings*). The first book of the Writings is the Psalms, and there is evidence that "Psalms" was sometimes used in the place of "Writings."[13] Thus, Jesus words are not arbitrary: they refer to the testimony of the three major groupings of the Old Testament. The same is true of the shorthand use of *Law* and the *Law and the Prophets*. Further confirmation can be found in Jesus's words in Luke 11:50,

> the blood of all the prophets, shed from the foundation of the world, may be charged against this generation, **51**from the blood of Abel to the blood of Zechariah, who perished between the altar and the sanctuary.

I am sure we have passed by this passage before without thinking much of it, yet we may wonder why Jesus has chosen these two figures, Abel and Zechariah. His choice is not chronological: though Abel was the first martyr, Zechariah was not the last. However, it is significant that Abel is the first martyr recorded in the Old Testament (Gen. 4:8) and Zechariah the last according to the Hebrew ordering of the books (2 Chronicles 24:20-22). Thus, Jesus is saying that all the blood of the prophets as recorded in the Old Testament, from Genesis to Chronicles, is against those to whom he speaks. This saying depends on the Hebrew order of the Old Testament. Following this order, our Bible looks like this:

---

[13] This is technically called *synecdoche*, where the name of a part is used in the place of a whole (e.g. referring to the actions of Great Britain by referring to London). We see this in the writings of Philo, the Qumran community, and various later Jewish writings such as the *Tosephta* and *Talmud*.

	Old Testament	
Torah	**Prophets**	**Writings**
Genesis	Joshua	Psalms
Exodus	Judges	Job
Leviticus	Samuel[14]	Proverbs
Numbers	Kings	Ruth
Deuteronomy	Isaiah	Song of Songs
	Jeremiah	Ecclesiastes
	Ezekiel	Lamentations
	The Twelve[15]	Esther
		Daniel
		Ezra-Nehemiah
		Chronicles
	New Testament	
Matthew - John	Acts	Romans – Revelation[16]

In answer to our second question, we have seen that the New Testament affirms three groups of books in the Old Testament. Earlier, we followed Van Pelt in labelling these: the Covenant (*Torah*), Covenant History (*Prophets*), and Covenant Life (*Writings*). It is interesting that as we turn to the New Testament, it bears a similar structure: the Gospels present the founding events of the New Covenant, Acts presents its successful history,

---

[14] The Hebrew Bible recognizes 1 – 2 Samuel, 1 – 2 Kings, Ezra – Nehemiah, and 1 -2 Chronicles as single books.

[15] The Minor Prophets were historically considered one book or compilation, *The Twelve*: Hosea, Joel, Amos, Obadiah, Jonah, Micah, Nahum, Habakkuk, Zephaniah, Haggai, Zechariah, Malachi.

[16] The earliest Greek manuscripts have the Catholic Epistles (James – Jude) before the Pauline Letters (including Hebrews). Some Western manuscripts also have the Gospels in a different order, Matthew, John, Luke, and Mark.

and Romans-Revelation gives various exhortations and instructions in living out this covenant.[17]

We see, therefore, that the Bible has an order or structure (i.e. three sections). We must now ask, is this ordered structure significant? Concerning the structure, our summaries of each section indicate that they each serve a particular function. These sections are relevant to our interpretation. We see this, for example, in the narratives of each section of the Old Testament. They look dramatically different in each section. Readers have often struggled with the vast differences between the history of Israel recorded in Samuel – Kings and the same period as recorded in Chronicles. We have seen that Samuel and Kings occur in the Prophets and Chronicles in the Writings; could this be the reason for their differences? Indeed, Samuel & Kings functions much like the rest of the Prophets: they expound the themes of God's indictment of Israel's sin, his judgment against them, and his present and future salvific acts towards them. The focus is intentionally negative in order to show that despite Israel's failures, God remains faithful to his covenant. The book of Chronicles does not shy away from recording negative aspects of Israel's history but has much more to say about the positive aspects of even the wicked kings. The reason appears to be theological: the author of Chronicles intentionally demonstrates the relationship between the righteous behaviour of the kings and their successes and the consequences that follow from their unrighteous behaviour. In this way, Chronicles presents a theological interpretation of Israel's history that is very similar to the teaching of the Wisdom literature, particularly the Proverbs. By doing so, it underscores the faithfulness of God to his promises and encourages the reader to live righteously, trusting God. In this way, it is perfectly suited for its context in the Writings.

Furthermore, attention paid to the connections between books also reveals insights. For example, consider Ruth in connection with Proverbs. Is it a coincidence that Proverbs and Ruth are the only books in the Bible that contain the phrase "excellent wife" (lit. "worthy woman": Prov 12:4, 31:10; Ruth 3:11)? In fact, Ruth bears a few close parallels with Proverbs 31 (Prov 31:15, Ruth 2:6-7; Prov 31:23, Ruth 4:1-12). Side by side, Ruth appears to be

---

[17] As with the Old Testament, there is some debate over the order of specific books, but the groupings remain the same no matter what our conclusions are on this issue.

an exposition of the "worthy woman" of Proverbs 31. Such parallels go on and on (consider thematic connections between Mal 4:1-6 and Ps 1-2). Because the Old Testament concludes with Chronicles, it ends on a cliffhanger: it records the people of God still in exile, awaiting the return God promises in Deuteronomy 30:1-14. Opening with a genealogy focusing on Jesus's relationship to David, Matthew alerts the reader to the fact that Jesus will take David's throne and usher in the return from exile anticipated in the latter parts of Isaiah (chapter 40 onward) and Jeremiah 30-33. Lastly, considering the Bible as a united covenant document, we find that Genesis 1 is carefully mirrored in the account of the new creation in Revelation 21-22. The end parallels the beginning yet is shown to be better. We see, then, that the Bible has an order and structure and that this ordered structure has interpretive importance.[18]

However, the groupings of literature (Law, Prophets, and Writings) and the book ends of each Testament (Genesis/Chronicles; Matthew/Revelation), the features attested to specifically in Scripture and clearly in the manuscripts we have, remain the most significant features to which we must pay attention. Variety among the order of books in each larger grouping should not be a concern. As I mentioned above, the order is important, but its loss is not catastrophic for the Bible. Identifying the structure of the Bible helps us to better interpret it. However, following the different orders of our English Bibles (and the alternate order of the Greek Septuagint) will not lead us astray. There is some benefit in all these orders, for they draw attention to different features of the text. Nevertheless, because the Bible does speak about its own structure and we can identify the purpose for it, we should give regard to its structure in our reading.

The Bible is a covenant document given to us by Yahweh, our covenant Lord. It is inerrant and authoritative, clear and sufficient, with an intentional structure.[19] Knowing these features of the Bible helps us to interpret it, but

---

[18] Covenant documents in the Ancient world similarly had specific orders that were meaningful. Consider the Torah; it has the same structure as these ancient documents and the results of moving Genesis, for example, around would be significant. The Bible shows us that it is intentionally ordered, and we can confirm that this is typical for covenant documents.

[19] Some readers at this point might ask where this order and structure come from. It is admittedly a lot harder to demonstrate the orderly structure of the Bible from

we need a little bit more. The last aspect of the Bible we will consider in this chapter is its purpose.

C. THE BIBLE GUIDES US IN FULFILLING GOD'S PURPOSE

As a covenant document, the Bible is given to govern our relationship with God, yet it is not yet clear what that means. We could consider the purpose of the Bible in two senses: first, it is intended to do various things, such as rebuke, instruct, or encourage (see Rom. 15:4, 1 Cor. 10:11, 1 Tim. 3:16-17). We are not considering here these purposes of the Bible. Instead, I want us to consider why the Bible does these things. Ultimately, for Christians,[20] the Bible is intended to lead us from faith to faith for the glory of God.[21] That is, it is intended to lead first to initial faith, believing in Christ Jesus and having life in his name (cf. John 20:30-31), and then growing faith manifest in good works (cf. 1 Tim. 3:16-17). We can consider this purpose from three different perspectives: Scripture is meant to lead us from faith to faith, meaning that

---

history than it is from the features of the Bible. Yet, I do not think this should be problem for Christians. If we can affirm that God guided the writing of Scripture and the recognition of its authority among the Jewish communities and then the Christians communities who received them, why could he not also have prepared them to have a specific shape. Consider this thought experiment.

Take a group of five proficient writers. If you assigned them five distinct yet related writing projects and specified that they must follow closely the outlines you provide and include certain key words at specific junctions, what would result? If you were careful enough in your planning, you could put together a final document that bore the distinct styles of each author yet was connected by the plan you conceived (maybe having poetic texts appear at key points) and the key themes or words you prescribed. Thus, unity and meaning as found in the Bible could be achieved without the need for a final redactor uniting the work. If we could conceive of its possibility, surely the omnipotent God could execute such a feat, even over an extended period of time and multiple languages.

[20] There is also a negative purpose of Scripture; though it is primarily intended to edify and build up the believer, it is also intended to harden the hearts of unbelievers as an act of judgment (e.g. Isa 6:8-13, Matt 13:10-17). We will focus on Scripture's purpose as it regards believers.

[21] John Piper's book *Reading the Bible Supernaturally* argues that the ultimate goal of reading the Bible the glory of God celebrated in the joyous worship of his people. I am considering the ways the Bible achieves that ultimate end.

we would become Yahweh's people, know and enjoy him more, and do his will.[22] Let us consider each of these in turn.

First, the Bible is intended to make the reader part of Yahweh's people. In the Old Testament, the Torah laid out complex rules for the life of the Israelites, distinguishing them from their neighbours. Birth into the community made someone part of the covenant, and the Law outlined what this looked like. The Old Testament was not so much concerned with what we would call "evangelism," getting people into the community, but how to be righteous before God and so receive his blessings and not his curses (Lev 18:5; Deut 27:9-28:68). Yet, this changed with the coming of the New Covenant. The Scriptures were written not only to show God's people what it means to be a Christian but also to lead the reader or hearer into faith (John 20:30-31; Rom 10:5-17). The Bible and its teaching has as its purpose the initiation of salvation, leading the reader to confess faith in Jesus and his accomplished work in order that they might be justified, counted right before God.[23] Becoming God's people means many things, not only being declared righteous before God but also being adopted into God's family (Rom 8:12-17; Gal 4:5), being in Christ and made part of his body (Col 3:2-4; 1 Cor 12:13), and being set apart for God's purposes—made "saints," those who are holy, set apart for God's purpose (1 Cor 1:2; 6:11).

Jesus tells us that the result of belief is eternal life, knowing God and Jesus whom he sent (John 17:3). Knowing God and worshipping him as the appropriate response to that knowledge is the ultimate end of faith. The way we know God, the way we grow in relationship with him, is through his self-

---

[22] Each of these is truly perspectival in that the whole of the Bible could be considered from any of these perspectives: everything is about knowing God, becoming his people, and following him faithfully.

[23] Though on the surface the Torah and the Gospel seems at odds, one offering justification through works and the other through Law, the contradiction is only apparent. God's people have been justified by faith throughout time (cf. Gen 15:6, Hab 2:4), yet God gave a Law that was impossible in order to imprison all under sin, to reveal human need until his answer arrived in Jesus Christ (Gal 3:15-39). Thus, the righteousness offered by the Law could never be attained, only a curse resulted. Yet this curse was removed in Christ, and we receive righteousness and the blessings of God through our Faith in Christ, who has fulfilled God's covenant on our behalf (Rom 1:16-17; Rom 3:21-31; Rom 5:12-21; Rom 10:1-5; Gal 3:10-14).

revelation in Scripture. God's Word is his very speech, so we encounter him as we read. He is present, and we grow in all dimensions of knowledge (cognitive, "I know things about him;" and personal, "I know Him") as we prayerfully read about God and his actions. All Scripture reveals God, not only teaching us about him but demonstrating his glory, the splendour of his majesty. As we read, we perceive his invisible attributes and character. The appropriate response to such revelation, to the glory of God, is worshipful awe and delight. As we get to know God through Scripture and encounter his glory revealed there, we will thus be led into joyous worship—the ultimate goal of creation.

Lastly, Scripture is intended to lead the Christian in the appropriate behaviour before God. By showing us God's will for our thoughts (Rom 12:2), our emotions (e.g. Deut 28:47), and our actions (1 Tim 3:16-17), Scripture transforms us into tools in his hands to do the good works he has created us for (Eph 2:10). We are equipped to love the Lord our God with all of our being (Deut 6:4-5).

We can see what these good works are by looking at Jesus' parting words to his disciples. According to Jesus, the purpose of a Christian as a part of his Church is to fulfil the great commission:

> Go therefore and make disciples of all nations, baptizing them in the name of the Father and of the Son and of the Holy Spirit, teaching them to observe all that I have commanded you. And behold, I am with you always, to the end of the age. (Matt 28:19-20)

This is not something any one person can do: this is Jesus's purpose for his people as a whole, for the Church and its local expressions. Each Christian has a role to play within this commission (1 Cor 12:1-31; Rom 12:3-8; Eph 4:11-16). Scripture thus equips each believer to be a part of the Church, using the particular gifts he has given them to build up the body and perform the work of ministry. We will consider the Church's work and so the believer's mission as part of it in the following chapters.

In this chapter, we set out to establish what sort of book the Bible is in order that we might read it accordingly. We have seen that the Bible is a covenant document possessing the attributes of the Lord who spoke it into being and an order that contributes to its interpretation. The purpose of the Bible, as a covenant document, is to govern the New Covenant between God and his New Covenant people, all those who believe in Jesus Christ. It does this by leading the reader to faith, growing them in the knowledge of God, and guiding them in the appropriate way to follow him.

To read the Bible we need eyes to see; to this point, we have considered the Bible as a book, the broad features of which each part partakes. Now we will turn to consider the content of the Bible, namely the worldview it teaches.

FURTHER READING[24]

The Bible

The Doctrine of the Word of God – John Frame [I]

The Structure of Biblical Authority – Meredith G. Kline [A]

*A Biblical-Theological Introduction to the Old Testament – Miles Van Pelt, pp. [23-41] [B]

*A Peculiar Glory – John Piper [B]

Reading the Bible Supernaturally – John Piper [I]

Systematic Theology – Wayne Grudem, pp. 47-138 [B-I]

The Biblical Canon

The Biblical Canon – David G. Dunbar, in *Hermeneutics, Authority, and Canon* eds. D. A. Carson and John D. Woodbridge [I]

*Canon Revisited – Michael J. Kruger [A]

The Question of Canon – Michael J. Kruger [A]

The Old Testament Canon of the New Testament Church and its Background in Early Judaism – Roger T. Beckwith [A]

---

[24] The following resources range from (relatively) easy to quite difficult in their readability, I mark the easier reads with a **B** for beginner, those a bit more difficult with an **I** for intermediate, and the most difficult with **A** for advanced. I adduce difficulty on the basis of the depth of content, knowledge presupposed by the author, and the clarity of the writing. An asterisk indicates a volume I particularly recommend.

2

THE BIBLE'S WORLDVIEW - THEOLOGY

> Hear Oh Israel, the Lord our God, the Lord is one; You shall love the Lord your God with all your heart and with all your soul and with all your might. – Deuteronomy 6:4-5

From the moment we wake up until we fall asleep, we are acting as interpreters. We interpret, for example, the objects in our homes through the lens of past experience in order that we might use them. We interpret the motives and actions of others, evaluating them as good or bad, a help or a hindrance. We are constantly interpreting; a worldview describes the interlocking web of beliefs that we use to make interpretations. Our worldview functions most of the time tacitly; it is there unnoticed behind our emotions, actions, and opinions.

Consider the basic belief in the trustworthiness of our senses: we believe that what we perceive through sight and sound corresponds to reality and act as if it does. We pay the amount we read on a bill or go through a green light but stop at a red. There may be another person who does not share this basic belief about traffic lights and who acts with paralysing caution or complete disregard, believing that his perception of a green light is a lie and stopping when he sees one. We all have a worldview; it is a gift of God's grace that he has provided us with a—indeed, the only—coherent worldview in Scripture.[1]

According to Romans 1:18-23, humanity has exchanged the proper interpretation of the creation granted to us by God for a lie, rejecting what is

---

[1] I discuss the coherence of the Biblical worldview and the incoherence of others when it comes to knowing in my book *The Gift of Knowing: A Biblical Perspective on Knowing and Truth* (Vancouver, Teleioteti 2019).

evident for a figment of our imagination. The Bible restores this worldview; it gives us the proper lens through which to see the world—and the Bible as a part of the world—correctly. We need to regain the biblical worldview if we are to properly interpret the Word and God's creation. A worldview is a network of beliefs concerning the objects of interpretation, the subject interpreting, and the way these interact.[2] For our purposes, we can focus on what the Bible teaches about the world we interact with—about "objects."

It will serve our purposes to consider first, in this chapter, key biblical teachings about the Creator and his creation, the objects with which we interact. Then, in the following chapter, we will consider the history and future of the Creator and his creation, the metanarrative that unites every event and object experienced in the creation. In Chapter 4, we will conclude this section by considering what the Bible teaches about humanity, specifically how God's people relate to God and his creation.

At every step, our primary authority is Scripture: as the Word of God, it is our ultimate standard of truth and the lens by which we interpret his creation. Regaining the biblical worldview lost in the fall is a progressive process; we are all growing in our knowledge of God and his world, yet we can jump-start this process by considering some of the major themes of Scripture.[3] I cannot hope to give more than a cursory summary of the doctrines of God, man, and the Kingdom of God. For those curious to go deeper, resources for further reading are provided at the end of this chapter

---

[2] From a different perspective, James N. Anderson helpfully summarizes the pieces of a worldview with the acronym TAKES, as in "What it TAKES to make a worldview." *T*: Theology, an absolute; *A*: anthropology, a view of man; *K*: Knowledge, a view of knowing and truth; *E*: Ethics, what is right or wrong, good or bad; and *S*: Salvation, what the problem of the world is and its answer.

This book and its companions, making up the first part of the series *God's Gift's for the Christian Life*, is an effort to unpack the second aspect of a worldview, the way by which subjects come to know objects. *The Gift of Knowing* provides the framework of how humans know; *The Gift of Reading* considers how we interact with the Bible, our authority for knowing; and *The Gift of Seeing* considers the relationship between the knowing subject and the objects of knowledge.

[3] This process is a spiral; it begins with faith, as God renews our heart and through the teaching of the Church gives us a foundation to start with. We then bring this foundational knowledge to Scripture and find it both challenged and enriched. Our understanding grows as we reject falsehood and adopt a greater understanding of the truth.

A. YAHWEH: THE GOD WHO IS

The 66 books of the Bible and all creation testify to the God of the Bible, so I cannot hope to sufficiently introduce the reader to God their creator. The Bible teaches that we all know God, yet in our rebellion we have suppressed this truth. Consider this, then, a refresher, an account of our God as he has revealed himself to us.

To his people, God has revealed himself as Yahweh, the one who is (Exod 3:13-14). By definition, God is the one who exists, the true God over against all false gods worshipped by man. In relation to his people, Yahweh is the LORD, the gracious Lord who has entered into covenant with us, who has offered mercy and salvation to rebels deserving of judgment. Yahweh is the one true God (consider Deut 6:4, 1 Sam 2:2; Isa 40:9-31). Without losing his oneness, Yahweh is also simultaneously three: the Father is Yahweh (e.g. Ps 110:1, cf. Mark 12:35-36), Jesus is Yahweh (Acts 1:34, 2:21, 9:10; Rom 10:9, 13; 1 Cor 2:16), and the Spirit is Yahweh (2 Cor 3:17, 18).[4] Scripture is clear that the Father, the Son, and the Spirit are in perfect unity, are one; so Yahweh is three (e.g. John 17:20-26).

This is ultimately incomprehensible for finite man: God in his grace Has revealed something truly beyond our comprehension. Traditionally, this doctrine has been known as the Trinity: God is simultaneously one yet three. In God, unity and distinction—fundamental characteristics of reality—are equally ultimate: Yahweh's oneness is not more ultimate, more "real," than his threeness.[5] There is simply too much to say about God's Trinitarian nature than we have space for. But in considering the depths of our Lord's self-revelation, we should feel in over our heads; we should feel as if we have touched upon things too great for us.

Yet, while our awe should be deep, we should also feel the joy that though limited, our knowledge is true. God is omnicompetent, competent to achieve all his purposes, so though we stand at the edge of the precipice of the depths of the wonders of God, we have the certainty that all we do know is true and

---

[4] In most English translations, the divine name Yahweh is translated LORD (all capitals). In the New Testament, the Greek word *kurios* translated "lord" is used in the place of the name Yahweh.

[5] I consider this further in the third volume of this series, *The Gift of Seeing*.

our source of joy—that we finite men and women are given a glimpse into the wonders and beauty of our infinite God.

Large theological treatments have the space to explore what Scripture teaches both about God's unity and threeness, giving separate consideration to God as Father, Spirit, and Son. We, however, will have to limit ourselves to God's unity. Beginning with God's Holiness, we will then consider God's relationship to us creatures in terms of his authority, control, and presence.[6]

a. *Yahweh is Holy*

Throughout the Bible, the theme of holiness is repeated: Israel is a holy nation, the Temple is a holy place, and Christians like Israel are a holy people. Yet behind and above all these holy things is Yahweh, the Holy One of Israel. All holiness attributed to created things derives from God's holiness. That God is holy means that he is separated from all his creatures by his complete and consistent dedication to manifesting the fullness of his character—to display his glory—in all he does.[7] That is, we can discern from Scripture that God's ultimate purpose in creating and redeeming is to magnify his glory, that is, to make his magnificent nature clear to his creatures, to reveal himself in all his splendour (consider Hab 2:14; John 17:24; Rom 9:22-24). That God is Holy means that all his interactions are intended to share his glorious beauty and the joy he has in himself with others. This is good news for the Christian, for we learn God himself is joyful, that this sharing of himself is the ultimate source of joy for his creation (consider Ps 16:11, Ps 84, Matt 5:2-12; 1 Tim 1:11). Out of this commitment flows all of God's actions.[8]

In contrast with this, the entire created order is twisted by sin away from this purpose for which God created the world. Man, who was supposed to

---

[6] "Authority," "control," and "presence" are terms John Frame uses in his work on the doctrine of God. He calls them "Lordship attributes," describing God's lordship over his creation. His discussion is invaluable and rich, yet I make no attempt to follow him closely: the terms avail themselves well to our purposes. I am indebted to Frame's work, so many similarities may be discerned in what follows, yet this largely follows from the fact that we both are presenting the truths of Scripture.

[7] On the meaning of Holiness as separation for a purpose, see my forthcoming book *The Gift of Seeing*.

[8] John Piper in my estimation has done more than anyone in recent years to draw our attention to this truth. However, he uses the term "holy" in the broader theological sense noted below. See especially his book, *Desiring God*.

worship the Creator, instead worships God's creation (cf. Rom 1:18-23). Men and women in this way are *unholy*: they are not devoted to God's purposes—indeed, they are set in complete opposition to them (cf. Rom 8:5-8). Humans, locations, and objects become Holy by consecration: God rededicates them to his purposes. Now, in theology, theologians often use "holiness" to refer more broadly to the way God is different from his creatures.

Yahweh is different from us in his unfailing commitment to uphold his glory in all he does, but he is also profoundly different in his very nature. In this sense of the word, Yahweh's holiness encompasses all of who he is considered as different from his creation. That Yahweh is holy means that there is no one like him (1 Sam 2:2). All that God is different from his creation. God is not, like the Greek "gods," an upgraded version of creation: he is not a more powerful version of us. God is bigger and better in those ways in which he is similar to us, this is true, yet he is the source of all these similarities. God is the reference point for goodness, love, kindness, etc.: we only know what is good, what is kind, what is love because of God. These only have meaning in reference to God, the ultimate measure of all that is good and the ultimate antithesis of all that is bad. In this way, God is different *qualitatively*, not just *quantitatively*: God is the original, we are the copy.

God's perfections are eternal; our reflections are merely derivative. That God is holy means that he is the Creator in distinction from the creation. In this way, Scripture teaches two categories of existence: there is God and all that is not God. God is distinct, separate from his creation. Visualizing this, we could follow Cornelius Van Til in picturing two circles that do not touch; one is labelled "Creator" and the other "creature." In this theological sense of the word, holiness means that the distinction between these circles, between the Creator and the creature, is never blurred. Even in the Incarnation, Christ never stopped being the infinitely Holy Creator while taking on the creation. This may be something we cannot comprehend. In the Bible, holiness refers primarily to God's utter commitment to his purposes, but "holiness" is most frequently used by theologians to refer to the distinction between the creator and the creature.

b. The Authority, Control, and Presence of Yahweh

We have said that God's Holiness is all that he is in distinction from his creation and consecrated for a purpose, yet what do we mean when we say, "all that he is." Traditionally, theologians have talked about the "attributes" of God, different perspectives by which we can consider God's nature. To be clear, God's attributes are not different parts of him (he is not part omnipresent, part omniscient, etc.) but different ways we can contemplate his character as revealed in Scripture. A helpful way to talk about these attributes is to consider God's attributes in terms of authority, control, and presence. These describe the united character of God, and so equally describe the Father, Son, and Holy Spirit. Yet, we can see that in different ways, the Father is particularly associated in Scripture with authority, the Son with control, and the Spirit with presence.[9]

The authority of God describes his character as expressed in authority over his creation. God has the authority to determine what is and will be: he is sovereign. God has the authority to determine what is true: he is omniscient. And God has authority to determine what is right and wrong: he is morally pure and just. According to Joseph, God was at work even through the malicious actions of Joseph's brothers to achieve his good purpose (Gen 50:20). Similarly, Peter identifies God hand working even in the crucifixion of Jesus (Acts 2:23). God is, according to Paul, at work in both good and bad events, working all things together for the good of his people (Rom 8:28). We can summarize this in Paul's words, "[He] works all things according to the counsel of his will" (Eph 1:11). God is not a distant God; he has authority over everything that conspires in his creation. The rise and fall of great nations, even the most wicked, happens according to his will (Hab 1:5-11, 2:6-20). It is not only humans that are subject to his sovereign governance; he is the source of rain and sunshine (Matt 5:45), and even the most wicked of storms (Gen 6-8; Josh 10:10-14; Job 38:22-30). It is God who provides food for our tables, brings forth the plants in the spring, and feeds the birds (Matt 6:25-34). God does this through means at times, such as human economies and jobs or the Church, yet all this happens only according to God's plan. God's sovereignty is the source of a Christian's hope and confidence. We can know that God will God be victorious over death and

---

[9] This is also an observation made by John Frame.

Hell in the final day, for all is happening exactly as he intends. I can have confidence that the death of my grandfather only a year ago was not a horrific accident but the perfect plan of our heavenly father who used him in the world for his good purpose and took him home at just the right time. We can have this confidence, for God works all things together according to his plan, good and bad for our good. I know that I will endure in faith only because God is in control, and nothing will catch him off-guard: nothing can separate me from the love of Christ (Rom 8:31-39). We can pursue his kingdom with selfless fervency because he has promised that he will never fail to provide for those seeking his kingdom (Matt 6:25-34).

God's authority also comprehends his knowledge and his moral purity. God, according to Isaiah and numerous Scriptures (e.g. Isa 40), is never caught off guard: he knows all things.[10] God knows the past, present, and future from all possible perspectives with perfect accuracy. That is, God does not only know about my existence, but he knows how everyone in my life interprets my existence, relates to me, views me. He even knows what a bee flying outside of the window beside which I am writing would perceive about me. God's knowledge is exhaustive: he has pre-interpreted all events and objects from all valid perspectives.[11] Not only is his knowledge exhaustively perfect, but it is also perfectly free from error. That is, God knows all true propositions (statements of truth) as true without knowing any false propositions as true. Because God knows all things perfectly, his interpretation of reality is the ultimate measure of truth: truth is that which corresponds to God's interpretation of reality. We have access to truth, therefore, through Scripture and God's creation as interpreted through the lens provided in Scripture. God's knowledge is thus the authority over our knowledge.

---

[10] This is, of course, an extension of sovereignty: if everything happens according to God's will, he knows everything that will happen. Yet there is reciprocity here: God's will is not mechanistic. He creates creatures and then plans their future and actions according to the way he has created them. He creates with consistency; his creative acts thus produce his foreknowledge by which he plans the course of his creation, and the course of his creation determines the nature of what he creates. Thus, there is a circularity here that we cannot quite comprehend: foreknowledge and predestination cohere perfectly in God in such a way that does not compromise his ultimate sovereignty.

[11] I discuss the relation between object and events and God's interpretation of them in *The Gift of Knowing*.

God is morally pure; he is good, just, free from wickedness. God's every action is good, free from imperfection: he can, in fact, do nothing wrong (1 John 1:5). God is therefore not just perfectly good; he is the standard for everything that is good. Something can only be called good if it corresponds to God's character and the revelation of that character in Scripture. Thus, God's moral purity is an attribute of authority: it is the standard by which all goodness in the world is measured. God's goodness means that we can have unfailing confidence that God will always act in ways that are ultimately good. Yet goodness is not defined as something that benefits man: goodness is defined by God's zeal for his glory. This not to say that what is good to God is not good for man. On the contrary, what God declares to be good is what is best for us, his creatures: he created us to benefit most fully from living in the world as he intended it. What is good is ultimately what brings God glory: mercy, for example, is good because it reflects God's merciful character; it is an act that glorifies God by demonstrating his character. Our actions are good only in as much as they mirror God's character on a creaturely level (that is, God can do some things that we as humans are not permitted to do).

God's authority describes God's attributes as they function as norms (or standards) for the world—for what is and will be, what is true, what is good, etc. But God does not only have authority; he is also a ruling Lord. He has control over his creation.

God's control comprehends all of his character. We will restrict our discussion of control to God's governance and omnipotence. God's governance refers to the active side of God's sovereignty: God has not only made a plan, but he is also at work in the world to accomplish it. Behind the scenes, God works through the hearts and hands of men and angels to accomplish all his will (cf. Exod 9:16, Hab 2:5-11). Furthermore, God not only actively achieves his will, but he also actively sustains his creation. According to the New Testament, all creation is held in existence by the word of Jesus Christ (Col 1:17; Heb 1:3); according to Genesis, the consistency of the natural order is because of God's oath to sustain it (Gen 9:8-17). What we call "natural laws" are, therefore, not impersonal processes but the activity of God within his creation to ensure things run as he so desires. We must then praise him each moment not only for the breath we breathe but the fact that our world remains together: we should not take for granted the stability of the chairs we sit on, the orbit of our planet—let alone the functioning of our vehicles. All this consistency owes itself to the faithfulness of God.

Governance describes God's acts of control in general; omnipotence describes his ability to control. That God is omnipotent means that his purposes will never be foiled: all that God desires he will bring about. We, as finite humans, often desire to do things we are unable to do; God does not face this struggle. Everything he desires he is able to and does accomplish. We could define omnipotence in many ways. One way is this: God is unhindered in the accomplishment of all his good purposes. Omnipotence does not mean that God can do *anything*, such as evil, but that he is unhindered. Consider whether or not God could do an evil act. In one sense, he could: most evil acts are quite simple. However, his goodness means that he never will. It would cause a contradiction in his very character, so we can be assured that this is indeed impossible for God. Yet such impossibility is not a hindrance to God, a limit to his perfection. Instead, it is the height of God's perfection that he will never desire anything contrary to himself and so will only ever desire what he can and will accomplish.

In Scripture, the primary way we see God's control revealed is his redemptive plan, which we will consider in the following chapter. Because God's control is primarily expressed in his plan to redeem a people for himself, we may consider mercy, compassion, love, and benevolence to be aspects of God's control. These are also expressions of God's presence among his creation and especially with his people.

God's presence is also known as his immanence, his nearness to the creation. God is omnipresent, meaning that there is nowhere in all creation where a creature could escape its God. In the depths of Hell, God is present; in the heights of heaven, God is there (Ps 139:8). God has probed the deepest depths of the created world and is present at the farthest reaches of the universe. God cannot be escaped: this brings great joy to God's people yet great fear to the unbeliever. God's presence for the believer is one of comfort and strength (e.g. 1 Sam 7; Phil 2:12, 1 Pet 1:5-8). God's presence with his people in the Old Testament was the greatest honour (Exod 33:15-16) but also a fearful thing (Exod 19-20); God is holy and majestic, terrifying to finite man (cf. Isa 6:1-7). For the Old Testament people of God, enjoying the presence of God required elaborate sacrifices to cover over their sin.

In the New Testament, God's presence can be a terrifying thing for the false believer (Acts 5:1-11) and is a work of judgment for the unbeliever (John 12:36-43), yet God's presence is the height of comfort for the believer (John 10:7-10, 25-29). The Spirit, God himself, is given to us as strength and comfort, and we are assured that we can safely draw near to God in our time of need through the blood of Christ (Heb 4:14-16). God's omnipresence for the believer means that God is an ever-present source of comfort, strength, and joy. Consider this: the joy which Israel sought in the courts of the Lord (cf. Ps 84) is present every day to the Christian, who is seated even now in the heavenly places with Christ (Eph 1:3), who draws near to the very throne of God—closer than any but the high priest in the Old Testament. The Christian is assured that through Christ, this presence, though at times painful (Heb 12:3-11), will never turn to white-hot wrath against our sin (Rom 5:9). The greatest implication of God's presence for interpretation is given in 1 Corinthians 2:9-16:

> as it is written,
>
> > What no eye has seen, nor ear heard,
> > > nor the heart of man imagined,
> > what God has prepared for those who love him—
>
> these things God has revealed to us through the Spirit. For the Spirit searches everything, even the depths of God. For who knows a person's thoughts except the spirit of that person, which is in him? So also no one comprehends the thoughts of God except the Spirit of God. Now we have received not the spirit of the world, but the Spirit who is from God, that we might understand the things freely given us by God. And we impart this in words not taught by human wisdom but taught by the Spirit, interpreting spiritual truths to those who are spiritual.
>
> The natural person does not accept the things of the Spirit of God, for they are folly to him, and he is not able to understand them because they are spiritually discerned. The spiritual person judges all things, but is himself to be judged by no one. "For who has understood the mind of the Lord so as to instruct him?" But we have the mind of Christ.

Thus, we have the Spirit with us always in order to discern the depths of the wisdom of God revealed in Scripture. The Spirit humbles us to receive what God has written and quickens our minds to better understand the meaning of what we read.

We could discuss the presence, authority, control, tri-unity, and holiness of God at endless lengths: all creation testifies to these truths! This has been my humble attempt to acquaint the reader with the contours of the doctrine of God revealed in Scripture, to complement our knowledge of God (personal, relational knowledge we have on account of our faith) with knowledge about God. As we interpret Scripture, we can only hope to grow in this knowledge and delight ever more in the splendour and glory of Yahweh, our Lord.

God and his character are the main content of Scripture: it is all about him and his redemption accomplished in Jesus Christ. Yet there is more than just truths about God in Scripture. To read it well, we also need to know something about humans, the primary characters in Scripture after God.

B. MAN: REBELLIOUS KINGS

For our purposes we can consider the doctrine of humanity, *anthropology*, in three different ways. We will consider, first, humanity in their ideal state, created in the image of God. But we obviously do not encounter humans in an ideal state. Every human we interact with is made in the image of God but does not manifest God nearly as well as he or she should. The reason for this is human depravity. We will thus consider, second, humanity's nature resulting from their rebellion against God. The image of God is the ideal of what humans could be, seen fully only in Jesus Christ; depravity is the depths to which we have dived, our dark, sinful nature that stains our actions. Yet Christians are new creations in Christ Jesus, no longer enslaved to sin and corrupted to the root of our hearts. Therefore, we must also consider, third, the state of believers, those who have been given new life through Christ.

According to Genesis 1:26-28, God created man in his image and commissioned them to rule the earth and multiply within it. Much has been written on what the image of God may or may not be, yet what we can say from this passage is that as God's image-bearers, we were created to represent him. This is realized partly in our physical constitution, how we are perfectly created for the ruling and representing task he has given us. This is realized partly also in the community that begins with one man and one woman in marital union, mirroring the oneness of the Trinity. It is realized thirdly in the representing function God assigned man.

Humans were not created to be passive paintings representing God but active vice-regents ruling the creation under God's authority. Humanity was created, in other words, to glorify God by extending and ruling over his kingdom on earth. This was essentially the calling of each human being, to extend the kingdom of God in submission to their Lord. In other words, we were created to be kings.

However, instead of being faithful to this call, Adam followed Eve in rebellion against God. Instead of ruling the creation under God's authority, humanity became rebels attempting to exert their own authority. The result of this was catastrophic: the creation was cursed, subjected to futility (Rom 8:18-25). Marriage was cursed with conflict: wives would strive to usurp the leadership of their husbands, and husbands would tyrannize their wives (Gen 3:16). Men and women were also individually cursed in the area of God's original commission for which they were most responsible: women, primary in "multiplying" (Gen 1:28), were cursed in childbearing (Gen 3:16); men, charged with a primary role in taking "dominion" (Gen 1:28), were cursed with toil in their labours (Gen 3:17-19). Humans were thus cursed in their relations to one another (cf. Gen 4:8), in their relations to God's commission in creation, and ultimately in their relationship with God.

In his curse on Satan, God speaks of a conflict that will take place between Eve's seed and that of the serpent (Gen 3:15). This foreshadows the coming division of humanity into the people of God and the World, the rebellious human race under Satan's dominion. We learn from the New Testament that Adam's sin had a deeper consequence than this external strife: the death promised for his rebellion was transferred to his descendants (Gen 2:17). According to Romans 5:12-21 and 1 Corinthians 15:20-24, Adam's sin bound us to sin and subjected us to death. All humanity followed in his footsteps, falling short of God's glory to which they were called (Rom 3:23). Every human, as a result of Adam's sin, is dead in sin, enslaved to sin, and hardened in rebellion against God (Gen 8:21; Deut 29:4; Rom 6:17-19; Eph 2:1-5). Far from the ideal, this is the state of fallen man: we are guilty before God and incapable of obedience towards him (Rom 8:6-7).

It is in the great mercy of God that this is not all Scripture has to say about humanity. After creation, we read of people who are not quite the ideal, yet neither are they totally depraved: Noah is favoured by God and is considered righteous (Gen 6:9), Abraham is granted a covenant by God and made righteous through his faith (Gen 12:1-3, 15:6). Among the people of Israel, there were many who were unfaithful to God but also some who were faithful (Hab 2:2-4). In the New Testament, the veil is pulled back, and we see that the cause of this faithfulness in some is God's merciful gift of regeneration (cf. Deut 30:6). In Ephesians 2, Paul writes that believers were once dead in their sins as the rest of humanity, yet God in his mercy raised us to new life (2:1-5). Jesus terms it as a new birth: it is only by Spirit-wrought birth that anyone may enter into, even see, God's kingdom (John 3:5-8, 6:44-45).

The result of this new birth is new life and a recommissioning. Christians, those who believe in Jesus Christ, are made new creations by the Spirit: we are emissaries of a New Creation dwelling within the Old (2 Cor 5:17, Gal 6:15). The call to be fruitful, multiply, and have dominion is changed slightly because the concept of the kingdom has changed. Jesus issues a new commission to make disciples (multiply) under Jesus universal authority (dominion) (Matt 28:18-20). Christians are those being made anew in the image of God perfected in Christ (Rom 8:29) and expanding his kingdom through the spreading of the Church.

Much more could be said about the doctrine of man, but these points provide a good foundation for understanding humanity as found in the Bible. Created good in God's image, we fell into sin; this resulted in what we could call an "antithesis." There are two branches in humanity, representing two kingdoms: every human being is born into sin, depraved and part of Satan's kingdom. Yet through God's mercy, a new humanity has been created in Christ Jesus (Eph 2:1-5). These two humanities are in conflict (cf. Gen 3:15), with the World persecuting those who are in Christ (John 15:18-25). Yet the victory of Jesus Christ, to bring all his sheep to himself and conquer the kingdom of Satan, is assured (John 10:14-16; 1 Cor 15:20-28; Rev 19). This brings us to the last theme we will consider, the Kingdom of God.

C. KINGDOM: THE RULE OF GOD

Though the phrase "the Kingdom of God" or "the Kingdom of Heaven" is not very frequent in Scripture, the concept is everywhere. "Kingdom" is rightly considered one of the key themes of Scripture. The phrase "the Kingdom of God" in the New Testament is very specific, yet Scripture makes it clear that God has a kingdom in a broader sense as well. To unpack this theme a bit, we will consider the Kingdom of God as heavenly, earthly, and eschatological.

a. *God's Heavenly Reign*

According to Scripture, God rules in Heaven and does all that he pleases (Psalm 115:3). Everything is under his authority (Matt 28:18). I am using the term "heavenly reign" to describe God's universal reign over creation. The world as we experience it is in conflict. We have already seen that there is a conflict between God's people and Satan's people, a conflict of two kingdoms. This is true, yet it is not the full story.

According to Jesus, he has been given all authority (Matt 28:18); having sat down at the right hand of the Majesty on high (Heb 1:3), Jesus is currently reigning over all creation (1 Cor 15:24-28; Col 2:15). In the Gospels and Revelation, Jesus's enemies are considered to be restrained while Christ reigns (Mark 3:23-27; Luke 10:18-20; John 12:30-32; Rev 12:8-9; Rev 20:1-6). There is a sense in which Christ is in complete control and Satan's "kingdom" is really rebellion kept tightly under reigns. Satan may roam about as a prowling lion (1 Pet. 5:8), but he only roams where the Lord lets him. Thus, viewing Jesus' reign from the perspective of Heaven, it is all-encompassing. Yet viewing it from the perspective of earth, it is unfolding. It is in this latter sense that "the Kingdom of God" is used in the New Testament.

b. *God's Earthly Reign*

When Jesus entered into his ministry, he preached that the Kingdom of God had arrived (Mark 1:15). Throughout the Gospels, the arrival of Jesus is associated with the inauguration of God's kingdom on earth. Yet, it was not the kingdom the Jews were expecting. They were looking for an earthly king to throw off the Romans and re-instate the glory of David and Solomon's kingdom. When the Jews welcomed Jesus with cries of praise as he entered Jerusalem, calling him the "son of David" (Matt 20:9), they were expecting the fulfilment of God's promises in an earthly kingdom. And they thought they had biblical warrant for believing so:

> Say to the daughter of Zion,
>
> > 'Behold, your king is coming to you,
> > humble, and mounted on a donkey,

on a colt, the foal of a beast of burden.' (Matt 21:4-5, cf. Zech 9:9)

It quickly became apparent that this idea was false: Jesus had no intention of instituting a kingdom like Rome or Israel at that moment. His intent was not to institute a kingdom with an identifiable physical location in competition with other nations of the world. When Pilate asks Jesus if he is a king, Jesus does not deny it (Matt. 27:11). However, he clarifies that what he means by "king" is not what the Jews thought: "My kingdom is not of this world.... You say that I am a king. For this purpose I was born and for this purpose I have come into the world—to bear witness to the truth" (John 18:36-37). If Jesus means by the "Kingdom of God" something other than an earthly empire like Rome, what does he mean?

It becomes quickly evident that what is meant is not the "heavenly Kingdom" we have already seen, for only believers belong to the Kingdom of God (e.g. John 3:3, 5). I have labelled it "earthly" for this reason: it is Jesus's heavenly rule as it is unfolding on earth. It is his rule over and through those the Spirit grants to recognize and embrace his heavenly rule. This contrasts Jesus's kingdom considered from the perspective of heaven, which is his rule over obedient and rebellious subjects alike. From the perspective of earth, we can identify the Kingdom of God as Jesus's rule over the Church, his people. John in Revelation 5:9-10 writes as much, "for you were slain, and by your blood you ransomed people for God from every tribe and language and people and nation, and you made them a kingdom and priests to our God, and they shall reign on the earth." Though they do not yet reign on the earth, Jesus has "made them a kingdom" already. According to Graeme Goldsworthy, a kingdom implies three things: a king, a people, and sphere of rule.[12] The Kingdom of God is the present rule of *Jesus Christ* over *Christians*—those who believe in him and confess his Lordship—*in the midst of a world in rebellion against its King*. That is, the sphere of Christ's

---

[12] Goldsworthy outlines the Kingdom of God as involving God's people in God's place under God's rule. Graeme Goldsworthy, *Gospel and Kingdom* in *The Goldsworthy Trilogy* (Colorado Springs, Paternoster Press 2000), 53-54.

rule is all creation, but it is manifest in the Church where his Lordship is proclaimed.

The Gospel and the Kingdom

A lot has been written in recent years on the connection between the Kingdom of God and the Gospel. Though a lot of this is very unhelpful, it is important to recognize that the idea of "kingdom" is an essential part of what we call the "Gospel." When we think of the Gospel, we usually think of historical events and their present consequences for those who believe: Jesus Christ lived a perfect life, died in our place bearing the punishment for our sins, and was resurrected to a position of authority having accomplished his work. For those who believe, this means that we receive the forgiveness of sins, the righteousness of Christ, and become his people (e.g. Rom 3:21-31; Rom 5:12-21; Gal 3:1-14; 1 Corinthians 15). This is where the emphasis in the New Testaments falls.

However, to understand how the New Testament relates to the Old Testament, we need to see that this is not the whole picture. When Jesus preached the Gospel, he declared that "The time is fulfilled, and the kingdom of God is at hand; repent and believe in the gospel" (Mark 1:15). This is also the way that Luke summarizes Paul's ministry, "He lived [in Rome] two whole years at his own expense, and welcomed all who came to him, **proclaiming the kingdom of God** and teaching about the Lord Jesus Christ with all boldness and without hindrance" (Acts 28:30-31, emphasis added). Romans begins on this note, Paul was "set apart for the gospel of God, which he promised beforehand through his prophets in the holy Scriptures, concerning his Son, who was **descended from David according to the flesh** and was declared to be the **Son of God in power** according to the Spirit of holiness by his resurrection from the dead" (Rom. 1:1-4, emphasis added). The kingdom of God is the goal of the historical events proclaimed in the Gospel and the transformation of persons achieved by the Gospel. We could, then, consider "kingdom" a third facet, or perspective, on the Gospel: the Gospel concerns historical events (Jesus's life, death, and resurrection) with present effects transforming persons (repent and believe and you will be saved) to be part of God's kingdom.

The kingdom of God in its earthly aspect thus corresponds to the second part of the great commission: Jesus says that he has all authority (Matt 28:18), which results in a commission for his people to go and to make and mature disciples (Matt 28:19-20). As there was an original commission to expand God's earthly kingdom in Genesis 1:28, believers have now inherited a command fitting Christ's present kingdom: expand the Church making disciples, baptizing them, and teaching them. Jesus died on the cross as a substitute for our sins and fulfilled God's law on our behalf in order that we might be delivered from this corrupt world (Gal 1:3-5) and be reconciled to God, having peace with him (Rom 1:16-18, Rom 5:1, 2 Cor 5:11-21). The goal of this rescue and the transformation that follows (sanctification and glorification) is that we might enjoy God forever under his benevolent rule and that we might fulfil his purpose for man as those who would rule under his authority over his creation.

This is the kingdom, but the kingdom is not passive: it is active; it is on mission. Christians are charged with extending this earthly kingdom—consisting of subjects of the King who confess his Lordship as part of the Church—in a world hostile to it. Because the success of this mission is guaranteed, there is one more aspect of the kingdom that is talked about in Scripture, its future consummation.

c. God's Eschatological Reign

According to 1 Corinthians 15:20-58, Christ is putting an end to the rebellion of his creatures through his people (cf. Rom 15:20). When he returns and puts an end to death and Hell, he will hand the kingdom over to the Father, and it will become the possession of all his people (1 Cor 15:24, 50). All sin and death will be crushed, and the people of God will rule over a new creation with Christ in the full enjoyment of the presence of God (Revelation 20-21). This is the hope of the Christian and all the creation (cf. Rom 8:18-25), when Christ returns, puts an end to sin and rebellion, and dwells bodily with his people. At that time, the kingdom will be fully consummated; at that time, the heavenly kingdom will be identical with the earthly kingdom of God.

In this chapter, we have considered three key teachings of the Bible, three essential pieces of the biblical worldview. We considered some of the glorious revelation of our God in Scripture, skimming quickly over the fathomless depths of his wonders. We also considered man as created, fallen, and redeemed. Finally, we considered the Kingdom of God in the various ways it is presented in Scripture. With this foundation in place, we will consider in the chapter that follows the **metanarrative** Scripture gives us.

FURTHER READING

*J. I. Packer – *Knowing God* [B]

John Frame – *Systematic Theology* [I]

*John Frame – *The Doctrine of God* [A]

Greg Gilbert – *What is the Gospel?* [B]

R. C. Sproul – *The Character of God: Discovering the God Who Is* [B]

R. C. Sproul – *The Holiness of God* [B]

Wayne Grudem – *Systematic Theology* [B-I]

Wayne Grudem – *Bible Doctrine* [B]

3

THE BIBLE'S WORLDVIEW - STORY

> Then God said, "Let us make man in our image, after our likeness. And let them have dominion over the fish of the sea and over the birds of the heavens and over the livestock and over all the earth and over every creeping thing that creeps on the earth."
>
> > So God created man in his own image,
> > in the image of God he created him;
> > male and female he created them.
>
> And God blessed them. And God said to them, "Be fruitful and multiply and fill the earth and subdue it, and have dominion over the fish of the sea and over the birds of the heavens and over every living thing that moves on the earth."
> – Genesis 1:26-28

So far we have considered the Bible as a united covenant document written for the New Covenant people of God, providing them with a worldview and with instruction so that they can know God, be transformed into the image of Christ, and pursue God's purpose in this creation. Historically, the Bible's teaching has often been expounded in a similar manner to the last couple of chapters, a systematic presentation of the vast teachings of Scripture. This discipline, known as systematic theology, takes the testimony of Scripture and applies it to the pressing questions and dilemmas of our age.[1] Systematic theology has a great historic pedigree and is essential to our use of the Bible.

In recent years, however, another aspect of the Bible has become the object of focus. It has been rightly observed that the Bible not only provides us with truths about the world but also gives a story that explains the world. The study of this story is often called biblical theology. Such a story is known as a metanarrative, an overarching story that gives meaning to everything within a worldview. Every worldview has a metanarrative; it presents an account of the beginning of time, prophecies about its end, and attempts to give a united account of all that transpires between the beginning and the end.[2] Like a novel, a worldview presupposes the there is a plot for the world: it presents a linear progression of events that move from something (the beginning) towards something else (an end). For the Christian, the comparison between a literary narrative and the biblical metanarrative is even more striking; as a novel is characterized by an author and a plot, so the biblical metanarrative is a plot authored by God—everything happens according to his preordained plan (Eph. 1:9-10). The biblical metanarrative is, therefore, the story that gives meaning to everything, that explains and gives significance to each object and action in the world.

The biblical metanarrative does not tell us anything different than a systematic account of the biblical data could but considers the Bible from a different perspective. We often talk about the features of the biblical metanarrative in non-narrative form, as we sometimes talk about systematic truths in narrative form. Yet we need both these perspectives. Systematic theology is great for bringing the whole Bible to bear on specific questions, yet in doing so, it is fragmentary. It so focuses on one aspect of the Bible's teaching that it must push aside the consideration of others. This is helpful and necessary, yet the resulting doctrines are sufficient to answer the question

---

[1] Systematic theology has been conceived in various ways, but I believe that John Frame's definition does the most justice to what we have already seen about the nature of the Bible: "theology is *the application of Scripture, by persons, to every area of life*," "*systematic* theology seeks to apply Scripture by asking what the *whole* Bible teaches about any subject." In *Systematic Theology*, pgs. 8-9.

[2] The metanarrative of many eastern worldviews is actually cyclical, where the end feedbacks into the beginning and the process is repeated endlessly. This remains a metanarrative, for it is essential to understanding how these worldviews attempt to give meaning to present events.

that raised them but not all the questions that could be answered. It is necessary to continually produce systematic theological treaties (in the form of sermons, letters, books, blog posts, etc.) as new questions arise or old answers are called into question. The result is fragmentary: it needs something to unite it. Thus we come to the narrative aspect of Scripture's teaching; the biblical metanarrative gives unity to the otherwise fragmented pieces of systematic theology. It answers "why questions"; it gives purpose to systematic theological endeavours.

The biblical story gives unity to the stories, events, truths, etc. given in Scripture. It is God's interpretation of created History, his narrative, given to us in Scripture. What, then, is this story? I think it is best summarized as *the story of God's kingdom extending throughout the creation through his covenants in order that the fullness of his glory might be displayed throughout the universe.*[3]

A. THE PROLOGUE: CREATION & FALL

We can identify four major movements in the history of God's created order. The first movement is the prologue; it sets the stage for God's redemptive acts to follow. The prologue to the biblical metanarrative features both the initial creation and then the fall. After the fall, God begins to redeem his creation. The first movement of redemption is the Old Covenant (or covenants). The Old Covenant refers primarily to the relationship between God and his people legislated at Sinai, but also to the covenants which preceded this, namely the relationship God enters into with Abraham and his descendants. These covenants govern a relationship between God and his people through which he intended to redeem the world. The second movement of redemption is the New Covenant; through Jesus Christ, God acts to achieve the redemption anticipated under the Old Covenant. The third movement of redemption is the consummation, when God will complete the work promised in the Old Covenant and achieved in the New Covenant. We will consider each of these in turn.

---

[3] For this formulation, I am heavily indebted to the work of Peter J. Gentry and Stephen J. Wellum in the book *Kingdom Through Covenant*.

a. Creation

The biblical metanarrative begins with the creation. Actually, the story begins before the creation. Before the foundations of the world were laid, God the Father, Son, and Holy Spirit dwelt in perfect unity and chose to create a world in which the fullness of their glory would be displayed. A world that would display the goodness of their wisdom in creation, the severity of their justice in judgment, and the magnitude of their mercy in redemption. According to this eternal plan, Yahweh spoke the creation into existence.[4]

In the beginning, God created everything that exists. His creation was good, and its pinnacle was man, a creature made in his image. On the sixth day of Creation, God personally formed and gave life to the first man and woman, Adam and Eve. Yahweh charged them with the task of expanding his rule in the world. They were to multiply and put the creation to service under their authority, to steward and use it to image him.

b. Fall

However, trouble was brewing even as God commissioned the first humans to expand his kingdom in the creation. Behind the scenes, a rebellion was unfolding. Though the details are few, it appears that one of God's angels led a cohort of others in rebellion against their creator. This devil, Satan, then entered earth in the guise of a snake in order to bring man into his rebellion. He found an opportunity in God's command given to Adam that neither he nor his wife was to eat of the tree of good and evil located in their garden home. With a clever twisting of God's word, the tempter presented Eve with the opportunity to seize autonomy, to determine whom she would trust. Faced with the choice between the word of her creator God and the promise of better things if only she ate what was forbidden, she chose to believe the lies of the serpent and disobey God. Her husband, having first allowed her to enter into temptation and sin, then joined in her rebellion and sided with the serpent against God.

---

[4] On God's plan and creation, consider especially Eph 1:10-14, Eph 3:7-13, Rom 9:19-24. For specific examples that show how God's actions are intended to magnify his character—demonstrate his glory—consider Hab 2:6-20 and its central verse 2:14; also, Exod 9:16 (quoted in Rom 9:17-18).

This was the fall, the rebellion of humanity's first parents; the consequences of this one event are incalculable. Judgment came quickly, yet not without mercy. God drew forth a confession of guilt from his sinful creatures, yet instead of pronouncing judgment right then and there, he showed mercy. Spilling the first blood of the created order, he himself slew an animal to cover over their sin. The good creation now felt the stain of sin in the loss of life, yet the death promised to Adam and Eve was suspended, transferred to the first sacrifice. Death was stayed for the moment, yet their sin would not be without consequences.

No longer would they have access to eternal life in fellowship with God, the promise of the garden; now they would face physical death and one day final judgment. No longer would their task of expanding God's kingdom go forth without impediment. Instead, their task would be characterized by conflict. First, the created order would rebel against them; for the woman, her role in multiplying heirs of the kingdom would be cursed with severe pain. For the man, the ground itself would impede his task, multiplying the toil of his labour to express dominion. Second, humanity would rebel against itself; as an example of every other human relationship, the closest human relationship, marriage, would be characterized by strife. No longer would a man lead in humble submission to God; instead, he would exert his own autonomy over his wife. In turn, instead of trusting submission, his wife would seek to usurp the role given to her husband by God.[5] Third, the kingdom of God would no longer expand without opposition. As those who love God expand his kingdom, they would be opposed by another kingdom, that of the serpent. The offspring of the woman and the offspring of the serpent would be engaged in warfare: humanity would be divided between the serpent's servants and God's servants. Almost immediately the war began, with the righteous Abel slain by his brother Cain. Because they aligned

---

[5] Cf. Gen 3:16. Though the word describing the husband's rule over his wife is not necessarily negative, the word describing the wife's "desire" for her husband definitely is. It is probably the case then that both are meant to be read as negative, "desire against" and "tyrannize over." Examples of מָשַׁל (*mšl*, to rule) used negatively are Judg 14:4 and Isa 19:4. תְּשׁוּקָה (*tᵉsûqāh*, desire) occurs several verses later describing sin's desire to rule over man (Gen 4:7), again with מָשַׁל. The New Testament calls for a reversal of this curse: husbands are still to lead, yet they are to do so in submission to God and as servants for the betterment of their wives. Wives are to submit to their husbands and give them respect as they lead according to God's word (1 Cor 11:2-16; Eph 5:22-33; Col 3:18-19; 1 Pet 3:1-7).

themselves with Satan, Adam and Eve's offspring would be born into the kingdom of Satan, not the kingdom of God. The multiplying that was to spread the kingdom of God would seem to spread the kingdom of Satan.[6] Represented by Adam in covenant before God, all mankind was condemned to death and given over to be slaves of sin (Rom. 5:15-20, 6:1-14; 1 Cor 15:20-22, cf. 42-49).

Yet, even in the midst of these curses, God's mercy shines forth in the promise of victory. From that which was cursed, the pregnancy of the woman, would come forth God's ultimate victory. An offspring would be born who would crush the serpent, though this victory would not come without a cost. Thus begins redemption, the true story of the whole world. God's kingdom would break into hostile territory and expand to encompass the creation. God's redemption of the world can be considered in terms of its beginning in the Old Covenant, accomplishment in the New Covenant, and consummation in the New Creation.[7]

B. REDEMPTION INITIATED – THE OLD COVENANT(S)

a. God's Covenant with Noah

The world that came forth from the fall was not a pretty one: it was characterized by rampant sin—debauchery and idolatry of all sorts. Humanity took its great gifts—gifts intended by God for the furthering of his kingdom—and put them to work in building their own kingdom. The kingdom of man flourished, with God's people a mere speck in an ocean of evil. A speck though they may be, in the hands of God and in light of his promise to Eve, hope remained.

The birth of Seth evoked hope in Eve (Gen 4:25), yet he was not the offspring she had hoped for. Godly, yes, but not sufficient to overturn the enemy's kingdom. Finally, after years of sin, God acted once again in judgment. A flood to wipe out the inhabitants of the earth was his tool, yet

---

[6] Cf. Eph 2:1-5

[7] This storyline has often been divided into only three or four moments: Creation, Fall, Redemption, and (sometimes) Consummation. However, my teacher Brad Copp has observed that glossing all of God's redemptive action as "redemption" fails to reckon with the significance of Jesus Christ. This formulation is my own, developed from Brad's feedback.

again his mercy shown forth. To one man and his family, redemption was granted, deliverance from the judgment to come. With Noah, God committed to withhold such judgment again and commissioned him as he had Adam. Yet Noah was not the offspring anticipated; he sinned, and his sons were cursed. However, hope was particularly attached to the line of Shem.

b. *God's Covenant with Abraham*

Years passed, and humanity again multiplied, yet this multiplication was once again at the service of the kingdom of the serpent. Committed to their own glory, man sought to ascend to the heights of heaven, to be where God was. In mercy and in commitment to his covenant made with Noah, God refrained from obliterating humanity. Yet he cursed them once again. Divided by the barriers of language and location, they would not be able to work together to build their kingdom.

However, God was not without a plan. From this multitude of mankind, Yahweh chose a descendant of Shem named Abraham. From this man and his barren wife would come forth the redemption of humanity and hope for the creation. God covenanted with Abraham, promising to multiply his descendants innumerably and to give him a kingdom that would bless all the other families of the earth (cf. Gen 17:6). Yet Abraham was again not sufficient to follow his obligations; obedience escaped him.

However, the world was not doomed to a cycle of covenants and covenant breakers. As God's promises to Noah—promises which would prevent a repeat of the flood—moved forth the story of redemption, so also would his promises to Abraham. Yes, Abraham sinned, but God promised to credit his faith—as imperfect as it was—to him as *righteousness*. The very thing that the rest lacked, a right standing before God—the freedom from curse and the reception of blessing—would be Abraham's. This would not come from perfect covenant obedience, for Abraham had failed like the rest, but from God's own initiative.

In Genesis 15, we read of something unheard of in the history of Creation. Entering his world for a short time, God walked through the midst of the severed carcasses of birds and beasts that Abraham had prepared for a covenant-making ceremony. Though seemingly inconsequential, this would change the course of history: by doing this, by performing an ancient covenant ceremony in Abraham's place, God vowed to take upon himself the curses due to Abraham (cf. Jer 34:8-22). Instead of stripping Abraham of the promised blessings and replacing them with a curse, Yahweh—the Lord of all creation—promised to take the curse on himself and become Abraham's righteousness.[8] Thus, with the covenant between Yahweh and Abraham, the contours of God's plan to redeem the creation begin to appear. God would take upon himself the covenant curses and earn the covenant blessings of Abraham so that his offspring and all the nations of the earth might be blessed. What remains to be seen is how the offspring promised to Eve could possibly factor into God's plan to be the personal redeemer of Abraham and all the nations.

c. God's Covenant with Israel

Fast forward several hundred years, Abraham's descendants have multiplied greatly, yet they appear to be in no position to bless the earth. Enslaved under a wicked Egyptian king, they laboured hard while Pharaoh attempted to eradicate their children—endangering the promise of an offspring. Yet God was not silent, acting once again with salvation accompanying judgment. This time, God would judge Egypt to magnify his name across the earth and bring forth his chosen people.

The events that transpired from Moses's exile in Midian until Israel's arrival at Sinai, known as the Exodus, is one of the most significant events in Scripture. God's salvific action to deliver Israel from Egypt and bring judgment on their oppressors becomes the paradigm of all God's later salvific activities, including his climactic work through Jesus Christ. The pattern exemplified here, of salvation (for Israel) accompanying judgment (for Egypt), is repeated throughout the Bible. The goal of the Exodus was God's covenant made at Sinai. God did not redeem his people without a purpose; he did so in fulfilment of his promises to Abraham and in order to move forward his redemptive plan.

---

[8] Cf. Jer. 34. My explanation of this passage can be found in my paper, "Towards a Biblical Theology of Imputation," available at https://teleioteti.ca/resources/technical-papers/.

The covenant that resulted was grand; God ordained an entire society devoted to himself. Ruled by his righteous Law, Israel was to be a beacon of his glory shining amid the surrounding nations. They were to be a kingdom of priests mediating God to all peoples. Yet a problem remained; sin was still dominant. At the centre of the Law was a way to deal with this sin, yet it fell short of the promises made to Abraham. God instituted a sacrificial system that enabled faithful Israelites to be forgiven of their sins and that would remind each generation of the consequences of sin, death.

However, God had promised Abraham that he would take his people's curse upon himself and to be their righteousness; this is conspicuously absent from the covenant at Sinai. In place of God were mere animals. Furthermore, the requirement of obedience was magnified; only perfect obedience would bring blessing, anything else would lead to horrific curses.[9] It appears that this law, which promised life, could only be a means of death. As the following accounts of the Old Testament record, Israel did not and could not obey perfectly. Their disobedience was devastating, ultimately leading to the destruction of their homes and the exile from their land. However, hope was again built directly into the covenant. In the midst of Law was the repeated call for a changed heart: this was what Israel needed. However, such a change would have to be a miracle. Yet God promised to one day work this miracle, to circumcise the hearts of his people, to put the law in their hearts so that they could obey him.[10] The Law was good yet could only enslave under sin; it could not bring the redemption God promised.[11]

d. God's Covenant with David

The inability of God's covenant with Israel to bring about redemption is clear from the accounts of Joshua and Judges. God's people only descended into deeper and deeper sin. Though commissioned to expand his kingdom over against the kingdom of Satan, they were looking more and more like their

---

[9] Cf. Lev 18:5, Deuteronomy 27-29

[10] Cf. Deut 30:6. Deut 30:1-14 anticipates the reversal of Israel's exile by God's sovereign action. Though not commonly recognized, 30:10-14 looks to God's future action. For my translation and exegesis of this passage, see my paper "Do Not Say in Your Heart: An Exposition of Romans 10:1-8" and the first appendix of my book *Prevenient Grace: An Investigation into Arminianism* (2016, Teleioteti). Both are reprinted as appendices in *The Gift of Reading – Part 2*.

[11] Cf. Galatians 3, Romans 7.

neighbours. Yet amid an ever-darkening picture (the unfolding of God's words in Deuteronomy 27-29, 32), a glimmer of hope was once more found. Throughout the Prophets and the Writings, hope was found in a glorious day of Yahweh, when he would act on behalf of his people, repeat the Exodus, and rule once again over his people through an offspring of David. The source of this hope is God's words recounted in 2 Samuel 7.

Both books of Samuel are essentially prophetic, demonstrating God's purpose to bring his kingdom to bear in the creation through a Davidic priest-king.[12] After bringing his people into the land he had promised, God eventually gave them a king in the form of David.[13] Though imperfect, David was chosen by God to be the channel through whom salvation would come.

If God's promise to Eve of an offspring leads us to anticipate a child who would destroy Satan and his kingdom, 2 Samuel 7 brings this hope to bear on a descendant of David. God would make a covenant with David's offspring, give him an eternal priesthood and kingdom, and would be to him a father and make him a son. This child would build Yahweh a temple. Though 1 Kings might lead us to think that this is fulfilled in Solomon, it is clear that Solomon and his temple were not the ultimate sources of hope.

God's action to redeem his people was still unfinished. In the years following David's reign, Israel continued its downward spiral, earning for itself destruction and exile. Though God gave great favour to his people and returned them from their physical exile, it is clear that their estrangement from him was never repaired. They remained under the law yet had sinful unchanged hearts. The temple they built failed to live up even to the glories of Solomon's. At the close of the Old Testament, God had not yet acted to bear their curse or give them the assurance of blessing. Though back in the land, God's people had not yet returned from exile.

---

[12] This is the subject of my master's thesis now printed as *God's Kingdom through his Priest-King* (Vancouver, Teleioteti 2019). This thesis is also available in its original form through the John Richard Allison Library (Regent College) and TREN, under the name James Rutherford.

[13] Saul, David's predecessor, was the king chosen by the people not by God. cf. 1 Samuel 8.

C. Redemption Accomplished – The New Covenant

Roughly 400 years after Israel returned from their physical exile in Babylon, something new began to happen. Though God seemed silent as his people languished under the rules of the Persians, the Greeks, and the Romans, change seemed to be happening. It began with a priest and his wife in their old age. Like Abraham and Sarah, God granted the gift of a child to a woman beyond the prime of her life. Elizabeth's unexpected pregnancy was accompanied by an astonishing encounter with an angel of the Lord. Zechariah's lack of faith when he heard the words of the angel resulted in a curse of silence; he was rendered mute. All wondered at the birth of their child John and the events surrounding his birth. Yet something even more amazing was happening within their family. God's plan continued to unfold through their relative Mary. God chose her to bear him a son, Immanuel, who would be conceived by the Holy Spirit, not a man. Immanuel, meaning "God with us," would be an offspring of David and God's presence with his people. Foreigners and Judeans were struck with wonder at the events unfolding in their midst.

Yet the kingdom of Satan would not stand by and be defeated without resistance. Through Herod came an attempt to wipe out the life of Mary's child. To escape his attempts, Mary and Joseph took Jesus, their child, to Egypt. For the discerning observer, how similar were these events to God's past actions! Though the enemy tried to wipe out the offspring of promise in Egypt and in Bethlehem, Israel and Jesus both survived. And as both came forth from Egypt to be God's people, so Israel and Jesus came forth to enter into God's purpose for them.[14] It seemed that God's purposes were finally coming to bear in history: God himself had entered into creation as a man to redeem his people.

In Jesus, the biblical metanarrative finds its climax. The promises made to David, that his son would sit on his throne, and the promises to Abraham, that God would bear the curse and bring the blessings of the covenant, found their fulfilment in him. In fact, all the promises of God found their fulfilment in him (2 Cor 1:20). We have already seen that his preaching ministry was focused on the proclamation of the kingdom; thus, in Jesus and his ministry,

---

[14] Matthew makes this connection in Matt 2:15.

the kingdom that had failed to expand under Noah, Abraham, Israel, and David began to expand in earnest. Beginning with twelve, it would spread in only short years to thousands and from thousands to millions. Jesus described it like a mustard seed; though beginning quite small, it would blossom into something huge. Yet if Jesus was to attain victory over the serpent, he would have to be struck; and if he was to fulfil the promises to Abraham, he would not only have to live a perfect life but die in place of Abraham and his descendants. In this way, his path to cross was laid long before his birth, and it transpired just as God's hand had ordained it to (Acts 2:23-24).

Jesus was a king, yet his path to the throne would be characterized by humble service, not violent rebellion. Eschewing every opportunity to seize his throne in other ways, Jesus intentionally set his face to Jerusalem and the cross he would bear there. His crucifixion was far from the glorious display of power Israel expected. Mocked, beaten, and spurned by the people he came to save, the Creator of the universe bore a wooden cross from Jerusalem to the hill upon which he would be slaughtered—buckling under its weight. The Lord of Glory, clothed in weakness, was nailed to a cross whose existence he planned before the foundations of the world, having brought into being the very tree from which it was hewn. Facing taunts to save himself as he had others, the eternal king hung bleeding from nails through his hands and feet. He was himself sustaining the very wood upon which he hanged as it sapped the life from him. Yet unseen to human eyes, something far more devastating was happening.

The only man who knew no sin was made sin for the sake of his people. He drank in full the cup of God's wrath they deserved. It was God's good will to strike him, and this he did (Isa 53:10). For the first time in all existence, something horrific happened between the members of the Trinity: God the Father forsake his beloved Son.

Yet that moment was not to last, having drunk fully from the cup of God's wrath, Jesus declared his task accomplished and gave up his life. The eternal God, dead at the hands of his creation. At that moment, the earth shook, the heavens darkened, and the dead were raised to walk the streets of Jerusalem.[15] Yet far more significant was an event not seen by the common

---

[15] On the rather bizarre occurrence of the dead rising, see Matt 27:52-53.

man. While the earth shook, the veil that closed the Holy God off from his people in Herod's temple was split. The heavy curtain was split from top to bottom: no more would God be separated from his people by their sin. In heaven, Jesus's work continued as he applied his own sacrifice just made to his people, cleansing them. Three days after his death, his victory was guaranteed by his resurrection. Coming forth from the dead, Jesus became the first of a new creation breaking into the old. After visiting and teaching his disciples, appearing to hundreds, he finally took his throne on High. Receiving all authority, he rules over the kingdom he created. By the blood of his sacrifice, something new began, a New Covenant to replace the Old. With this New Covenant came a new form of God's kingdom.

The New Covenant in Jesus blood brings all the promises of the Old Covenant(s) to his people; the full forgiveness of sins anticipated by the sacrificial system, new hearts enabling obedience to God, final victory over Satan, and an eternal kingdom over a new creation under the rule of a Davidic priest-king. However, though these were all bought completely through Jesus' life, death, and resurrection, they were not inaugurated fully at his ascension. Before ascending to sit at the right hand of the Father, Jesus commissioned his disciples to expand his kingdom on earth by making disciples. The New Covenant thus changed the nature of the kingdom and guaranteed the success of its expansion, but it did not yet usher in its fullness. Its promises are already here, yet they are not yet completed.[16] God's people have been given a strategic role in fulfilling this purpose, in expanding his kingdom.

After Jesus ascension, the story continued on the trajectory he set. His people went out and preached the Gospel, making disciples and expanding the kingdom in Judea, Samaria, and to the ends of the earth. At the close of the New Testament, the Gospel had spread throughout the known world, at least as far as Rome, maybe even to Spain. And wherever the Gospel spread, the Kingdom of God manifest itself in churches, in local groups of his people united in their purpose to see the great commission fulfilled. Though no single local church was or is perfect, Jesus's kingdom has progressively expanded through the preaching of the Gospel until the present age, where his name is proclaimed on every continent. Yet the biblical metanarrative

---

[16] In New Testament studies, "Already-Not-Yet" is a common way to refer to this suspension of fulfilment.

does not end with the last events of the apostles as recorded in Scripture; it also speaks of what is next.

D. Redemption Consummated – The New Creation

According to Jesus, his absence would not be long. He told the apostle John that he was coming quickly to finish what he had begun. He would come back, raising his people to new life, delivering final judgment, and beginning the new creation. From our perspective, his return has been delayed; almost 2000 years have passed, and he has not yet returned. Do not be deceived, warns Peter, though all things appear unchanged, God is not slow to fulfil his promises (2 Pet 3:1-13). God's patience is great as he gives men and women one final chance at repentance, yet we are not to count this patience as an opportunity for sin. Jesus has for 2000 years stood at the threshold: considering the plan of God in terms of major events, only one remains. All of God's promises have come to pass except the return of Christ to bring judgment and final salvation to his people, to recreate all things and dwell with his people. Therefore, history stands in tension: we are at its end, yet that end has not yet arrived. At any moment Jesus could cross that threshold and usher in glory. All creation is at the razor's edge of the passing of ages, with the consummation of all things a hairsbreadth away. And when that threshold is crossed, no word suffices to give an account of that future.

Far from a boring life sitting upon a cloud picking at harps, the consummation of Christ's kingdom will not end time but transform it. With all opposition ended, God's kingdom will extend unabated for endless ages as his people delight in him, in his glorious presence with his people. They will endeavour to bring him glory through the labour of their hands, no longer cursed to futility by sin.

This is my sketch of the story that unites all history and all the events of the Bible. It is only a sketch; much more could be said about all the events recounted, the characters that experienced them, their significance, and the God who orchestrated them. For this, we must turn to the Bible. The story just recounted will help us make sense of the events of the Bible and the purpose behind them, but one question remains before we can turn to the skills we need to read the Bible well: what is our place in all of this?

FURTHER READING

Graeme Goldsworthy – *According to Plan* [B]
Stephen G. Dempster – *Dominion and Dynasty* [I]
*Peter J. Gentry and Stephen J. Wellum – *Kingdom through Covenant* [A]
*Peter J. Gentry and Stephen J. Wellum – *God's Kingdom through God's Covenant* [B-I]

THE PEOPLE(S) OF THE BIBLE

And I will make of you a great nation, and I will bless you and make your name great, so that you will be blessing. I will bless those who bless you, and him who dishonors you I will curse, and in you all the families of the earth shall be blessed.
– Genesis 12:2-3

Considering the theology and story of the Bible as we have in the last two chapters should raise some questions. Namely, where do we fit into the biblical worldview? How does the story of the Bible and the theology recounted earlier relate to us? What is the place of those who believe in Jesus Christ, the New Covenant people of God? Such are the questions we will consider in this chapter. We are those upon whom the end of the age has come, those for whom the Bible was written (1 Cor 10:11). Living in the time between Christ's first and second coming, we are called by God to be ambassadors of a new creation, of Christ's kingdom as it breaks into this hostile World. In a word, *Christians are God's chosen and redeemed people who are called to be transformed into the image of Christ as they seek to expand God's kingdom on earth.* Our identity, our place in the world, can be considered from these three perspectives—as those redeemed, commissioned, and becoming like Christ.

Yet the unique place of Christians in this world, especially as it will impact our reading of the Bible, needs to be understood in light of the Old Testament people of God. Because God's acts to redeem Israel and then Christians, through the Exodus and then the Cross, established them as a distinct people in relationship with him, I will consider God's work to redeem Israel and then the Church as their establishment as his people. Therefore, I intend for us in this chapter to consider first the establishment, commission, and nature of the Old Covenant people of God. Then we will, in contrast, consider our place as the New Covenant people of God.

A. THE OLD COVENANT PEOPLE OF GOD

> You yourselves have seen what I did to the Egyptians, and how I bore you on eagles' wings and brought you to myself. Now therefore, if you will indeed obey my voice and keep my covenant, you shall be my treasured possession among all peoples, for all the earth is mine; and you shall be to me a kingdom of priests and a holy nation. – Exodus 19:4-6

As God began making covenants with those whom he chose in the Old Testament, his covenant people took on a definite shape. The Old Covenant people of God was Israel, the descendants of Abraham, Isaac, and Jacob. Made up of all those born into the community or who joined themselves to it, Israel was constituted as God's covenant community at Sinai after the Exodus. At Sinai, God entered a covenant with them (he would be their God, they would be his people) and delineates in great detail the nature of their relationship. As I suggested above, we can consider Israel from the perspective of how God prepared them as his people (establishment), what God has called them to (commission), and their particular character (nature).

a. *The Establishment of Israel*

Israel was at first distinguished from its neighbours by Yahweh's relation to them. Beginning with their ancestor Abraham, God chose Israel to be his people and continually acted in history on their behalf. The most significant act he performed on their behalf was the Exodus from Egypt. In fulfilment of his promises to Abraham, Yahweh performed a great act of redemption, bringing forth his people while judging Egypt. Through this act, he would establish them as his people under his covenant.

Yahweh acted towards them in a distinct manner from his interactions with nations around Israel; he made them his people. By redeeming them from Egypt and then binding himself to them in covenant, God set them apart from their neighbours and gave them a divine commission to be his people.

b. *The Commission of Israel*

God's people were distinguished from the rest of the nations by their unique calling. Israel was not chosen by God to be a stagnant blob on a map, to be a comfortable kingdom content with secure borders. They were redeemed for a mission. In the last chapter, we saw how the nation of Israel was part of the plan to fulfil God's promise to make Abraham a blessing to the nations. They were created to be "a kingdom of priests and a holy nation" (Exod 19:5), a nation set apart for God's purpose and mediators between God and the surrounding nations.

The first thing that may come to mind when we think of Israel's commission is the holiness aspect: we may recall seemingly endless pages of law indicating how Israel was to be distinct from its neighbours (not eating certain foods, acting in peculiar ways, avoiding certain practices). Even the most obscure of these laws functions to visually demonstrate Israel's calling to be a holy people dedicated to God. Consider, for example, the law to not wear garments made of mixed fabrics: the purity of fabric provides a visual reminder of Israel's nature as a community distinct from all others, not mixed (Lev 19:19). The same can be said of the food laws; they were to eat animals that did not mix features, again a reflection of Israel's separation from their neighbours (Lev. 11:1-8).[1] Yet what we may miss in the sea of legislation is that they were not only set apart *from* the other nations but ultimately *for* the other nations.

As God's people on earth, Israel was (intended to be) God's representatives on earth. In all their behaviour, they were to radiate his character to those around them. Sometimes this representation was fulfilling God's goals on earth, such as enacting his judgment. Examples of this may immediately leap to mind, such as Israel's commission to bring God's judgment on the Canaanites by wiping them out (cf. Gen 15:16, The Book of Joshua) or the commission God gave Saul to wipe out the Amalekites (1 Sam 15:1-23).[2] However, the emphasis of the Law is not on such actions or on any explicit actions to reconcile the other nations with God. Instead, they were to live their lives individually and nationally as an image of God in the

---

[1] This insight is from Bruce Waltke, from a class he taught on Biblical Theology.

[2] I discuss accounts of God's acts of judgment recorded in the Old Testament at greater depth in my Habakkuk study guide, *Believe the Unbelievable: A Study in Habakkuk* (Teleioteti, 2018).

creation: they were to be holy as he was holy (Lev 11:44). This is why the reason frequently given for the particular laws governing Israel was "for I am YHWH" (e.g. Lev 18:4-6, 21).[3] God brought them forth from Egypt to make his name known and constituted them as a nation to do the same.

If they were obedient to his commands, they would image him in his creation and receive blessings upon their land and lives, showing his power and beneficence. In this way, other nations were to be drawn to the God of Israel: this is seen at some points throughout Israel history (Josh 9:1-27; 1 Kings 10:1-13). Yet, instead of being obedient to God and remaining distinct from the nations, Israel began even from the time it first entered Canaan to conform itself less to God's Law than to the surrounding nations (consider The Book of Judges). They ultimately failed to be holy as God was holy and so failed to be light to the nations.[4] This brings us to on last important perspective by which we must view the Old Testament people of God.

c. *The Nature of Israel*

To this point, we have seen how Israel related to those around it, how the Exodus distinguished and established them and that their commission was to image God over against their neighbours. However, we have not said anything about Israel's "salvation." Salvation broadly conceived of in the Bible is a right relationship with God and the enjoyment of the blessings that follow from this relationship. Israel's experience of salvation was not completely different from ours as New Testament believers, yet it is important to observe that it was not a universal experience. In Paul's words, not all Israel was true Israel, the inheritors of God's promises (Romans 9). Israel was what is sometimes called a mixed community: the **covenant community** consisted of both those who loved and believed in God *and*

---

[3] In Biblical quotations, I prefer to transliterate the Hebrew name of God instead of translating it LORD or Yahweh. Among many reasons for this, two are important for our purposes here. On the one hand, Yahweh is God's personal name given to his people so they might know him; on the other hand, because of the history of translations, God's name is found in the New Testament as "The Lord." By transliterating God's name, I hope to lead the reader to think of God's personal name while at the same time making the connection to the New Testament use of Lord.

[4] The Book of Jonah appears to be an indictment of the inward focus of Israel, their ignorance of God's greater purpose to make them a blessing to the nations.

those who were ambivalent or against God.[5] In the language of Habakkuk, some were righteous but others wicked (Hab 1:13, 2:4).

Salvation was available to Israel: they could be right with God, be righteous, but not all Israel had this salvation. According to Deuteronomy and Leviticus, to enjoy the blessings of God's covenant, Israel and the people within it needed to be flawlessly obedient (e.g. Lev 18:5; Deut 28:1-2). It is quickly evident that even the best of them could not do this, yet we learn throughout the Old Testament that a right relationship with God could not and so did not come from perfect obedience to the Law and through the sacrificial system (e.g. Psalm 51). At the height of Israel's sin, Habakkuk makes explicit that like Abraham before them, the righteous of Israel were not identified by their perfect obedience but by their belief in God, even when he acted in unbelievable ways (Hab 2:4, cf. 1:5). Thus, Israel was a community of believers (the righteous) and the unbelievers (the wicked) united in a relationship with God. This mixed nature ultimately led to their exile; the nation as a whole was characterized by wickedness and unbelief—only a remnant of righteous ones remained (e.g. 1 Kgs 19:18).

Israel as a whole lacked hearts of obedience towards God. Such a heart was something only God could grant them, and he had not yet done so. Yet he promised that a day would come when he would (Deut 30:6). This became the great hope of the Prophets. Jeremiah spoke of a day when Yahweh would

> make a new covenant… not like the covenant I made with their fathers on the day when I took the by the hand to bring them out of the land of Egypt, my covenant that they broke, though I was their husband, declares the LORD. For this is the covenant that I will make with the house of Israel after those days, declares the LORD: I will put my law within them, and I will write it on their hearts. And I will be their God, and they shall be my people. And no longer shall each on teach his neighbor and each his brother, saying, "Know the LORD," for they shall all know me, from the least of them to the greatest, declares the

---

[5] **Covenant community** refers to a body of people represented together in covenant. Under the New Covenant, the covenant community consists of all those who truly have believed, believe, and will believe in Jesus Christ (past, present, and future). Under the Old Covenant, all ethnic Israel (or at least those who were circumcised or connected to a male who was circumcised) and the sojourners who attached themselves to Israel were part of the covenant community.

LORD. For I will forgive their iniquity, and I will remember their sin no more. (Jer 31:31-34)

No longer would the people of God be mixed like Israel in the Old Testament, promised Yahweh. They would no longer be a community of the faithful and the unfaithful; no longer would anybody have to labour to get their brother to know God, for everyone in the covenant would know him.

Israel was a redeemed earthly nation called to image God among their neighbours, to be holy as he is holy, yet they failed this mission. They were not consistently a faithful people; they were perpetually marked by the presence of the faithful and the unfaithful in their midst. Though there always remained a remnant that trusted in Yahweh, their numbers were small, and they were surrounded by wickedness (cf. Hab 1:1-4), but God promised that a day would come when this would change. The Law that governed them would no longer be external; instead, it would be inside them (Jer 31:31-34; Isa 54:13; Ezek 36:25-27; cf. Deut 30:6-14 (in Hebrew)).[6] When this covenant came, a new covenant community came into existence.

B. THE NEW COVENANT PEOPLE OF GOD

> But you are a chosen race, a royal priesthood, a holy nation, a people for his own possession, that you may proclaim the excellencies of him who called you out of darkness into his marvelous light. – 1 Peter 2:9

As one reads the New Testament, it becomes evident that the Church bears some continuities with Israel: for one, we receive all the promises of God through Christ (2 Cor 1:20), and Paul places us in continuity with the true "Israel" (cf. Rom 9-11, Gal 6:16). Yet discontinuities also appear: the hope of Jeremiah is fulfilled in the Church, meaning that his picture of a believing community is realized in the Church (e.g. John 3:5-8, cf. Ezek 36:25-27; John 6:44-45, cf. Isa 54:13; Rom 10:5-17, cf. Deut 30:6-14; Heb 8, cf. Jer 31:31-

---

[6] For Deut 30:6-14, see the first appendix of my *Prevenient Grace* and my paper "Do Not Say in Your Heart," reprinted in the appendices of *The Gift of Reading – Part 2*.

34).[7] In addition, the New Testament is clear that Christians are not bound by the regulations of the Torah in the way Israel was (e.g. Acts 10:9-33; Gal 2:15-21, 3:1-6, 4:1-7, 5:1-2). This change is responsible for some of the greatest difficulties facing Christians as we seek to apply Scripture to our lives.

All Scripture was written for us, yet we are not simply Israel 2.0. We are a different community established in a different manner, with a distinct commission and nature, meaning that our obedience to God looks differently. The Old Testament was written for us, yet instructions that revealed God's character as it would be expressed through an earthly kingdom will look very different when applied to a community defined spiritually, not physically.

a. The Establishment of Church

Israel's Exodus was physical, from slavery to freedom in the promised land. Christians also undergo an Exodus, yet this one was spiritual: from slavery under sin to freedom in Christ Jesus (Romans 6, cf. Gal 5:1). The formative event for the Church was not the physical defeat of Egypt and the Canaanites but the crucifixion and resurrection of God on their behalf. As physical redemption established a physical nation and physical kingdom, so spiritual redemption established a spiritual nation and spiritual kingdom.

This is the first fundamental distinction between the Church and Israel: though Israel was a physical kingdom with land and distinct physical presence, the Church is the manifestation of an invisible kingdom without a land (at least not in this age) and without a distinct physical presence. That is, if one were to gather all the local churches together, this would not be the Church, nor would an earthly "Christendom," a nation-state defined by Christian values, be the Church. The Church is an exiled people sojourning in a foreign land (cf. 1 Pet 1:1; Hebrews 11).

b. The Commission of Church

---

[7] This is not to say, of course, that everyone in a local church really believes in Jesus. This is, unfortunately, not always the case. There are unbelievers and believers who both claim Christ as their own, yet God's covenant is only with the believers—the "invisible Church"—and thus his promises towards them and the success of his mission through them is guaranteed.

As exiles in a strange land, Christians also have a different commission than Israel. They are not to expand the Kingdom of God in a physical manner, radiating his image as a nation in the midst of other nations. Instead, they have been commissioned to "Go... and make disciples of all nations, baptizing them in the name of the Father and of the Son and of the Holy Spirit, teaching them to observe all that I have commanded you" (Matt 28:19-20). Thus, though both Israel and the Church were commissioned to extend God's kingdom, the way this commission manifests is different. Christians are told to "seek first the kingdom of God and his righteousness" (Matt 6:33), yet this looks dramatically different than the instructions originally given to Adam and Eve and legislated for Israel.

The great commission is a command to multiply and solidify the kingdom of God as it is expressed in the Church. That is, the Church is commissioned to make disciples and mature them. We can consider the form this takes in the New Testament in terms of three contrasts between the Old Covenant and New Covenant people of God: internal versus external holiness, church versus political polity, and exilic versus secure existence.

i. Internal Versus External Holiness

Concerning holiness, what in Israel was external holiness becomes for the Church internal holiness. Christians, like Israel, are called to be holy as God is holy (1 Peter 2), and this holiness has consequences for the relationship of Christians with those outside the Church. Yet, instead of radical physical separation (i.e. do not associate in any way), the New Testament calls for radical spiritual separation while being physically present among unbelievers.

Jesus, praying to the Father, is clear that his desire is not for Christians to separate from the world; in fact, he sent them into the world (John 17:15, 18). He stresses that Christians are foreigners in the world, sent into it from the outside: "the world has hated them because they are not of the world, just as I am not of the world" (John 17:14). Paul makes the same point,

> I wrote to you in my letter not to associate with sexually immoral people— not at all meaning the sexually immoral of this world, or the greedy and swindlers, or idolaters, since then you would need to go out of the world. But now I am writing to you not to associate with anyone who bears the name of brother if he is guilty of sexual immorality or greed, or is an idolater, reviler, drunkard, or swindler—not even to eat with such a one. (1 Cor 5:9-11)

Christians are commissioned to exist in the world, to be present and active among those who do not believe—how else will they hear the Gospel! Yet, Christians are never to forget that their presence in the world does not mean that they are part of the world. The spiritual separation signified by the Christian's non-worldly nature manifests throughout the New Testament as a radical commitment to the Church and the kingdom at the expense of worldly pursuits.

Consider several examples. A Christian's primary relationships in the world are with the Church even over their relationship with biological family (Matt 10:34-39; 12:46-50; Luke 14:26-27). This even transforms marital commitments: Christians are to hold fast to their spouse even if they are an unbeliever, but if an unbelieving spouse leaves a believer, the latter is not bound to the usual laws concerning remarriage after divorce. And for those unmarried, Christians are only permitted to marry believers (1 Cor 7:10-16, 39-40). Not only are Christians called to separate in these ways from intimate family, but Christians are also commanded to abstain from aligning their purposes with an unbeliever:

> Do not be unequally yoked with unbelievers. For what partnership has righteousness with lawlessness? Or what fellowship has light with darkness? What accord has Christ with Belial? Or what portion does a believer share with an unbeliever? What agreement has the temple of God with idols? For we are the temple of the living God; as God said,
>
> > I will make my dwelling among them and walk among them,
> > > and I will be their God,
> > > and they shall be my people.
> > Therefore go out from their midst,
> > > and be separate from them, says the Lord,
> > and touch no unclean thing;
> > > then I will welcome you,
> > and I will be a father to you,
> > > and you shall be sons and daughters to me,
> > says the Lord Almighty.
>
> Since we have these promises, beloved, let us cleanse ourselves from every defilement of body and spirit, bringing holiness to completion in the fear of God. (2 Cor 6:14-7:1)

In this text, Old Testament holiness laws are applied to the spiritual separation to which Paul calls Christians. As the church lives out this spiritual separation, they shine for the world to see. Jesus puts it in this way,

> You are the light of the world. A city set on a hill cannot be hidden. Nor do people light a lamp and put it under a basket, but on a stand, and it gives light to all in the house. In the same way, let your light shine before others, so that they may see your good works and give glory to your Father who is in heaven. (Matt 5:14-16)

ii. Church Versus National Polity

As the change in the nature of the Church shifted the manifestation of holiness, it also changes the focus of many features of national life in the Old Testament. In the Old Testament, Israel, as a physical kingdom, had legal legislation to reflect God's character towards those in need. There were laws to regulate slavery and indicate where it was appropriate, instructions for leaving food at harvest for those who could not afford it, and instructions for carrying on the family line and inheritance in light of unexpected deaths. All of these had a function analogous to modern social welfare, only they were to be performed by individuals towards the rest of the nation of Israel and not by the state.

In the New Testament, similar provisions are made, yet their focus shifts from the national sphere to the local church. Paul leads the churches in making provision for widows (1 Tim 5:3-16), for the poor (e.g. 2 Cor 9:1-5, cf. Rom 15:25), and instructs slaves to use their slavery as a Gospel opportunity (e.g. Eph 6:5-9). Even work is encouraged towards these ends; it is encouraged so that the ministry of the Church is not burdened but supported (Eph 4:28, cf. 2 Thess 3:6-12). This church focus is summarized in Galatians 6:10 in this way, "So then, as we have opportunity, let us do good to everyone, and especially to those who are of the household of faith." The focus of allegiance and societal structures which had a national character under the Old Covenant are shifted to the Church and its local manifestations.

iii. Exilic Versus Secure Existence

Lastly, Christians are called not to the security of an earthly home like Israel had in the promised land. Instead, they are called to live as exiles within an alien land. In Hebrews 11, the author presents the heroes of the Old

Testament as examples of those who endured the hardships of life by setting their hope on a secure inheritance awaiting them in the future, a secure heavenly Jerusalem:

> By faith Abraham obeyed when he was called to go out to a place that he was to receive as an inheritance. And he went out, not knowing where he was going. By faith he went to live in the land of promise, as in a foreign land, living in tents with Isaac and Jacob, heirs with him of the same promise. For he was looking forward to the city that has foundations, whose designer and builder is God. (Heb 11:8-10)

Like Abraham, who sojourned in alien lands, and Jesus, who found no home among his people and suffered outside Jerusalem, the author of Hebrews exhorts Christians, "let us go to [Jesus] outside the camp and bear the reproach he endured. For here we have no lasting city, but we seek the city that is to come" (Heb 13:13-14). Peter uses this image to set the tone of his first epistle, writing, "To those who are elect exiles" (1 Pet 1:1). Because Christians do not find a home in this world, it frees them to become what is necessary to see the Gospel spread (1 Cor 9:19-23), to go wherever is necessary (Rom 10:14-17), and to bear the reproach that comes with proclaiming Christ (Matt 5:2-12, 1 Pet 4:12-19).

These are some of the ways that the commission of the Christians defines them in ways that differ from Israel. One last perspective remains for us with which to consider the New Covenant People of God, their nature as a people being transformed.

c. *The Nature of the Church*

As a covenant community, Israel was characterized by a mixture of believers and unbelievers, meaning that some of the community possessed the Holy Spirit and obedient hearts while others did not. This has changed under the New Covenant; every Christian has received the Holy Spirit empowering them for ministry (cf. Joel 2:28-29, Acts 2:14-21), and everyone who believes in Jesus does so because they have received the promised new or circumcised heart (Deut 30:6; cf. John 3:1-8, John 6:44-45).

Because the Church is a believing covenant community, its nature is not defined by a mixture of unbeliever and believer. Instead, it is composed of believers who are being progressively transformed by Holy Spirit, setting aside their old selves to don the new self in Christ. Now, though everyone who is part of the covenant community is truly a Christian, the covenant community is not identical to the local church. The covenant community is the invisible Church, the sum total of all who truly believe throughout time. The visible church is composed of all who *claim* to believe, though not all who are part of the visible church are truly saved. Though God knows the scope of the invisible Church, it is impossible for us to identify at all times who have genuinely believed in Jesus Christ. The local church will strive to recognize only those who have truly believed as its members, yet it will not do so perfectly. Despite this qualification, this distinction is clear in Scripture and is relevant for church teachings concerning discipline and the nature of the church, among other things.

The continuing result of this transformation is the mutual ministry characterizing the Church. Israel was called to be a holy priesthood but failed in this. Christians are likewise a holy priesthood. Each Christian is enabled and equipped by Holy Spirit to walk in Spirit, performing good works towards the Church and then towards the outside world (Gal 5:1-6:10). This is especially manifest in ministry to one another as the Spirit equips (e.g. Rom 12:1-8; 1 Cor 12:1-31; Eph 4:11-16) and to the outside world so that they might hear the Gospel (Rom 10:14-17).

In a way, Christians are called to a more radical life than Israel. Israel was separate from the nations and would have enjoyed security and comfort in their own land if only they were obedient. Christians, on the other hand, are sent into a world that hates them in order to be instruments in God's hands as he saves that world. They live in a way that clearly distinguishes them but does not separate them; they are therefore open to ridicule as they live among other people in a way that is remarkably different. They exchange the allegiances of the world and its comforts for radical commitment to Christ and his Church.

The New Testament paints a picture of the Christian covenant community as one that is radically inward focused in order to be effective in reaching the world. Working together, they take care of one another's needs and see that everyone is growing up into the fullness of Christ. By doing this, they show the World their light shining like a city on a hill. The World is shown the heavenly Jerusalem imaged in the earthly church in order that they might give glory to God. This inward focus also provides the training and resources necessary to send Christians into other communities, cities, and countries in order that they might be an effective witness there. The commission to go out and make disciples, the outward focus, is thus inextricably tied to the inward focus of teaching them to obey Jesus's commandments. This is our place in the biblical story: we are God's people united in the local church on a mission to expand God's kingdom through the making and maturing of disciples.

Knowing our place, especially in contrast with God's Old Covenant people, will help us find our way as we apply Scripture, as we seek to understand how the biblical instructions direct us in living our New Covenant identity. When seeking to apply Old Covenant teaching to our New Covenant context, we must first understand what it meant for the Old Covenant people, identify the differences between the two covenants that are relevant to the application, and use the New Testament's explicit teachings as a guide to identify how this text applies to our new situation. For example, the holiness laws in Leviticus were meant to highlight the physical separation that characterized Israel. As the New Testament people of God, we are not called to be physically separate but spiritually separate. How, then, does this command to holiness apply to us today? Paul, for example, teaches that Christians should neither marry nor closely align themselves in purposes with unbelievers (1 Cor 7:39, 2 Cor 6:14-7:1), they should maintain a sort of separation; yet they are not to remove themselves entirely from these relationships (e.g. 1 Cor 5:9-13). We will consider the task of applying the Bible, including the Old Testament, further in the next part and in *The Gift of Reading – Part 2*. This should suffice for us now.

Understanding our place in Scripture is intimately connected with the metanarrative taught in Scripture; this narrative helps give us purpose and brings unity to the teachings and stories of the Bible. This narrative shows how all the events in Scripture and the lives of contemporary Christians are working together towards the fulfilment of God's purposes in the new creation. Knowing the theology of the Bible helps us begin to answer the questions raised in our reading of Scripture and to answer the questions raised as we interact with the Bible. Having these glasses, seeing the Bible as it is, will help us read the Bible profitably and not to distort it to fit any agenda other than the one for which God created it. However, having an idea of what the Bible teaches is not enough for reading it well. For this, we need to build good reading skills: we need ears to hear what the Lord is speaking.

FURTHER READING

John Frame – *The Doctrine of the Christian Life* [A]

Bruce Waltke – *Old Testament Theology* [A]

Peter J. Gentry and Stephen J. Wellum – *Kingdom Through Covenant* [A]

J. Alexander Rutherford – "Biblical Themes that Define Us," [https://teleioteti.ca/2017/11/01/biblical-themes-that-define-us-two-kingdoms/ [B]

J. Alexander Rutherford – "Christians and the World," https://teleioteti.ca/2017/11/29/christians-and-the-world-the-ethics-of-a-city-on-a-hill/ B]

J. Alexander Rutherford – "Is There a Cultural Mandate for Christians" https://teleioteti.ca/2018/01/31/2306/ [B-I]

—Part 2—

We Need Ears to Hear

5

KNOWING WHEN WE HAVE READ WELL

> And whoever will not listen to my words that he shall speak in my name, I myself will require it of him. – Deuteronomy 18:19

When God's people Israel did not listen to him, when they did not understand and obey, God "gave them over to their stubborn hearts, to follow their own counsel" (Ps 81:12). The result of this obedience was judgment culminating in exile. The fool in the Book of Proverbs is the one who ignores the voice of God, who rejects the fear of the Lord (e.g. Prov 1:7). His end is destitution and death (e.g. Prov 10:8). In Matthew, those who called on the name of Jesus but never submitted to him, who never obeyed his Father's commands, heard the devastating words, "I never knew you; depart from me, you workers of lawlessness" (Matt 7:23). To ignore the Word of the Lord, to fail to listen, results in destruction. We who believe in Christ do not want this end; we love our Lord and want to hear from him, "Well done, good and faithful servant" (Matt 25:23). It is imperative, then, that we recognize and obey the voice of our Lord as he has spoken in Scripture. Of course, in these passages "listen" focuses primarily on our response to the words, yet such a response has several preconditions. We need the proper framework to understand the words: we need the appropriate lens to clearly see what is being said, or we need to be tuned to the right frequency to hear it. We also need an obedient, humble heart to desire to respond to what we hear. But a right response is contingent on us not only receiving the message and having willing hearts but also listening carefully so that we understand what the Lord would have us do or believe.

As we will consider in the final part of this book, having a right heart is essential to listening well, yet it is not sufficient. What good would it do if our hearts were in the right place, but we were unable to understand who God is, what he has done for us, and how he has called us to live? In Deuteronomy 18, God speaks of a future prophet like Moses, a prophet God would raise up to speak his truth once more. When this prophet came, his words would be considered God's words, so obedience was essential—God would deal with disobedience (Deut 18:19)! We must, therefore, pay close attention to the words God has spoken; we must ensure that we hear appropriately so that we might obey.

In the beginning of this book, I said that to read the Bible, we need *eyes to see, ears to hear, and hearts to understand.* In the last four chapters, we considered the lens we need to read Scripture; we looked at what the Bible is and sketched its teaching. Using the analogy of sight, Part 1 has given us the right lens to bring the text of Scripture into focus. However, the right lens is useless if we have no idea how to interpret the images we see, how to string together the symbols on a page into a meaningful sentence. In this second part, I want us to consider the actual act of reading, interpreting the words we find on the pages of Scripture.

Switching analogies, Part 1 has helped us tune in to the right frequency so that we can make out the words God is saying; now we need to focus on our ability to listen to what he is saying. In this chapter, we will consider what we aim for as we read and study the Bible and how to discern when we are reading well. In the following chapter, I will outline a methodology for reading the Bible in order to understand and be changed by it. The following four chapters will then go through different challenges that arise as we read the Bible and explore tools to help us overcome these challenges. In chapter 7, we will look at the different styles of writing in the Bible and how we can adopt different approaches for reading narrative texts (e.g. Samuel and the Gospels), poetry (e.g. found in Psalms and Proverbs), prophecy (found in most prophetic books, such as Isaiah and Revelation), and didactic prose (e.g. Romans, Hebrews, 1 Peter).[1] In Chapter 8, we will consider Bible translation and the uses of the different English Bible translations that are readily available to us. Chapter 9 will take us a little bit deeper, looking at the use and abuse of the biblical languages (Hebrew, Aramaic, and Greek) in studying the

---

[1] There is some overlap here with the usual discussion of genre in interpretation, but I am intentionally deviating from the standard discussions here. For a further discussion of genre, see *The Gift of Reading – Part 2*, Chapter 4.

Bible. We will conclude in Chapter 10 with a survey of the various resources available to help us read better and in Chapter 11 with how to evaluate what we read in these resources and our own conclusions about the text.

The question of evaluation brings us back to our first purpose in this chapter: what is our aim when we read or study the Bible? We considered in Chapter 1 the grand purpose of the Bible and what we are to expect from it: the Bible is meant to lead us from faith to faith in the fulfilment of God's purposes. But this is not where our troubles lie. That is, this book is necessary because we often struggle when we read the Bible, but it may not yet be clear what we are actually struggling with. It does not seem like we struggle with accepting and responding to the Bible's general purpose: as Christians, we are progressively growing in faith in order to fulfil God's purposes. Our struggle is with understanding what we are reading, with specific texts.

Sometimes we read and do not struggle, but other times we find ourselves confused. And at other times, we understand the general meaning of the words, but we fail to connect what the text is saying with our lives. Our struggle in all these cases is moving from a general comprehension of the words on the page to *understanding*. When a passage confuses us, it is not because we cannot explain what each individual word means but because we cannot quite understand how they work together. In other words, we do not understand what we are supposed to do with what we have read. Our goal when we read the Bible must be to understand so that we can give a right response to what God is saying: we need to listen so we can obey. The response we need to give may be an emotion, to feel sadness or anger; a thought, to believe something; or an action, to do something.[2]

---

[2] In some treatments of biblical interpretation, authors divide what I am calling "understanding" into two different categories, meaning and significance. To understand is, then, to grasp the meaning and to apply is to get the significance. I am not convinced that these can be so easily separated. It seems to me that to understand a text is to grasp how it applies in one way or another. John Frame argues that we do not know what "You shall not murder" means unless we can identify circumstance that are prohibited and others that are not. Would we say someone understands what it means to say "you shall not steal" if they think it is okay to commit tax fraud? Sometimes meaning is said to be the proposition (statement of truth) made by the text, yet this is again an instance of application or use: we are applying the text to our thinking, learning what truth we should believe from it. I discuss this issue at length int *The Gift of Reading – Part 2*. See further John M. Frame, *The Doctrine of the Knowledge of God*, A Theology of Lordship (Phillipsburg: P&R Publishing, 1987),

This second part of the book is about being able to listen to God's voice as he communicates to us through the Bible; in this chapter we will look at how we know we have heard God's voice, that we have read well. We can define reading well or hearing God's voice in Scripture as understanding the right responses to a text. To read well is, therefore, to know what to do with a text. What to "do" can be many different things: we understand a text if we are able to translate it into another language (e.g. לֹא תִרְצָח, *lō' tirṣāḥ*: "You shall not murder", Exod 20:13)—though translations can be better or worse, reveal more or less understanding of a text. We understand a text when we can paraphrase it (e.g. You shall not murder = it is normally wrong for a person to kill another human through intentional action or negligence, except where permissible by God's law). We understand a text if we know when it applies and when it does not: "You shall not murder" means that it is a sin before God to kill another human being in cold blood (cf. Gen 9:5-6), it is a sin before God to act negligently or fail to act with the result that human life is lost (cf. Exod 21:29), but it does not mean that capital punishment or taking a life in war is sinful (e.g. Deut 7:24, 9:3, 13:6-11; cf. Rom 13:1-5).

To say that reading well is understanding the right response to a text implies that reading badly is to misunderstand or fail to understand a text and to have a wrong response to that text. It is wrong to respond to the portrayal of the utter sinfulness of Israel in The Book of Judges (e.g. Judges 19) with joy or mirth. We fail to read well when we read the 6th commandment and think that all killing in the post-fall world is sinful or think that killing is never sinful.

So if we are going to read well, we need to know how to come to a right understanding of the text—to know the proper response—and how to avoid misunderstanding the text. In the following chapters, we will look at the "*how*" of reading well. In the rest of this chapter, I want us to consider the "*what*," three perspectives by which we can identify right and wrong responses to a text.

67, 93–98; J. Alexander Rutherford, *The Gift of Reading - Part 2: A Biblical Perspective on Hermeneutics*, God's Gifts for the Christian Life Part 1 - The Christian Mind II (Vancouver: Teleioteti, 2019).

A. IDENTIFYING THE RIGHT RESPONSES TO SCRIPTURE

A right response to Scripture is, of course, one that is consistent with a proper understanding of the text. But this is a circle, for we only know we have properly understood the text when we have properly applied it. We must now ask the important question; how do we identify if our application of the text is right? In other words, we need at this point to know what a justified application or response to the text is. To be "justified" means that the application or response is firmly grounded, it is based on good reasons, and so is right. I think the best way to identify a justified application or use of a text is by the criteria of *validity*, *appropriateness*, and *fittingness*.[3] We could say that an application is justified when it is a *valid* use of the text that is *appropriate* for the function of the text and *fits* its field of reference. Let's look at each of these individually.[4]

a. Validity

The first criteria to determine a justified use of a text is *validity*. Validity refers to the meaning of the words we read. A use of a text is valid when it does not twist or distort the words on the page and their relationship with one another. Positively, an application is valid when it represents a right understanding of words and their relationships (phrases, sentences, and paragraphs). To know if our application is valid, we must ask questions like, "does my interpretation of the words of the text fit their context?" "Am I interpreting the relationship between these sentences appropriately?" Some examples should serve to illustrate what I mean.

Consider, for example, the 6th commandment: "You shall not murder" (Exod 20:13). A valid application will be one that is consistent with the

---

[3] This is based on a section of my master's thesis "God's Kingdom through his Priest-King," which I expand upon in *The Gift of Reading – Part 2*. The discussion in the latter volume is supplementary to this. Rutherford, *The Gift of Reading - Part 2*, J. Alexander Rutherford, *God's Kingdom through his Priest-King: An Analysis of the Book of Samuel in Light of the Davidic Covenant*, A Teleioteti Technical Study 1 (Vancouver: Teleioteti, 2019), 93–99.

[4] Though we are addressing validity, appropriateness, and fittingness as three different criteria, they are truly only three different perspectives by which we can view a text and test our application against it. If one were to fully understand a text and all its implications, as God does, every valid use would also be appropriate and fitting, and vice versa.

meaning of לֹא (lō', not) and רָצַח (rāṣaḥ, to murder). Consider the following five examples:

1) It is sinful (a crime against God) to kill a human being without God-given authority to do so.
2) Humans are under a serious obligation to murder.
3) It is sinful to kill another human in war.
4) It is sinful for a government to kill another human in punishment for a crime.
5) It is sinful for a human to act in a negligent manner or fail to act with the result of the loss of human life.

I contend that only examples 1 and 5 are valid applications of Exodus 20:13; examples 2-4 are invalid. Example 1 is valid because the word translated "murder" doesn't merely mean "kill" but to kill in unauthorized circumstances. There are dozens of cases where killing is divinely authorized; these are not instances of "murder." However, example 1 is vague, for it does not specify under which circumstances it is appropriate to kill. Example 5 is valid because the case laws in the Torah apply the command in this way (e.g. Exod 21:29).

Example 2 is clearly invalid, for the adverb translated "no" has been interpreted as an intensive adverb, adding emphasis to the action. Instead of "shall not," it has been applied as "must do so." This is invalid because it does not fit within the range of meanings for לֹא (lō'), the Hebrew word for "no." We will explore the concept of "range of meanings" below, in Chapter 9.

Example 3 is also invalid; in this case it takes the word translated "murder" too broadly. It is clear from Deuteronomy and elsewhere in the Old and New Testaments that God permits, even commands, people to kill others in war (e.g. Deut 7:24).

Example 4 is likewise invalid; it also takes the word "murder" too broadly (cf. Deut 13:6-11, 18:20; Rom 13:1-5).

In the rest of this part of the book, we will be looking at strategies for reading the text better, for understanding the flow of thought and interpreting the words correctly. These are the ways we determine if our application is valid or not. Chapters 7 and 8 will deal with the issue of validity to a greater depth, looking at how Hebrew, Aramaic, and Greek words (the original languages of the Bible) are translated into English and how to determine the appropriate meaning of these words. In the above cases, the validity of these interpretations could have been tested by consulting English translations (cf. example 2), searching up the word "murder" in a concordance or רָצַח (*rāṣaḥ*, to murder) in a Hebrew-English lexicon (i.e. dictionary) (cf. examples 1, 3-5), or using cross-reference notes and bible dictionaries or topical bibles to look up the theme of killing in the Old Testament (cf. examples 3-5).

Validity deals with the meaning of the text, asking the question, "does our application respect the meaning of the words of the text in their contexts (in the paragraph, in the book, in the canon of Scripture)?" Validity is essential to any justified application of a text, but it is not by itself sufficient. We can imagine uses of the text that appear valid to us yet are not *appropriate* or *fitting*.[5]

For example, using Exodus 20:13 to argue that a person should be joyous when they murder another human being would be inappropriate. Nothing in this statement contradicts the words on the page, it is not misusing the word "murder" or "not." However, the text is intended to discourage murder: the text gives us God's command that murder is sinful and will be punished. The appropriate response to such a command is obedience and horror when it is transgressed. It would, therefore, be inappropriate to derive an application that is valid yet does not acknowledge the purpose of the text—that twists it to its own service.

A valid use may also not be *fitting;* that is, it may misunderstand what the text refers to. For example, it would be *valid* to interpret "Seize him and lead him away under guard" (Mark 14:44) as a command; this is what the grammar indicates. However, it would not be *fitting* to take this as a command for you and your friends to arrest a stranger walking down the street. It is not fitting because "him" refers in context to Jesus, and the command is directed towards the crowd coming to arrest Jesus, not anyone else. Though these

---

[5] It may interest the reader to consider that it is only from our perspective that *validity, appropriateness,* and *fittingness* do not fully overlap. That is, because none of us understand all the implications of the text we read and perfectly grasp its relationship to the Biblical context in which it is found, we may identify some valid applications that turn out to be inappropriate. However, from God's perspective these three criteria all agree perfectly and are merely different ways of looking at the meaning of the text.

examples may seem ridiculous, illegitimate interpretations like these occur more often than we would like to think. So, in addition to being *valid*, an application must also be *appropriate* and *fitting*.

b. *Appropriateness*

Let's first consider what it means for a use or application of a text to be appropriate. We will then consider fittingness. "Appropriateness" refers to the goal or function of a text, what sort of behaviour, thinking, or emotions it ought to produce. Validity considers *what* the text says; appropriateness considers the sort of response we are to have to what is said. For example, a command is intended to produce an obedient response: we obey commands. A narrative, especially a parable, or poem is intended (among other things) to produce an emotional response, make us feel one way or another about a character or subject. A didactic text, a text intended to teach, is intended to make us believe something to be true or false and then to have an appropriate response in our actions and emotions. Appropriateness thus relates to the effect a text should have on our doing, feeling, and thinking and how our application successfully or unsuccessfully manifests this effect. Appropriateness also encompasses the scope of an application. If a promise is made, we ought to interpret—it is appropriate to interpret—that promise as the promiser's intent to bring about the state promised. Yet this is not the case with a proverb from the book of Proverbs. In the latter case, it would be inappropriate to read a proverb about diligence as a promise that diligent behaviour will result in wealth (e.g. Prov 12:27). A careful study of the proverbs in light of the rest of Scripture and the book itself—along with our experience—reveals that they have a different purpose, that they are not meant to be promises. Therefore, it would be inappropriate to take Proverbs 12:27 as a promise of wealth for those who are diligent.

> ### *The Proverbs and Appropriate Application*
>
> In *The Gift of Reading – Part 2*, I explain much of the approach developed in this book as an expression of the "analogy of faith," reading Scripture in light of Scripture. The Proverbs are a good example of the necessity of this approach. If we were to take a proverb such as 12:27 out of context, it would lead us to conclude that God has broken his promises or to work ourselves to death attempting to be "diligent," for

obviously that will bring us wealth. However, reading the Proverbs in light of the rest of Scripture, we see that there is no simple equation such that hard work brings wealth. God does promise blessing to his Old Covenant people if they perfectly keep his ways, but this blessing is not individual wealth and it is clear that none of his people were able to keep this law and earn this blessing perfectly. A close look at the book of Proverbs and the rest of the Wisdom literature, especially Job, yields a different picture of the function of the wisdom sayings found in these books.

The function of wisdom literature, including the Proverbs, is to instruct the People of God in the right way to live before God in his world and discourage wrong living. All life is to be lived with reference to God—in the fear of him. A proper understanding of God and his creation will result in certain behaviours, such as honesty, hard work, faithfulness, etc. The Proverbs teach this way of life by contrasting it with ungodly or foolish behaviour and juxtaposing their results: if you want blessing, you should act in one way; to do otherwise will result in horrid consequences. The blessings and consequences attached to right and wrong behaviour are a mixture of covenant blessings and the natural consequences of such behaviour—for example, hard work generally will bring success whereas idleness will lead to failure. However, it is evident from the wisdom literature and elsewhere that there are many exceptions to these general rules. They remain true enough to motivate right behaviour and so are a convenient tool for communicating God's will.

However, there is a greater perspective in the wisdom literature, one we could call "eschatological," or focusing on the end of this age. This is especially seen in Job; Job is the quintessential righteous man and initially receives the blessings of God. Yet for reasons unknown to him, God strips away all his blessings and leaves him destitute. God does restore him in the end, but The Book of Job reveals that there is no one-to-one correlation between earthly prosperity or destitution and God's blessings or curse. There is a tension in this age, we often ask "why do the wicked prosper when the righteous suffer?" The answer is found in the age to come, the new creation, when all of God's people will enjoy the fullness of life with God for ever and the wicked will reap the consequences they have sown. Reading a text in its immediate context and the analogy of faith, reading Scripture in light of Scripture, is essential to determining the appropriateness of an application.

Taking our example in Exodus, "You shall not murder," an appropriate application is one that prohibits behaviour or identifies an implication of such a prohibition: "It is wrong to murder," "I should not murder people," "I should feel bad about murder," "God does not condone murder," etc. Some applications will be appropriate but invalid, such as "it is sinful to kill in war." This application is appropriate to the nature of the command yet misunderstands the word translated "murder." Inappropriate applications of this text would be those that misidentify the intended effect of the text. "It is right to murder," "I should feel good about murdering," and "Murder is not a sin" are all inappropriate applications of the text. Each of these examples misses the proper response to a command from God. However, if the speaker was not commissioned by God, these might be appropriate applications. For example, if the speaker is Satan saying, "throw yourself down from here" (Luke 4:9), the appropriate response is not obedience, for the Bible does not expect its readers to obey such a command (this command is also directed to Jesus, so any application that applies it to us as a command is not *fitting*, which we will address below). Our applications are appropriate when they correspond to the intent of the text, discerned by paying attention to who is speaking and what they are saying. The last perspective that we need to use to determine the validity of our application is fittingness.

c. *Fittingness*

Fittingness ask the question, "Does my application fit with the text's referents?" A **referent** is the textual or, most often, extra-textual (i.e. in the real world) object to which a symbol such as a word may refer.[6] For example,

---

[6] Not all words have a "referent," but some do. Proper nouns, for example, refer to a person or place. The referent of a proper noun may not exist outside of the text in question—it may refer to a character earlier in the story—or it may be a person in a T.V. show, merely a product of human creative activity.

It may be helpful to observe that the *referent* is not the *meaning* of the word. For example, "Israel" has a specific function in the context—it means something specific. The nation of Israel does not *mean* anything. A word does not replace the thing it refers to but speaks about it to communicate something. In other words, words interpret reality, so a word interprets in one way or another its referent. It may

the word Israel often—though not always—refers to the historical people of Israel; the proper name Jesus Christ refers to the Son of God, born of the Virgin Mary in the last decade BC. It is important to ask if our application or use of a text reflects a right understanding of the referents in a text.

For example, a text such as Exodus that concerns the historic nation of Israel refers to this nation and not anything else that bears the name "Israel." If we were to derive from this text a statement of historical truth, for example, "God brought Israel forth from oppressive slavery to Egypt," our application would only be fitting if the referents are those of the text. That is, if by "God" a pagan idol such as Marduk is meant, this application is not fitting. If by Israel, the spiritual people of God—including us Christians—or Jesus is intended, this application is not fitting. If "Egypt" is used to refer to the city in Arkansas, USA, instead of a historical nation in northern Africa, this application is not fitting. Fittingness is not concerned with the meaning of the words but the correspondence between the symbol and the thing it signifies.

Surprisingly, this is where most errors in application occur. The problem is usually not in the historical application but in personal application. That is, we usually do not mistake the historical nation Israel for Jesus or "Egypt" for the United States of America. We do, however, often mistake the Old Testament people of God for the New Testament people of God or specific characters in a narrative for ourselves. For example, you may have heard someone cite 2 Chronicles 7:13-14 saying that if we repent, God will deliver our nation (maybe America or Canada) from a particular crisis:

> When I shut up the heavens so that there is no rain, or command the locust to devour the land, or send pestilence among my people, if my people who are called by my name humble themselves, and pray and seek my face and turn from their wicked ways, then I will hear from heaven and will forgive their sin and heal their land.

---

speak to the referent, about the referent, or the referent may be a piece of scenery designed to evoke some response. When we consider referential words, we concern ourselves with meaning: why has the author referred to this here? What does he mean when uses this word and what does that—his use of the word—tell us about the referent?

This seems to be a *valid* application: this is what the words say. It also appears to be an *appropriate* one: this is indeed God's intent. But it is not a *fitting* application, for God is not addressing Christians in America or in any earthly empire. In this context, God is speaking to Solomon after he prayed to dedicate the newly built temple to Yahweh. God is not speaking in a vacuum; he is drawing upon the curses given in Deuteronomy that would come upon those who broke God's covenant with Israel (Deut 28:1-29:29). He is saying that he would respond graciously if his people repented and relent from calamity. Christians are not under the Old Covenant made at Sinai, so its curses and blessings do not apply to us. Also, Christians are a different sort of people than historical Israel; we do not have a "land." According to Peter and the rest of the New Testament, we are sojourners and exiles among all the nations (e.g. 1 Pet 1:1). This means that no nation on earth bears the relationship this text describes with God.[7]

Or maybe you have heard it said that as a Christian, you "Lack one thing; go, sell all that you have and give to the poor, and you will have treasure in heaven; and come, follow me" (Mark 10:21). This is again a *valid* and *appropriate* application, but it is only a *fitting* application for the rich young man in this passage. In the narrative, Jesus is addressing a specific person in specific circumstances. For this reason, the command of the text is *fitting* only for that specific person in those specific circumstances. Indeed, if this man repented of his greed, sold everything, and then read this passage 20 years later, it would not necessarily be *fitting* for him to go and sell all he had again. We saw already that all Scripture is given by God to be useful for all Christians, so this passage must have some application for us today, yet that application may not—and often will not—be identical to what the text says.

We first must understand what Jesus is saying and why he is saying it, then we can understand what Mark (who recorded Jesus words to make a point)

---

[7] Some would argue that this text reveals a general pattern of God's faithfulness, that he is inclined to bless those who live in obedience to him—including nations. I am not convinced that this is an appropriate understanding of God's relation to the world in this age. But even if it were, this would not be an application of this text but of a general theology of God that is manifest in this text and others. So I would say that as concerns the application of *this text*, we cannot identify our nations as fitting referents. This text does however reveal the faithfulness of God to his promises, so we can derive confidence from it that God will uphold his promises to us, such as that found in Matthew 6:33.

wants us to learn and do. If I were asked to apply this text to my church and life right now, I would say something like this.

> Christians are called to be committed wholly to Jesus Christ and follow him at any cost, giving up all things that stand in the way of pure and whole-hearted devotion to God. If wealth is an idol in your life, something that causes you to worship a created thing (money, security, etc.) instead of the Creator, you must choose God over your wealth. Indeed, God may be calling you to give up everything for his name's sake. Are you willing to count all as loss for the sake of Christ, to give up comfort and ease for, maybe, life as a missionary to the tribes of the Amazon rainforest?
>
> It may not be wealth, though, that holds you back. Is it that home you just paid off? Maybe the risk of moving and taking out a new mortgage is keeping you from going where God has called you. Is it that girl or boyfriend that is drawing you away from Christ who called you? How about your image—and this one hits home for me—do you horde up the praise and adulation of others as a sort of wealth from which you derive security and peace? Does this hold you back from confessing your sin, repenting for your wrongs, and from joyfully enduring suffering with thanksgiving instead of drawing attention to yourself through it?

On Matthew's version of this passage, R.T. France writes, "The demands of discipleship will vary for different individuals and situations. But they will never be less than total availability to the claims of Jesus, however differently these apply in practice."

Let's consider one more example of "fittingness." Have you ever heard an exhortation to "Pray for the peace of Jerusalem!" That is, have you ever heard Psalm 122:6 used as a call to pray for the peace of present-day Jerusalem, located in modern-day Israel? I humbly suggest that, though *valid* and *appropriate*, this application is not *fitting*. Such an application—you ought to pray for present-day Jerusalem—confuses the present Jerusalem with the historical capital of Israel and confuses the Old Covenant people of God to whom this was first addressed with the New Covenant people of God who now sing this psalm.

Considering the identity of Jerusalem: it is true that modern-day Jerusalem sits on the site of historic Jerusalem, so there is continuity in name and location. The inhabitants then and now are also ethnic Jews, among others. However, there are important differences. Jerusalem in Psalm 122 was the capital of the Old Testament people of God; it was the centre of God's power on earth expressed through the Davidic monarchy and his presence in the tabernacle and later the temple. This Jerusalem represented all God's people at that time; its peace meant the blessings of covenant faithfulness, its demise the curses of covenant unfaithfulness. Much has changed in 3000 years. Jerusalem is no longer the home of God's people; Christians are exiles in the earth awaiting a heavenly Jerusalem (1 Pet 1:1; Heb 11:1-40; Rev 21:1-27); and the Old Covenant is no longer valid, having passed away with the coming of the New Covenant (Heb 8:1-13, Gal 3:1-21). Present-day Jerusalem is home to the State of Israel but not to the covenant people of God, which Jerusalem represents in this Psalm. Indeed, the end of that city with its role representing God's people came in AD 70, when it was utterly destroyed by the Romans (cf. Matt 24:1-2).[8] The Psalm was addressed to the covenant people at that time, for whom it would be appropriate to pray for the Jerusalem that then existed.

If it is not *fitting* to apply this Psalm in such a straightforward manner, how then shall we "Pray for the Peace of Jerusalem"? Essentially—arguing this would take some time—the role Jerusalem plays in this Psalm is replaced by the Church universal and its local expressions. I suggest, therefore, that a *fitting* application for a Christian would be to pray that the Jesus' Church would experience relief from persecution and suffering so that it can accomplish its mission. Also, Christians ought to pray for unity within the Church, that God's people would seek to emulate Christ's character in their relationships with one another—as brothers and sisters. In his commentary on the Psalms, Derek Kidner puts it this way,

> What Jerusalem was to the Israelites, the church is to the Christian. Here are his closest ties, his *brethren and companions* [v. 8], known and unknown, drawn with him to the one centre as fellow-

---

[8] This is not to say that God is done with ethnic Israel; this is not the case. Romans 11 indicates that God will draw to himself a large majority of Jewish people at some time in the future, before Jesus returns. Cf. Romans 11:1-36.

It is important to observe that God does not save them as Israelites, those under the Old Covenant, but through faith in Jesus Christ. Jews will be saved as Christians under the New Covenant, thus there is urgent need of evangelism to Jewish people (cf. Paul's approach in Romans 1:16).

pilgrims.... And whatever limitations of its citizens, Jerusalem was where God saw fit to build his house. The simple response to this, *I will seek your good* [v. 9], was the least that such a fact demanded; and it had no upper limit. For the Christian it has, besides, no territorial boundary. For the inspiring implications of this, see Hebrews 12:22-24; for its immediate application, Hebrews 13:1-3.

Fittingness asks, who is this text about, who is it directed to? Once the subject of the passage is identified, we then need to ask: am I, or the one whom I am applying the text to, identical with the subject? If not—if we are not Israelites or the rich young man—how are we different, how are we similar? By looking at what was fitting for the subject and identifying how we are different and similar to the subject of the passage, we can identify what a fitting application might be for us. This takes practice, but be encouraged that for many passages, it is pretty easy: "you shall love the Lord your God with all your heart and with all your soul and with all your mind and with all your strength" (Mark 12:30; cf. Deut 6:4-5) applies to us as it did to the Israelites, only the particular ways we do this have changed. Learning what fitting applications look like in clear passages trains us to identify them in more difficult ones. This holds true for learning to identify valid and appropriate interpretations also. Knowing about the storyline and peoples of the Bible, as we discussed earlier, is also helpful.

Fittingness and Typology

There are cases where questions of fittingness are not so easy. The discussion above may appear to say that when a text has a referent, there is only one. However, there are significant instances throughout Scripture where this is clearly not the case, where two or more non-textual objects or individuals are referred to with the same symbol (word or phrase). There may be a couple of places where the author intends overlapping referents, analogous to instances where both senses of a word are clearly valid in context (cf. John 3:7, where the word translated "again" can also mean "above"). However, I know of none. There are, however, many places where multiple referents are in view through corporate solidarity or typology.

Corporate solidarity refers to the union (however the connection is conceived) between various members of a group, such as a nation, family, or covenant party. Where there is solidarity, what is true of the group is true of its members. For example, because God is the covenant Lord of Israel in the Old Testament—a corporate group—he is the covenant Lord of every Israelite—one who is part of the group "Israel." A particularly important case of corporate solidarity occurs between a group and its representative: for a covenant group, there is often a covenant head; for a nation, there is a king. In our day, analogous relationship exists between a CEO and a company or a president/prime minister and a country. In both cases, the representative (CEO or national leader) has the ability to make decision that will be binding upon the entire corporation or nation. In the Bible, corporate solidarity is found among family, between heads and children (Abraham and his descendants, cf. Heb 7:4-10); among covenant heads and the covenant people, namely Adam and the creation and Jesus and the New Covenant people of God (Rom 5:12-21; 1 Cor 15:22, 42-49); and between kings and their people (2 Sam 24:1-25). Where corporate solidarity exists, both a representative and the entire people could be referred to in the same text. For example, in Daniel 7:13-16, the son of man figure appears to refer both to Christ Jesus and the saints (cf. Matt 16:27-38, 24:30-31, 26:64). This is true because what is true of Christ in this case will be true of the saints, for they will inherit his kingdom with him. A similar relationship is found in Isaiah 40-53 concerning the servant of the Lord, who is clearly Jesus and yet also the people of God. This also probably explains how Malachi 1:2-5 can use "Esau" and "Jacob" simultaneously to refer to historical individuals and the nations that descended from them. Solidarity accounts for many instances where a text seems to have more than one referent in view; another possibility is the use of typology.

Typology has been the subject of much discussion throughout the history of interpretation, so there are many competing ideas concerning what typology is. However, for our purposes we could define typology as a divinely ordained correspondence between historical events or persons.[i] Every instance of typology is, first, divinely ordained: typology refers to a relationship God has ordained to exist between events or persons across history. It was God's intention, for example, that

Melchizedek—the enigmatic figure of Genesis 14—would prefigure Christ (cf. Heb 6:2-7:28). Second, it is a correspondence between historical entities: typology refers to an intentional relationship where one item prefigures or points to another, as Melchizedek who was the priest and king of Jerusalem pointed towards Christ who was the ultimate priest-king of Jerusalem. It is similar to prophecy, for both anticipate and tell us about something ahead of themselves; yet whereas prophecy is clearly forward looking, typology is retroactive, we see and learn from the correspondence only after the type (that which points to something) and the antitype (that which is pointed to, or the fulfilment of the type) have both appeared.

It is because of such a relationship that Matthew can identify Jesus coming forth from Egypt as the fulfilment of Hosea 11:1, "out of Egypt I called my son" (Matt 2:15). In its context, "my son" clearly refers to Israel, so an application to Jesus would appear to not be fitting. However, Matthew sees Jesus as fitting into and being the fulfilment of the historical pattern of God's relationship to Israel. Jesus came out of Egypt as they did, was tested in the wilderness as they were, yet he was not disobedient like them; he fulfils this pattern by being the true and faithful son Israel was called to be. Matthew rightly sees Jesus as a referent in this text, in addition to historical Israel, because the entire pattern of Israel's history was meant to point to Jesus. It is debated whether we are able apart from Scriptural guidance to identify types, but at the very least we can say that in those cases where Scripture makes such an application, multiple referents will be "fitting."

---

i. Cf. G. K. Beale, "Positive Answer to the Question: Did Jesus and his Followers Preacher the Right Doctrine from the Wrong Texts? An Examination of the Presuppositions of Jesus' and the Apostles' Exegetical Method," in The Right Doctrine from the Wrong Texts?: Essays on the Use of the Old Testament in the New, ed. G. K. Beale (Grand Rapids: Baker Books, 1994), 394.

d. *Examples*

In this chapter, we have considered what makes a good application of a text. I have attempted to answer the question, "What does a justified application of Scripture look like?" My answer was threefold: we could say that an application is justified when it is a *valid* use of the text that is *appropriate* for the function of the text and *fits* its field of reference. An application is valid when it is consistent with the text interpreted in its context. An application is *appropriate* when it is consistent with the force or intent of the text. An application is fitting when it is consistent with the referents of a text. Instead of jumping immediately into the next chapter, this is a good time to put into practice what we have just learned.

Below I have provided several applications of Romans 8:28; many of them are applications I have encountered in conversations, read in books, and used in my own teaching. Considering the text and its context (pay particular attention to 8:28-39), which of the following applications of the text are justified? Ask yourself why it is justified; is it valid, appropriate, and fitting? If it is not justified, why not? In the footnotes, I have provided what I think are the appropriate evaluations of these applications. If you disagree with me, ask yourself why. Why have I evaluated them the way I have? How have you evaluated them differently?

> And we know that for those who love God all things work together for good, for those called according to his purpose (Rom 8:28)

1. Because God works all things for the good of Christians, I am free to do whatever I want—maybe get drunk and drive home—knowing that it will work out for my good.

2. As a Christian I can have the confidence that even when I sin, God will work this out for my good.

3. As a Christian, I can be confident that no matter what I do or what happens to me, I will receive wealth, peace, and prosperity in this life.

4. As a Christian, I can have the hope that every horror in my past, every present and future suffering—including those brought on by my own sin—will contribute to God's good purpose in making me more like his Son.

5. I can be confident that whatever I do will turn out for good because God is good.[9]

---

[9] **Not justified:** **#1** is not justified because it is inappropriate: it uses a text meant to give confidence in God's gracious sovereignty as an excuse for sin. **#3** is not justified because it is invalid: it misunderstands the word "good," failing to interpret good within the New Covenant context of the New Testament and v. 29 in particular. **#5** is not justified because it is neither fitting nor valid. It appears to be a non-Christian speaking, so the text does not refer to him: it is not fitting to apply the text to someone who does not love Yahweh. It is also invalid because the statement that God's goodness is the reason for this promise is not taught in this text, regardless of whether or not it is true.

Justified: **#2** is justified because the text is directed to all Christians (so it is *fitting*), "all things" encompasses sin (so it is *valid*), and it is a promise from God in which we can have confidence (so it is *appropriate*). **#4** is also justified, for much the same reasons as #2. Furthermore, in contrast to **#3**, **#4** is valid because it rightly identifies "good" as the conformity to Christ mentioned in v. 29.

6

KNOWING HOW TO READ WELL

> This Book of the Law shall not depart from your mouth, but you shall meditate on it day and night, so that you may be careful to do according to all that is written in it. For then you will make your way prosperous, and then you will have good success. – Joshua 1:8

To this point we have mostly talked theory: we have looked at the big picture of the Bible in Part 1 and then looked at the immediate goal of reading the Bible, understanding and its application, in the last chapter. What we have yet to touch upon is the act of reading the Bible, the methods and means by which we arrive at our applications of the text. In this chapter, we will begin looking at the act of reading, often called exegesis. My main purpose in this chapter is to give an overview of the steps involved in reading the Bible. In our discussion of each step of exegesis, of interpreting the Bible, I will go over the basics of reading a text well. In the following chapters, we will take up the more technical yet sometimes necessary aspects of biblical interpretation.

Each step discussed in this chapter is essential to sound biblical interpretation, but the order in which I present them will not necessarily be helpful for every reader. If you are new to reading the Bible in a reflective and thoughtful manner, I suggest that you follow the method as I outline it and then tweak it as you become more comfortable in your study of the Bible. Some readers will find that they do these things reflexively, without deliberate thought, and others will probably find that what I identify as one step may be two or vice versa. All this to say, reading the Bible is more of an art than a science; others can share from their experience and provide time-tested tips, yet bible study will look different for every reader.

I break the method of exegesis, or Bible reading, into the following eight steps: (1) Pray, (2) identify the passage for study, (3) identify the contexts, (4) identify the translational difficulties and establish the text, (5) observe the text, (6) identify the passage's relation to its context, (7) apply the passage, and (8) check your understanding.

A. (1) Pray

> and take… the sword of the Spirit, which is the word of God, praying at all times in the Spirit, with all prayer and supplication. – Ephesians 6:17-18

The first thing we need to do when we begin to read the Bible is not reading. If reading is a moral act, as I have suggested in the introduction and will unpack more in the last part of this book, we need to pray for a right heart as we read the Bible. In this sense, reading the Bible is not like reading any other book, or at least it is not like reading any other book calmly at home in peace and quiet.

Instead, it is like reading in the middle of a war zone—akin to taking a seat outside a bombed-out building and opening your favourite book while machine guns are being fired around you and bombs are exploding a few meters away! And I do not mean it is difficult to focus because of the endless distractions available to us; this is true but not the most perilous danger facing us as we read the Bible.

The picture the Bible paints of the Christian life is one of warfare; it is not by accident that Paul calls his young compatriots "fellow soldier" (Phil 2:25, Phlm 2). As Paul famously writes in Ephesians, "we do not wrestle against flesh and blood, but against the rulers, against the authorities, against the cosmic powers over this present darkness, against the spiritual forces of evil in the heavenly places" (6:12). He does not have to argue *that* we are in a war; he only seeks to identify the proper nature of this warfare. It is not flesh and blood combat but spiritual warfare waged by spiritual means. Because we are at war, writes Paul, we need to equip ourselves; one of the key pieces of equipment we need is "the sword of the Spirit, which is the word of God" (6:17). If reading the Bible arms us to do battle for the glory of God, we cannot think our enemies will let us arm ourselves without opposition.

We must be praying at all times—notice how Paul connects prayer with the whole act of equipping ourselves for battle (6:18). We pray that God would protect us from the various strategies the enemy would use to make our time in the Word of God ineffective. He may bring distraction, but his most effective tool may very well be stirring up our sinful hearts to blind us to what God wants us to hear. Indeed, before God saved us, we were in complete blindness—for "the god of this world has blinded the minds of the unbelievers, to keep them from seeing the light of the gospel of the glory of Christ" (2 Cor 4:4). Satan veiled our eyes from truly seeing what God wanted us to see. By the grace of God, this is no longer the case: God "has shone in our hearts to give the light of the knowledge of the glory of God in the face of Jesus Christ" (2 Cor 4:6). Though this total blindness is gone, it is still the case that we face times of blindness caused not by hearts totally sold out to sin but by the sin that still tempts us.

That is, Satan has an ally—an inside man—in his efforts to make our reading of the Bible ineffective. According to Paul, the Christian life from now until Christ's return is characterized not only by this external battle but also by an internal one, a battle between the vestiges of our old self and the new life we have in Christ through the Holy Spirit. In Galatians 5:16-17, Paul calls the Galatians to walk by the Spirit and not their sinful passions, "for the desires of the flesh are against the Spirit, and the desires of the Spirit are against the flesh, for these are opposed to each other, to keep you from doing the things you want to do" (5:17). If we are going to be effective in reading the Bible, we need to be doing battle on both these fronts—internally, against sinful desires, and externally, against spiritual opposition. This begins with prayer. We pray that the Spirit would reveal our sin, lead us to repentance, and defeat the deceit of the enemy. We will consider this aspect of Bible reading further in the final part of this book. But there is one other reason we begin our reading and continue it with prayer.

To put it plainly, it would be stupid to do otherwise—and I confess I am guilty of this stupidity more often than I care to admit. Not only is the Spirit our greatest ally in defeating the deceit of the enemy and our sinful flesh, but he is also the author of the Bible. How often have you come upon an interesting or difficult part of a book and wished you had the author there beside you to help you understand. I have definitely wished this. Would it not be utterly dumbfounding to witness someone struggling with a difficult text all the while ignoring the author sitting right beside them, never once asking for a little help?

Paul argues that the natural man, someone apart from the Spirit of God, considers the Scriptures to be foolish and cannot accept them. He does so because he does not have the Spirit who reveals the Scriptures to us as the wisdom of God (2 Cor 2:6-16). In this passage, Paul argues that the Spirit, as God, has a full understanding of God's thoughts and words. This makes sense. This means, because we have the Spirit always with us, we have access always to the author of the Scriptures—the one who knows exactly what God intended to say through the human authors of Scripture and how this applies to us today. Therefore, it makes sense to ask him to help us as we read his Word. It is not as though he is going to give us a key to understanding the text that is not in the text itself; no, the Bible is sufficient and clear. However, he can call to our minds others passages that may shed light on what we are reading or help us to notice something we missed. We pray that he would quicken our minds to perceive what was there the whole time.[1] With the Psalmist, we need to pray,

---

[1] I know some authors, and maybe some of the readers of this book, have dismissed this aspect of illumination. They argue that every passage that refers to the Spirit helping us understand and obey God refer to his help overcoming our sinful blindness. I suspect this is a misunderstanding of the Spirit's work as portrayed in the Bible and a subtle—though unintentional—capitulation to the naturalism of our day. Though the Spirit's primary work in Scripture is spiritual, associated with giving us believing, obedient hearts (regeneration) and helping us live out our faith in obedience to God (sanctification), this is not the only work he does. In 1 Corinthians 12:4-11 and Romans 12, the Spirit is said to gift people with particular skills or abilities for the sake of the Church. We often focus on the so-called supernatural gifts, but several gifts in both lists are what we would usually call "natural" (e.g. wisdom, knowledge, distinguishing between spirits, teaching, serving). It is not as though the Spirit codes these things into our DNA and lets them play out in our lives; on the contrary, in Philippians 2:12-13 Paul tells us Christians "work out your own salvation with fear and trembling, [13]for it is God who works in you, both to will and to work for his good pleasure." God accomplishes the "doing" in our lives. If we look at the Old Testament, we see that the Spirit's work was not only Spiritual: he empowered Samson with supernatural strength (Judg 14:6, 15:14) and specific Jewish individuals—especially Bezalel (Exod 31:1-5)—with artistic skills and craftmanship (Exod 28:3). In these instances, the expression of these "natural" abilities is in explicit conjunction with the filling of the Spirit (e.g. Exod 31:3, Judges 14:6). I conclude that it is wrong to restrict the Spirit's work to the spiritual realm and that it is perfectly acceptable—indeed, necessary—to ask for the Spirit to

> Deal bountifully with your servant,
>   that I may live and keep your word.
> Open my eyes, that I may behold
>   wondrous things out of your law.
> I am a sojourner on the earth;
>   hide not your commandments from me! (Ps 119:17-19)

B. (2) IDENTIFY THE PASSAGE FOR STUDY

After praying, we need to identify the text which we will study. In many contexts, this will be given to us. However, there will be times when we want to study a passage or are given the freedom to teach or preach on a passage of our choosing. In these situations, we need to be able to identify the contours of the passage that we will study. No sentence, verse, or passage in the Bible exists in isolation; every word, sentence, paragraph, etc., is intimately related with what precedes and follows it. For this reason, we cannot arbitrarily pick a block of text to study. Instead, we need to identify the boundaries of a paragraph, verse, or scene/pericope (smallest textual unit in a narrative).

Doing so will help us to understand what the text is saying and to not artificially take a chunk of text out of context (as if you could study "blessed are those who mourn, for they shall be comforted" [Matt 5:4] apart from the speech in which it falls). It will also keep us from doing an unnecessary amount of work. This second problem arises when we realize that every word is related to every other word, every sentence to every sentence, and so on until our study of a passage encompasses the whole Bible—a task too great for any of us! By carefully identifying our passage for study, we keep our study to closed units of a text, such as a full paragraph, scene, or poetic verse.

---

quicken our intellect, eyesight, and memory so that we might understand the Scriptures.

I hope the emphasis on Scripture so far would caution against the movements today that would encourage seeking the Spirit's leading above and beyond Scripture. Though I would not disavow some form of prophecy continuing today, it is clear that the primary way God speaks to us is in Scripture and that whatever prophecy may look like today, it will never be contrary to Scripture. Furthermore, because Scripture is sufficient for the Christian life, prophecy and other supernatural works of the Spirit should be understood as God giving insight into our situations and circumstances in order that we might be better equipped to live obediently to his Word.

The passage we study may not be identical with the passage we teach, for we may be given only a single verse to teach, yet our passage of study must encompass both the text we teach and the surrounding material that makes a complete thought or textual unit.

Though it doesn't match how we write, completed texts can be visualized as a string of blocks that are put together like Lego pieces to make a whole. A clause is made up of several different types of "blocks" (verbs, adverbs, adjectives, nouns, prepositional phrases). A sentence (or line in poetry) is made up of several forms of these clauses (independent and dependent clauses). Paragraphs are made up of different sentences, sometimes connected by conjunctions (e.g. "and, or, but, for") and sometimes not (asyndeton). Paragraphs are strung together to form larger blocks of text, and these are strung together to form books. To establish the boundaries of our study, we are looking for the larger blocks made up of sentences or lines of poetry that form a unit. For example, the ESV considers Galatians 6:1-10 to be a single section, assigning it the heading "Bear One Another's Burdens," and it divides this section further into two paragraphs (6:1-5, 6-10). The whole section or either paragraph would serve well as a passage for study. In poetry, the smallest completed unit is a series of lines called a colon (e.g. Hab 3:2 is divided into one bi-colon, made of two lines, and one tri-colon, made of three lines). These groups of lines, colons, are then put divided into larger sections.

A unit of text will look different for each style of text we study—e.g. whether it is narrative or poetry. In the following chapter, we will look at the different styles of texts in the Bible and the units that make them up, with techniques to better understand how the text is shaped and how to identify and relate the units of text that make up a passage. It is important to remember that verse and chapter numbers, though helpful, are not sure guides to the divisions of a text or to identifying the units of thought that make it up. These divisions were added in the last millennia (13th-16th cent.) and represent an interpretation of the text. Many translations and original-language Bible's will provide paragraph divisions and section headings; these are helpful but not inerrant.

C. (3) IDENTIFY THE CONTEXTS

Every passage we study is embedded in various levels of context. It is essential to identify these layers at the beginning of our study and consider them throughout it. Context is the literary setting, the textual environment, in which a passage resides. The immediate context is those blocks of text—sentences, paragraphs, scenes, lines, chapters, etc.—that precede and follow our text. It is most intimately related to these, yet it also has relation to the chapter, book, canonical section, and testament in which it is found.

Consider, for example, the book of Habakkuk. If our passage of study is Habakkuk 2:2-4, the immediate context will be God's response to Habakkuk given in 2:2-20. The greater context is the discourse between God and Habakkuk introduced in 1:1 and extending to 2:20. It is part of the book of Habakkuk, which is part of the Minor Prophets or the Twelve, which is part of the *Nevi'im* or The Prophets—the second division of the Hebrew Bible. It is part of the Old Testament, and it is part of the Bible.

One particular feature of the biblical context that we must observe is where our book fits in the metanarrative or story taught by the Bible (cf. Ch. 3). We must ask where in the story of God's unfolding work does this book take place: considering the big movements of this story, is this before or after Christ? It is also helpful to observe where it fits more precisely: for example, Habakkuk takes place sometime near the end of the kingdom of Judah, so it is similar in themes and addresses a similar period of time as the book of Jeremiah and the end of the books of Kings and Chronicles.

When we first consider the context of our passage, we only want to identify the broad features that will help us understand our passage. We need to understand how the Old Testament differs from the New, but also that our passage fits into the whole Bible, which testifies about Jesus. As part of the Twelve, Habakkuk serves to communicate with the rest of the Minor Prophets a picture of God's indictment of sin, judgment of sinners, and future salvation for his people. It is helpful to observe that its place in The Prophets means it is going to provide an authoritative revelation from God concerning the relation his people have to him and how he has or will deal with them.

The most important piece of context will be the book itself. At this stage of study, it is important to read the entire book—ideally in one sitting—and make observations about the book as a whole. Consider, for example, the main theme or themes of the book (e.g. Habakkuk focuses on *faith*, *judgement*, *righteousness*, and *salvation*; Romans likewise focusing on these four themes in addition to other things). Observing repeated words—especially word roots (see Ch. 9)—is helpful in identifying key themes, but at times a theme will be introduced without any specific vocabulary to identify it. It is also important to observe the contours or flow of the book; how does the author unfold his argument, lay out his narrative, or structure his poem? What parts are most closely connected to each other? This part, outlining a book, will probably require you to consult secondary resources, such as a good commentary or biblical introduction (see Chapter 10 for more on these resources).[1] As you read the book, especially an epistle, consider the purpose the author has for writing. Given what he says, what is the goal he is hoping to achieve—to correct false doctrine, provide encouragement, give specific instruction, etc.? Habakkuk, for example, appears to be written to encourage the believing community of Judah to hold fast to God in the midst of horrific conditions, to trust him for salvation even when salvation looks worse than the problem. Romans appears to be written to help reconcile Jewish and Gentile believers in the Roman church. Identifying the purpose of the book helps us to trace its argument, understand our text's role within the book, and identify its key themes.

Identifying themes and outlining the flow of a book helps us answer the key question we need answered to interpret books of the Bible: why is the author writing this? Careful attention to these features reveals, for example, that Habakkuk is writing to encourage believing Jews to trust God despite his unbelievable deeds—namely, the Babylonian invasion of Judah. Galatians is written to persuade the Galatian Christians to turn from false teaching and persevere in the true Gospel, namely that all of God's promises are given through faith in Jesus Christ and not through obedience to the Law.

At this stage of exegesis, we are merely getting a general feel for the contexts in which our text falls. After looking closer at our passage of study,

---

[1] As discussed in *The Gift of Reading – Part 2*, identifying the shape or flow of book is more important for some forms of Biblical literature, such as narratives, than for others, such as poems. With didactic prose, such as the New Testament epistles, it is less important to grasp how the author might group his thoughts (such as having a thanksgiving section and a body) than to see how his argument unfolds.

we will then revisit these contexts and ask more intentionally how our passage relates to them (see step 6).

D. (4) Identify the Translational Difficulties and Establish the Text

Having identified the passage of study and the contexts in which it is embedded, we must now turn to consider the details of the text. The first thing we need to do is identify the best text to use. That is, translations will sometimes differ from one another; we need to identify which translation best represents the original biblical text—what is often called the *autographa*.[2] This will look differently depending on whether you are reading the original language texts (Greek, Aramaic, or Hebrew) or a translation. There are two issues that need to be considered when establishing the text. There are issues, first, of translation difference and, second, of textual difference. The latter issues are relevant mostly to readers of the original text. Generally, for most readers of the Bible, it would be best to trust the translation you are using unless you are given a significant reason otherwise.

When it comes to differences in translation, there are many helpful tools that can guide readers in resolving the issue. However, when it is necessary to resolve a textual difference—even for those who have the knowledge base and skills to resolve a significant textual difference (namely, reading ability in the original languages)—we will be highly dependent on the work of scholars who specialize in the field of text criticism and who know the original languages. For these reasons, it is necessary to use secondary resources—such as commentaries or study Bibles—in this step of exegesis. Though we will discuss both types of issues here, this book will mostly address issues concerning different translations. The recommended reading in this chapter

---

[2] The *autographa* are the original canonical texts—the texts given to us by God under the guidance of the Holy Spirit to act as a covenant document for his people—not necessarily the original text that left the named author's hand. For example, the *autographa* of the Pentateuch involve various editorial details that were added after the text was written by Moses; these editorial editions (such as the notice about Moses' death or notices about changes in place names) should be considered part of the *autographa*.

and later chapters will provide additional resources for those who want to pursue text-critical issues.[3]

a. *Translation Differences*

When you are reading a translation—or translating the text—you must identify what the best translation of particular words or phrases is. For most of us, our concern will not be with every word in a text but only with those places where one English translation differs from another. Consider, for example, Habakkuk 3:13:

> You *went* out for the salvation of your people,
>> for the salvation *of your anointed*. (ESV, cf. NASB, emphasis added)
>
> You *come* forth for the salvation of your people,
>> for salvation *with your anointed*, (my translation, cf. KJV, emphasis added)[4]

I have chosen the ESV and NASB translations for comparison because, as we will see in Chapter 8, the more literal translations are the best translations to use when studying the Bible. There are two differences here that need to be considered if we are going to properly interpret this passage. First, is it "salvation *with*" or "salvation *of*" God's anointed? Second, is this text referring to Yahweh's past ("went") or present ("come") action?

If you are not familiar with the original language of the passage (Hebrew in this case), this may be a difficult difference to resolve, yet there are helpful resources that will guide you in making a decision. We need to figure out, first, why the translation is different. Namely, we must ask if there is a difference in the underlying text or if the translations are disagreeing on the translation of the same underlying text. To identify the problem, the use of a study Bible or some sort of interlinear text will most likely be necessary.[5] Again, for many readers of the Bible, this step will be unnecessary. If such a

---

[3] If you are going to be studying in the original languages, especially in Hebrew, it will be necessary to learn the basics of text criticism.

[4] My translation is taken from my Habakkuk study guide, *Believe the Unbelievable* (Teleioteti, 2018).

[5] We will look at such resources and there use in Ch. 10.

question arises, it may be wisest to seek the help of a pastor or language expert in your church.

Study Bible's will often have a footnote stating alternate translations and why they are different. They will often give a source, such as a different text (e.g. LXX, the Greek translation of the Old Testament) or an emendation (a deliberate correction made by the translator) for the difference between the footnote translation and the one in the text.[6] Looking at an interlinear for both translations or using Bible software (see chs. 9 and 10) will also show someone with basic knowledge of Hebrew whether translators are translating the same text or different ones.

If there is a disagreement over the underlying text (if one translation says it is word-A but the other word-B), the way to resolve this disagreement is textual criticism, which we will consider briefly below. But if translations agree that it is the same word, only differing in how to translate it, several steps can then be taken. The first is to identify the word in question (in Habakkuk 3:13 it is אֵת (*'et*)) and do a word study (see Ch. 9). A word study will, in this case, reveal two things; first, there are far too many instances of this word to study. Second, this word is actually a homonym, two different words spelt in the exact same way. One word is a preposition meaning "with"; the other is a textual marker that indicates which word receives the action of a verb (called the marker of the definite direct object; that is, it is used to indicate two grammatical categories, that a word is *definite* and the *direct object* of a verb). The question is, which word is Habakkuk using? A good commentary will discuss the pros and cons of each translation, and a Hebrew Grammar or lexicon (i.e. dictionary) will give examples of how each word is used.

In this case, a commentary may argue that the marker of the definite direct object (DDO) is not often used without a verb and that "for salvation," though resembling a verb, is clearly a noun with the preposition "for" (לְ) attached to it. Furthermore, it will be observed that Habakkuk, like most Hebrew prophecy and poetry, very rarely uses the marker of the DDO (3x,

---

[6] Consider Hab 2:5, the ESV footnote on "wine" says "Masoretic Text; Dead Sea Scroll, *wealth*." That is, the standard Hebrew Text (Masoretic Text, MT) has a Hebrew word meaning "wine," but the Dead Sea Scroll has a Hebrew word meaning "wealth." By putting "wine" in the text, the translators indicate that they think this is most likely to be the original.

1:4, 6; 2:14). From this evidence, we could then conclude that the most evident reading of the text is "with your anointed," unless the context indicates that this is not correct. However, a close study of the context reveals that this makes great sense.

Regarding the tense of the verb, "went" or "come forth," a scan of several commentaries should reveal that the Hebrew verbs behind this whole chapter (Habakkuk 3) are ambiguous: they could refer to a past or future event. Considering the events Habakkuk is describing in Chapter 3 in light of the first part of the book (cf. 1:5 and 3:2, 3:16-19), I think that the present translation is far more likely.[7]

b. *Textual Differences*

In other cases, the difference between two translations may not be a question of grammar or word meaning but of which words the biblical author intended. That is, the Bibles we read today are obviously not the original pages written by the biblical authors, nor are they translations of the originals. Instead, what we have are copies and translations of copies—and we have a lot of copies (20,000+ NT manuscripts)![8] When we read the Bible, we are interested in hearing what God is saying, what he led the authors of Scripture to write. So we are interested in the original words of the authors.[9] None of these copies is perfect, so the discipline of *text criticism* was developed to recover the original text from the copies we have. None of our English Bibles represents a single manuscript. The texts usually printed as the Greek New Testament (Including the Nestle-Aland, UBS, and Tyndale Greek New Testament) are known as critical texts, produced from comparing the

---

[7] I discuss this example further in my study guide *Believe the Unbelievable* and in my commentary on Habakkuk (Teleioteti, 2019). Essentially, Habakkuk is portraying the coming Babylonian invasion—in all its horror—as a salvific act of God.

[8] This number includes Greek language manuscripts and early translations into Latin and other languages.

[9] To be specific, we are interested in the canonical *autographa*. That is, the original texts that God has ordained to govern his people. In the time between the original writing of some books, such as the Pentateuch (Genesis-Deuteronomy), and the writing of the last book by the end of the 1st century AD, some editorial comments were added but are considered authoritative—part of the *autographa* (these include, for example, updated place names in the Pentateuch).

manuscripts we have in order to reproduce what was most likely the original text. The Hebrew Old Testament text as it is usually found (including the BHS and similar editions) is known as a diplomatic text: it presents the content of a single manuscript, the Leningrad Codex, and presents the alternative evidence in the critical notes (i.e. notes that offer alternative textual readings and the evidence for them).

Sometimes translations disagree on which textual reading—which manuscript text—best represents the original. For instance, in 2 Thessalonians 2:13, the ESV translates "because God chose you as *the firstfruits* to be saved" (emphasis added) but the NASB "because God has chosen you *from the beginning* for salvation" (emphasis added). This is a textual difference; firstfruits translates the word ἀπαρχὴς (*aparchēs*) and "from the beginning" the phrase ἀπ' ἀρχῆς (*ap' archēs*). As you can see, these are very similar, only a space differentiating them. The manuscript evidence is strong for both readings. Therefore, to make a decision in such a case, text critics use what are called internal evidence. That is, they ask how the context help us identify which one of these is most appropriate. In my own study, I have concluded that Paul's intention here and use of both these words (or lack thereof) supports the manuscript evidence in favour of ἀπ' ἀρχῆς, "from the beginning."[10]

A more significant difference is found in the book of Mark. English translations make some sort of break between Mark 16:8 and 16:9-20, noting that the later verses are not found in the earlier and generally more trustworthy manuscripts. In this case, a text-critical decision is not over which word is original but over whether a section of text (cf. John 7:53-8:11) is part of the original text. In both of these cases, Mark 16 and John 7:53-8:11, the current consensus is that these are later additions to the text, inserted by scribes in the years after the canon was closed—after the last biblical book was written. This decision is made primarily on the basis of manuscript evidence, evaluating the testimony of the manuscripts for and against each reading, both their age and quality. But internal considerations are also made.

If you intend to read and study the Bible in its original languages or study the Bible for teaching, it would be wise to familiarize yourself with the basics of text criticism, at the very least so you can evaluate the arguments presented

---

[10] *Prevenient Grace: An Investigation into Arminianism* (Teleioteti, 2016), 192-193.

by different commentators. See the Further Reading section at the end of this chapter for resources to help in this area. In conclusion, it should be remembered that though there are differences in translations and manuscripts, there is far more agreement than disagreement and the most common differences between copies are insignificant for meaning and interpretation. There is good reason to trust the Old Testament text we have and the New Testament critical text that stands behind our English translations.

E. (5) OBSERVE THE TEXT

At this point, we have prepared our hearts, identified our passage and its context, and begun to resolve differences between translations of the text. With this foundation laid, it is now time to turn and consider the text itself. The best thing to do is read, read, and read some more. Read in several translations or work to translate the text yourself—this will help you clarify what you think the text is saying. As you read, observe connections between the text, what words are repeated, themes are revisited. Consider if the author is using quotations from or allusions to the Old Testament; if so, read those texts and ask yourself why he is drawing on these texts. Some of us find it helpful to mark up our Bibles—draw lines between repeated or connected words, highlight or mark different words and their relationships, etc.—or to print out the passage on a piece of paper and do the same.

The point is to pay careful attention to the text, to make sure you understand what is being said and why it is being said. It is only by understanding clearly what is being said that you will know how to make an application of your passage. This step should take the most amount of time. There are several tools that you can use to read better, depending on the type of passage you are reading (poetry, narrative, or letter); I will discuss these tools in the following chapter. At this point, all I want to do is hammer in how important it is to read the text well, to read it carefully, and do so repeatedly. A good technique for looking well is asking good questions; instead of staring blankly at the text, ask why this word is used instead of that one, ask why this sentence follows that one or this conjunction is used. Asking good questions will reveal far more than just looking will do.

In our culture, we are used to quick fixes—5-minute oil changes, 30-second commercials, and Google searches. We are not trained to work our way patiently and slowly through a text to ensure we understand it. If we are going to be good readers of the Bible, we need to train ourselves to do this. When I was taught exegesis in Bible College, my teacher used the following story to illustrate this:

a.   Agassiz and the Fish

It was more than fifteen years ago that I entered the laboratory of Professor Agassiz, and told him I had enrolled my name in the scientific school as a student of natural history. He asked me a few questions about my object in coming, my antecedents generally, the mode in which I afterwards proposed to use the knowledge I might acquire, and finally, whether I wished to study any special branch. To the latter I replied that while I wished to be well grounded in all departments of zoology, I purposed to devote myself specially to insects.

"When do you wish to begin?" he asked.

"Now," I replied.

This seemed to please him, and with an energetic "Very well," he reached from a shelf a huge jar of specimens in yellow alcohol.

"Take this fish," he said, "and look at it; we call it a Haemulon; by and by I will ask what you have seen."

With that he left me.... I was conscious of a passing feeling of disappointment, for gazing at a fish did not commend itself to an ardent entomologist....

In ten minutes I had seen all that could be seen in that fish, and started in search of the professor, who had, however, left the museum; and when I returned, after lingering over some of the odd animals stored in the upper apartment, my specimen was dry all over. I dashed the fluid over the fish as if to resuscitate it from a fainting-fit, and looked with anxiety for a return of a normal, sloppy appearance. This little excitement over, nothing was to be done but return to a steadfast gaze at my mute companion. Half an hour passed, an hour, another hour; the fish began to look loathsome. I turned it over and around; looked it in the face—ghastly; from behind, beneath, above, sideways, at a three-quarters view—just as ghastly. I was in despair; at an early hour, I concluded that lunch was necessary; so with infinite relief, the fish was carefully replaced in the jar, and for an hour I was free.

On my return, I learned that Professor Agassiz had been at the museum, but had gone and would not return for several hours. My fellow students were too busy to be disturbed by continued conversation. Slowly I drew forth that hideous fish, and with a feeling of desperation again looked at it. I might not use a magnifying glass; instruments of all kinds were interdicted. My two hands, my two eyes, and the fish; it seemed a most limited field. I pushed my fingers down its throat to see how sharp its teeth were. I began to count the scales in the different rows until I was convinced that that was nonsense. At last a happy thought struck me—I would draw the fish; and now with surprise I began to discover new features in the creature. Just then the professor returned.

"That is right," said he, "a pencil is one of the best eyes. I am glad to notice, too, that you keep your specimen wet and your bottle corked."

With these encouraging words he added—

"Well, what is it like?"

He listened attentively to my brief rehearsal of the structure of parts whose names were still unknown to me; the fringed gill-arches and movable operculum; the pores of the head, fleshly lips, and lidless eyes; the lateral line, the spinous fin, and forked tail; the compressed and arched body. When I had finished, he waited as if expecting more, and then, with an air of disappointment:

"You have not looked very carefully; why," he continued, more earnestly, "you haven't seen one of the most conspicuous features of the animal, which is as plainly before your eyes as the fish itself. Look again; look again!" And he left me to my misery.

I was piqued; I was mortified. Still more of that wretched fish? But now I set myself to the task with a will, and discovered one new thing after another, until I saw how just the professor's criticism had been. The afternoon passed quickly, and when, towards its close, the professor inquired,

"Do you see it yet?"

"No," I replied. "I am certain I do not, but I see how little I saw before."

"That is next best," said he earnestly, "but I won't hear you now; put away your fish and go home; perhaps you will be ready with a better answer in the morning. I will examine you before you look at the fish."

This was disconcerting; not only must I think of my fish all night, studying, without the object before me, what this unknown but most visible feature might be, but also, without reviewing my new discoveries, I must give an exact account of them the next day. I had a bad memory; so I walked home by Charles River in a distracted state, with my two perplexities.

The cordial greeting from the professor the next morning was reassuring; here was a man who seemed to be quite as anxious as I that I should see for myself what he saw.

"Do you perhaps mean," I asked, "that the fish has symmetrical sides with paired organs?"

His thoroughly pleased, "Of course, of course!" repaid the wakeful hours of the previous night. After he had discoursed most happily and enthusiastically—as he always did—upon the importance of this point, I ventured to ask what I should do next.

"Oh, look at your fish!" he said, and left me again to my own devices. In a little more than an hour he returned and heard my new catalogue.

"That is good, that is good!" he repeated, "but that is not all; go on." And so for three long days, he placed that fish before my eyes, forbidding me to look at anything else, or to use any artificial aid. "Look, look, look," was his repeated injunction.

This was the best entomological lesson I ever had—a lesson whose influence was extended to the details of every subsequent study; a legacy the professor has left to me, as he left it to many others, of inestimable value, which we could not buy, with which we cannot part....

The fourth day a second fish of the same group was placed beside the first, and I was bidden to point out the resemblances and differences between the two; another and another followed, until the entire family lay before me, and a whole legion of jars covered the table and surrounding shelves; the odor had become a pleasant perfume; and even now, the sight of an old six-inch worm-eaten cork brings fragrant memories!

The whole group of Haemulons was thus brought into review; and whether engaged upon the dissection of the internal organs, preparation and examination of the bony framework, or the description of the various parts, Agassiz's training in the method of observing facts in their orderly arrangement, was ever accompanied by the urgent exhortation not to be content with them.

"Facts are stupid things," he would say, "until brought into connection with some general law."

At the end of eight months, it was almost with reluctance that I left these friends and turned to insects; but what I gained by this outside experience has been of greater value than years of later investigation in my favorite groups.[11]

F. (6) IDENTIFY THE PASSAGE'S RELATION TO THE SURROUNDING CONTEXTS

In step 4, I suggested that you identify the contexts in which the text is found before beginning to study the passage itself. At that point, you learned about the context, then in steps 4 and 5, you learned about the passage. Now it is important to bring these two together. In this sixth step, we identify why our passage is where it is. For example, why does Paul begin the main argument of Romans with an exposition of the fallen state of humanity (Rom 1:18-3:20)? Or why does Mark tell the story of Jesus cleansing the temple between the cursing of the fig tree and its effect (Mark 11:12-25, cf. Matt 21:19-22)? Why does it matter that you study Mark's account of an event and not

---

[11] There are several versions of this story available around the web, this one is from the Gospel Coalition, https://www.thegospelcoalition.org/blogs/justin-taylor/agassiz-and-the-fish/.

Matthews? Does Mark have a different purpose that will affect your understanding of the passage? Answering such questions will teach you more about your passage and reveal some of its significance, ways in which it applies.

Consider Romans 1:18-3:20; by thinking about its place in the book of Romans, we see that it has a fundamental role in establishing the truth that all humans need the salvation God makes available through the Cross. We understand, then, that the negative picture Paul paints of God's wrath against sin is intended to point Jews and Gentiles alike—all people—to their need for Jesus Christ. On such a foundation, there is no legitimate ground for Jews or Gentiles to look down on one another. The following passages (3:21-4:25, 5:1-21) show us that on the day "God judges the secrets of men by Christ Jesus" (Rom 2:16, cf. 6-11), our hope for a positive verdict will be in what Christ has accomplished and not in any works we have done (Rom 3:21-5:21; cf. Rev. 13:8, 20:11-15). For the passage in Mark, studying the context of Mark 11:12-25 would reveal that Mark frequently splices a story in the midst of another (forming an A1, B, A2 pattern) in order that the middle story would interpret the surrounding material or vice versa. In this case, the cursing of the fig tree—a tree which appeared to have fruit but had none—reveals God's verdict upon the temple, which ought to have produced the fruit of righteousness but was instead found to be a den of robbers (Mark 11:17). In Habakkuk, the location of Chapter 3 at the end of the dialogue between God and Habakkuk in chapters 1-2 leads us to interpret this song (chapter 3) as a response to God's revelation of the Chaldean invasion, given in 1:5-11 and discussed in 1:12-2:20. For this reason, the "anointed" in 3:12[12] is best understand as the Chaldean leader raised up by God (1:5), and the "work" mentioned in 3:2 is to be correlated with the other two instances of this word root in 1:5 ("For *I am doing* a *work* in your days").

In addition to questions of the immediate context, also identify what difference the greater canonical context makes. You may ask, for example, what difference it makes that the Psalms are in the Old Testament and not the New. How will your application have to take into account its location? Also, why is Chronicles in the third section of the Old Testament (the

---

[12] This verse ought to be translated, as in the KJV and my commentary on Habakkuk, "You went out for the salvation of your people, for salvation with your anointed."

Writings)? Does this shed light on its purpose and give you ideas on how it applies? Why does the phrase "worthy woman" appear only in Proverbs and the book of Ruth? Does the close connection between Proverbs 31 and the book of Ruth shed light on the application of the latter? For passages appearing in the Old Testament, we will have to consider what has changed between the Old and New Covenants in order to make an appropriate application.

Interpreting Chronicles in light of the 3rd section of the Old Testament explains why it differs in its presentation from Samuel and Kings and may point us to more explicitly ethical applications, using the stories of righteousness reward and unrighteousness punished to illustrate God's faithfulness to uphold his promises to bless and to curse certain behaviours. However, we will also have to take into account the difference between Testaments and the rest of the biblical teaching. Doing so, we may see instances of a curse as ultimately pointing to final judgment and blessing pointing to our hope in God's faithfulness, whether we see it fulfilled to some extent in this life or wait for the fulness of his promises fulfilled in the new heavens and the new earth.

Considering the differences between covenants will lead us to apply the passages in Exodus, Leviticus, and Deuteronomy about physical separation from unbelieving nations as examples and illustrations of the spiritual separation we are called to under the New Covenant (2 Cor 6:14-7:1). Though God's will and character remain the same across both Testaments, the difference in the covenant community (cf. Ch. 4) will lead us to apply texts concerning God's promises and his will differently than the ancient Israelites would have. We may eat bacon, but we will be reminded that God cares about the purity of his people, that they would not be a mixture of holy and unholy, torn between the Kingdom of God and Satan's kingdom (cf. Lev 11:2-33).

Intertextual connections such as that between Proverbs 31 and the book of Ruth will draw our attention to the exemplary behaviour of Ruth. Though the idealization of the faithful woman in Proverbs 31 seems unattainable, Ruth illustrates how the godly characteristics extolled in these proverbs play out in real-life circumstances.

G. (7) APPLY THE PASSAGE

Once you are satisfied that you have understood the passage—not exhausted it but have enough understanding of what it is saying—apply it to yourself or those to whom you are ministering. Ask questions like; how does God want me to change my thinking in light of this passage? For example, Romans 9 may require you to reconsider your understanding of how you were saved. Ask, how does God want me to act in response to this passage? Maybe Paul's conviction to remember the poor in Galatians 2:10 will lead you to use your wealth to meet the needs of those in your congregation who are lacking. Or ask, how does God want me to change my attitude, the way I feel? In reading the Psalms, the appropriate response may be mourning over sin or rejoicing over salvation. Reading Philippians 4, the response may be to battle anxiety with thanksgiving and the truth of God's Word.

As you seek to apply the text, remember the categories we discussed in Chapter 5 (validity, appropriateness, and fittingness). Make sure that your application is valid in light of the text's wording, appropriate to its intent, and fitting for its referent—e.g. that you are not applying an injunction solely for Israel to the Church today. As you formulate and clarify your application of the passage, it often happens that you come to a better understanding of the text and must revise your application. This is part of the process of understanding the text well.

H. (8) CHECK YOUR UNDERSTANDING

The last step in interpretation is to check your understanding. So far, you should have been checking your work against the text itself and your application against your previous study of the text. Now, seek the input of others to verify or challenge your work. This can often happen effectively in dialogue with someone else studying the same passage. It can also be helpful to talk to your pastor or lay leaders, if they have time, about your understanding of the text.

In addition to those in your church or school community, commentaries, theological studies, and good web resources can help you better understand the text, see things that you missed, and revise or confirm your application. We will discuss these resources further in Chapter 10, but now is the time when you would use them.

I. Conclusion

Though I have divided exegesis, or Bible study, into these eight steps, you will probably discover that you would do it a little differently. You will also discover that this list is more of a circle than a line; each step often forces you to go back to the beginning and move through the steps again. The important thing is that we must be good readers of the text; each of these steps is necessary, though you may do them a little bit differently than I do. We must also never leave our work at step 6, understanding what the text says; we must always press on to application, asking why it matters that the text says this. It is our responsibility as those seeking to be faithful to Jesus Christ to read closely and respond appropriately. Only when we have responded to the text in a right manner have we completed our task.

Further Reading

Fee, Gordon – *New Testament Exegesis: A Handbook for Student's and Pastors* [I]

Stuart, Douglas – *Old Testament Exegesis: A Handbook for Student's and Pastors* [I]

Text Criticism[13]

Black, David Alan – *Rethinking New Testament Textual Criticism* [A]
*Jongkind, Dirk – *An Introduction to the Greek New Testament* [B]
Wurthwein, Ernst – *The Text of the Old Testament* [I]
Metzger, Bruce M. & Bart D. Ehrman – *The Text of the New Testament: Its Transmission, Corruption, and Restoration* [I]

---

[13] Many of resources on this subject are not written by Evangelical Christians and need to be approached with considerable care. Dirk Jongkind's book is a good place to start for an Evangelical perspective.

KNOWING THE STYLES OF BIBLICAL WRITING

> "Hear my words: If there is a prophet among you, I the Lord make myself known to him in a vision; I speak with him in a dream. Not so with my servant Moses. He is faithful in all my house. With him I speak mouth to mouth, clearly, and not in riddles, and he beholds the form of the Lord. Why then were you not afraid to speak against my servant Moses?" – Numbers 12:6-8

As we read texts—books, essays, blog posts, etc.—we learn quickly to identify relationships between related types of text. For example, we classify books as fiction and non-fiction according to their intent. We can relate essays according to the style of writing and the amount of knowledge they assume. Technical essays assume a lot of pre-understanding and often involve difficult style; popular essays, on the other hand, do not assume the reader is fluent in the topic and try to write in a more common vernacular.[1]

Beyond these general types or genres of literature (books and essays; popular and technical), we can also identify styles of writing shared among bodies of writing. For example, though it is difficult to draw a solid line between them, poetry and narrative texts can be distinguished. In English,

---

[1] The reader who has previously studied Biblical exegesis and hermeneutics will notice that some divergence in this chapter from the standard evangelical approaches to "genre." I explain in *The Gift of Reading – Part 2* why I take issue with contemporary genre theory and how the approach taken here is helpful. The second section of this series ("God's Gifts for the Christian Life") will provide much of the content concerning genre usually found in hermeneutics textbooks. What is said here is meant to lay a foundation for interacting with these other resources and the Biblical text.

the former are identified by their rhythm and often vivid imagery, the latter by its coordinating style (where events are relayed one after another with explanatory detail revolving around these events). Furthermore, we can distinguish broadly didactic prose texts, texts that communicate hypotactically—that is, they use lots of conjunctions to subordinate sentences (e.g. because, for, therefore, so that, etc.)—and favour logical organization rather than temporal (they relate ideas logically not events in temporal order).

This book is an example of didactic prose (though the story of Agassiz and the Fish was narrative, and the prayer in the introduction was poetry). In the Bible, we can identify four broad text styles used by the authors to communicate. There are narrative, poetic, didactic prose,[2] and prophetic styles. It is usually the case that a book will mix these styles, having both narrative and poetic texts, for example. In this chapter, we will consider key features of these styles and techniques that can help us observe texts of a particular style better. Having categories for recognizing different styles of texts will help us in many of the steps outlined in the previous chapter. I cannot hope in a book this size to give a sufficient account of the following styles found in the Bible; instead, I intend to lay a foundation upon which the reader may build with online and print literature or by learning from a mentor or teacher. However, like every aspect of exegesis, knowledge of the styles of biblical texts emerges from careful attention to the texts themselves, so readers who have not had formal training yet have spent much time in the Word may very well recognize the various textual features I group together as "styles."

A. Narrative[3]

Now when they had departed, behold, an angel of the Lord appeared to Joseph in a dream and said, "Rise, take the child

---

[2] The term "discourse" is often used for what I am calling "didactic prose." I admit that discourse is a lot less clumsy and technical sounding, yet "discourse" is in many ways too broad of a category. All communication is "discourse," not just one style of it. My terminology is weak because outside of Biblical literature, "didactic prose" does not need to be a form of teaching (such as a love letter). However, I think this accurately captures the style as it is found in the Bible.

[3] Some of the content and many of the examples in what follows are adapted from my master's thesis on 1 & 2 Samuel, *God's Kingdom through his Priest-King*.

and his mother, and flee to Egypt, and remain there until I tell you, for Herod is about to search for the child, to destroy him." And he rose and took the child and his mother by night and departed to Egypt and remained there until the death of Herod. This was to fulfil what the Lord had spoken by the prophet, "Out of Egypt I called my son." – Matthew 2:13-15

The most common style in the Bible may be narrative; many books are narratives, and many books that are not narratives contain narrative segments (e.g. Job 1-2; Isa 36-39). We could define a narrative as a text that is characterized by a narrator and a plot.[4] That is, it is characterized by a person telling a story—a narrator—and progressing set of events. A plot has elements of progression—it moves somewhere—and this progression is based on the temporal succession of events. Narratives will predominantly use a narrative style, as discussed below, yet will integrate sections of didactic prose and poetry. For example, the book of Samuel is a narrative; it has a single narrator and a plot. Yet the book contains texts in non-narrative style, such as the songs in 1 Samuel 2:1-10 and 2 Samuel 1:19-27. For this reason, we need to distinguish narrative texts, characterized by plot and a narrator, from narrative style, the predominant style of writing within narrative texts. The same distinction is true for didactic prose texts and style; a didactic prose text, such as an epistle, will often contain sections written in narrative, poetic, or prophetic style (e.g. Galatians 2:11-16).[5]

Every style uses basic units to communicate—for example, didactic prose (such as this book) is driven by sentences organized into paragraphs. The basic building blocks of a narrative are actions and scenes, a set of actions accompanied at times by a setting or interpretation. In the example above (Matt 2:13-15), there are seven actions that comprise the scene. The final

---

[4] This is based on the definition employed by Jean Louis Ska, *"Our Fathers Have Told Us": Introduction to the Analysis of Hebrew Narratives*, Subsidia Biblica 13 (Roma: Editrice Pontificio Instituto Biblico, 1990), 6.

[5] In such cases, these texts need to be analysed according to their style; so a poem embedded in a narrative needs to be analysed as a poetic text. However, a poem will play a role in the narrative in which it is embedded. They will often provide a narrator or a character's interpretation of the surrounding events. For example, Hannah's song in 1 Sam 2:1-10 provides a lens through which to interpret all the following events.

sentence is an example of a narrator interpreting the scene. Narrative is also distinct from other styles in the way it communicates its message. Instead of directly explaining what is meant or using symbolism and metaphor, narrative employs description. In literary theory, it is often said that narratives *show;* they do not tell. If, for example, the narrator wants to impress upon the reader the seriousness of murder and its consequences, he would not say, "You shall not murder" (Exod 20:13). Instead, he would tell a story showing the severity and consequences of murder (Gen 4:1-16).

Recognizing these basic features of narrative (its temporally based plot, descriptive character, and basic division into scenes) helps us learn to read specific narratives better. For the rest of this section, we will consider how the author of a narrative uses plot and the order of scenes to communicate, how an author uses description to convey meaning, and how the technique of storyboarding can help us look closer at narratives.

a. How Narratives Communicate: Plot and Scene Arrangement

Though a narrative is based on a linear series of events (Bob leaves the house, shuts the door, locks the door, walks to his car, and drives to work), narratives are not necessarily told in a linear fashion. Sometimes the narrator will rearrange a series of events to communicate something, to make his point. There are many examples of this throughout the Bible, but a particularly prevalent device used is called "interpolation" (this is especially common in the Gospel of Mark, earning it the nickname "the Markan sandwich").

Interpolation occurs when an author begins a scene but introduces another scene or segment of narrative before concluding the first scene. This forms an A1 – B – A2 pattern, where A1 is the first part and A2 the second part of a scene interrupted by B. An example of a significant interpolation is found in 2 Samuel 11 and 12. In 2 Samuel 11:1, the narrator introduces the siege of the Ammonite city Rabbah. The success of this siege is not recorded until 12:26-31. This raises a significant question: is the author merely interested in plot, recording events in their proper order, or is he making a point by separating the beginning of the siege from its conclusion? If you read the events that occur between this sandwich, you might observe their significance. 2 Samuel 11:2-12:25 recounts David's adultery with Bathsheba, a key point in the story of David. More significantly, this incident is closely related to God's promise to David in 2 Samuel 7. God promises to give David peace from his enemies and an offspring who would rule forever after him. Implicit in the covenant God makes with David is the demand for obedience. When we read of David's horrific acts, we should be drawn back to the covenant and wonder how David's behaviour will affect it. Indeed, the author invites us to do so by putting off the record of the defeat of the Ammonites until after the crisis resolves. By splitting the account of the defeat of the Ammonites, the author of Samuel places the promise of rest from David's enemies in danger. Careful attention to the structure of the narrative, and the technique of interpolation, helps us understand what an author is telling with his story.[6]

Authors use the arrangement of their narratives to teach the reader in many ways; interpolation is only one of them. Another arrangement to be aware of is a chiasm, where an author creates an A-B-C-B'-A' pattern by shaping his later material to reflect the first part of his narrative. In such an arrangement, the emphasis lays on the central point, C. Learning to identify and interpret such devices will only come with practice, but some basic principles can guide us in identifying them. If plot is the linear succession of events that lays behind a narrative (Plot = events A, B, C, D, E, F: Bob leaves the house, shuts the door, locks the door, walks to his car, and drives to work), we can discern the use of narrative devices when this temporal arrangement is changed. Narrators must necessarily exclude some events of a plot from their story (e.g. the story may only have events A, D, E, and F), for they cannot recount everything that happens; sometimes, these omissions are important. For example, in our story of Bob leaving his house to go to work, omitting the action "he locked the door" may foreshadow a future event, such as a home robbery. It is also significant when the narrator deliberately changes the order (Plot = A, B, C, D, E, F : Narrative = A, C, B, D, E1, F, E2). Sometimes a narrator will recount an event and then revisit it from another angle, shedding further light on its significance (Genesis 1, cf. Genesis 2). When this happens, we need to ask why the narrator has changed the order of events? What is he trying to communicate? What tension is he trying to create?

b. How Narratives Communicate: Description

---

[6] This example is taken from Rutherford, *God's Kingdom*.

The use of narrative arrangement could be called a macro-level tool narrators use to tell their stories; it involves the arrangement of scenes.[7] But zooming in to the scenes themselves, the narrator also has several tools at their disposal to tell the story.

When a narrator tells a story, he or she is not able to recount every detail of an event; to do so would be impossible and would make for horrible reading. Instead, they offer an interpretation of an event. They are selective about which details they include and which they exclude. Because they are selective about the details, carefully reading a narrative is key to understanding it. We must observe what the author includes—nothing is by accident—and what he excludes.

For example, consider the description the author of Samuel provides for Saul. In 1 Samuel 9, he includes, among other details, that Saul is the son of a wealthy man named Kish (9:1), a handsome young man (9:2)—indeed, the most handsome (9:2). Furthermore, he is tall (9:2). Coincidently, this tall (גָּבֹהַּ, *gābōah*) man is also from Gibeah (גִּבְעָה, *Gib'āh*), a tall place (10:26). The details about his height may seem pointless and disconnected from the details about his status, yet after closer examination, they may not be after all. Consider first that the word גָּבֹהַּ only occurs four times in 1 & 2 Samuel, all in 1 Samuel. In explicit contrast to 1 Samuel 9:2, God tells Samuel not to anoint a future king on the basis of "the *height* of his stature" (16:7, emphasis added). The most significant instances are in 1 Samuel 2:3, "Talk no more *so very proudly*," literally "very highly" (גְּבֹהָה גְבֹהָה, *gᵉbōhāh gᵉbōhāh*). In context, this line begins a contrast between the rich and lofty who are brought low and the lowly who are exalted by Yahweh. The point of the song in which 2:3 is found is to anticipate the work of God to exalt a future of king of Israel from a lowly state to the throne (cf. 2:10). For this reason, the way the narrator portrays Saul in 1 Samuel 9-10 is incredibly significant. By portraying Saul as a man of prominent physical presence and social status, the narrator subtly demonstrates that this man will not be the king God intends to give his people.

---

[7] Scene, as I am using it, is an imprecise descriptor. A scene is a complete narrative unit, composed of one or more major narrative actions and usually distinguished by some sort of scene transition or descriptor (e.g. 2 Samuel 11:2, 11:6, 11:14).

Paying attention to the details of a narrative takes time and practice, but there are several things to look for. Look for repeated words in scenes and across entire narratives; consider which characters the narrator describes and names—they are probably important—and which are barely considered, for they are often just part of the scenery (e.g. 2 Sam 11:2-5); and identify key themes that are repeated (e.g. Gen 11:30, 25:21; Judg 13:2; 1 Sam 1:5-6; Luke 1:7) or events that are closely related (e.g. Gen 12:1-20; 20:1-18; 26:6-11). Pay particular attention to the comments the narrator makes. If a narrator takes time to provide a comment evaluating the behaviour or motives of a character, it will be highly significant (e.g. 2 Sam 11:1).

Entire books are dedicated to the different techniques narrators use to communicate. We do not have space to explore these techniques, but I have provided several resources at the end of this chapter that do so. Though there are many books that will lay out different features to pay attention to, the best approach I have found is to read lots of narrative texts, getting a feel for how different narrators tell their stories. To breakdown a scene in a narrative and pay closer attention to its details, the technique of storyboarding may be helpful.

c. *Study Strategy: Storyboarding*[8]

Storyboarding is a technique for visually breaking a narrative down into its basic parts and thinking more slowly and carefully about it. To start, you need to identify the scope of your narrative. If you are dealing with a single scene, you will map out each major action of the scene. If you are dealing with a string of scenes, you will map out each scene. The idea is to identify those main actions or events that drive the story and how the narrator recounts these actions or events. The main action of a scene will often be accompanied by sideline actions; for example, for Jesus to heal someone, he sometimes stretches out and touches them (e.g. Mark 1:41). There will often be an introduction to a scene, presenting the circumstances in which the main actions occur or introducing the characters (e.g. Job 1:6). Sometimes individual actions are given background, such as a narrator's description of the circumstances preceding the action (Mark 4:38a). Place dialogue or clause

---

[8] I have adapted the idea of storyboarding for Biblical narratives and the format below from my teacher, Brad Copp.

of direct perception (he saw *that they were there*) beside your storyboard; the board is focusing on the actions themselves. However, dialogue is often essential to interpreting the actions of the scene. Here is a template:

Consider the account of David and Bathsheba (2 Sam 11:1-27). We could break this narrative down into five major scenes or moments (each made of several scenes) and an introduction (or exposition). The exposition or introduction is a narrative scene that serves to set the background for the events to follow; in these verses, it is verse 1. Storyboarding the exposition (2 Sam 11:1) and the three scenes (2 Sam 11:2-3, 4, 5) of the first narrative section (2 Sam 11:1-5) might look like this:[9]

Background information: here you will put any information concerning the setting of the main action (Hebrew: often nominal clauses, clauses beginning with a noun, or וַיְהִי (*vayhî*, and it happened)
Main actions: e.g. they saw that, they said, he touched, they fought (Greek: indicatives)
Sideline actions: e.g. they got up, packed up, embarked, walked (Greek: participles, infinitives)
Narrative Clues: Record any implicit or explicit clues the narrator provides for interpreting the scene. Implicitly, does this scene have repeated words, does it juxtapose with a preceding or following scene? Explicitly, does the narrator offer any evaluation of the events, any comment on their nature or purpose (e.g. Mark 1:41a)?

---

[9] We could divide 2 Sam 11:2-5 into 3 scenes. 2 Sam 11:2-3 gives the introduction and initial action of David. 2 Sam 11:4 gives the narrative climax of the account. 2 Sam 11:5 provides the conclusion of the narrative, the result. This transitions to the next narrative, in which David responds to the resulting situation. 2 Samuel 11:1 could also be divided into three small scenes.

Verse 1

Background information: Time: "In the spring of the year, the time when kings go out to battle" (1a-b)	
Main actions: David sent Joab... They ravaged... And besieged them...	**Sideline actions:**
Narrative Clues: "the time when *kings go out to battle*" - David, the king, does not go out to battle (1b). "David sent Joab, and his servants with him, and all Israel.... *But David* remained at Jerusalem" (1c-e). The last sentence (1e) focuses on the status of David; it is not a main action. The narrator is alerting us to a key piece of the story: everyone BUT David went to battle.	

Verse 2-3

Background information: Time and circumstance: late one afternoon, David was walking on the roof. Inciting incident: he saw a woman bathing. Characterization: she was very beautiful (11:2).	
Main actions: David sent And inquired (11:3) One said (11:3)	**Dialogue:** said "is not this Bathsheba, the daughter of Eliam, the wife of Uriah the Hittite?"
Narrative Clues: repetition of *sent* (11:3) from verse 1. 11:3 anticipates Uriah, a major character in the following narrative (11:6-13). We are shown that David knew she was married, highlighting his sin. In 11:2, the narrator notes that the woman was bathing, anticipating the narrators explanation of her bathing in 11:4.	

Verse 4

Main actions: So David sent messenges And took her And she came to him And he lay with her Then she returned to her house.
Narrative Clues: "sent" appears again, perhaps portraying David as aloof, separate from the rest of the characters (cf. 12:15-23). The narrator tells us, "She had been purifying herself from her uncleanness." That he provides this information indicates it is of some interpretive importance. Elsewhere, the narrator draws attention to ways David breaks the Torah; this may be one such instance (cf. Lev 18:19).

Verse 5

Main actions:	Dialogue: told David, "I am pregnant."
The woman conceived	
She sent	
And she told David	

Narrative Clues: "sent" appears again. Though we have been given a name, the narrator identifies her as "the woman." This is consistent with the way the narrator characterizes Bathsheba throughout the narrative.

A few notes should be made on these storyboards. The narrator indicates something is wrong in the introduction (or exposition) by contrasting the custom of the day, "kings go out to battle," with David's inaction. This is emphasized by the contrast between David and his troops in 1c-e, "But David remained…." Our suspicion, aroused by the narrator's comments, is confirmed by the following story. I have not marked any sideline actions in these narratives; Hebrew often presents all actions as coordinated, on the same narrative level, even where one action is logically more prominent.

In verses 2-3, David viewing Bathsheba bathing is part of the setting for the main actions David takes to pursue adultery. That the narrator gives us information about Bathsheba, both her name and her husband's name, indicates the importance of both characters for the following narrative. In contrast, the messenger David sends is merely "one."

In verse 4, the author mentions that Bathsheba was cleansing herself from impurity; we need to ask why he would include this information. Some commentators suggest that the narrator is indicating she is fertile, thus anticipating the statements in verse 5, but this hardly seems worthy of the narrator's attention. However, throughout the book of Samuel, the narrator holds Saul and David up to the standard of the Law revealed in the Torah, a pattern that fits here. If Bathsheba was cleansing herself from her menstrual impurity (11:4), it would have been against the Torah to sleep with her (Lev 18:19). This hardly seems worth mentioning in light of the adultery and murder, which are the focus of the narrative, yet that David would transgress in the minutiae of the Law underscores the point that David is not at this time acting as God's king ought to (cf. Deut 17:18-20), a point that the author repeatedly makes.

In verse 5, we also see Bathsheba treated as a secondary character, merely "the woman." She is presented primarily in relation to David and Uriah. When she is finally identified as "[David's] wife, Bathsheba" in 12:24, this serves to indicate the resolution of the tension throughout the narrative. So it appears that the author's reluctance to name her and identify her as David's wife from 11:2-12:23 is a tool he uses, perhaps to focus on David as the narrative's focus and to reveal the favourable outcome of the incident in 12:24, where God recognizes their marriage and grants them a son.

B. Poetry[10]

> How lovely is your dwelling place,
>   O LORD of hosts!
> My soul longs, yes, faints
>   for the courts of the LORD;
> my heart and flesh sing for joy
>   to the living God.
>
> Even the sparrow finds a home,
>   and the swallow a nest for herself,
>   where she may lay her young,
> at your altars, O LORD of hosts,
>   my King and my God.
> Blessed are those who dwell in your house,
>   ever singing your praise! *Selah*
> – Psalm 84:1-4

Poetry permeates Scripture. The longest book in the Bible consists of poetry, as does most of the third part of the Old Testament. Many of the narratives, epistles, and prophetic books in Scripture also contain texts written in poetic style. Though they come in many different forms (such as song, poem, and proverb), all the poetic texts in the Bible share several basic features that help

---

[10] Some of what follows is adapted from my study guide, *Believe the Unbelievable* (Teleioteti, 2018), and commentary (Teleioteti, forthcoming) on the book of Habakkuk. Habakkuk is one of the most poetic books of Hebrew prophecy, making it well suited for poetic analysis. Many of the examples that follow will be taken from Habakkuk, especially chapter 3, but the reader can see the same sort of features in other poetry, such as Psalm 23 and 84. Habakkuk 3 is explicitly a Hebrew poem, not an example of prophetic style.

us identify and interpret them. Understanding the basics of biblical poetry is essential to reading the Bible well. Even in narratives, poetic texts are often key to interpreting the work (e.g. 1 Sam 2:1-10).[11]

Poetry comes in many shapes and sizes, and the lines between poetry and prose are at times blurred (especially in prophetic literature). However, I think we can distinguish poetry as a style of literature that uses various devices to create a *conceptual rhythm*, often to great emotional effect. Whereas prose strikes the reader with its profundity and narrative draws the reader into its tensions, poetry incites the passions of the reader with despair and hope, anger and joy, etc. By "conceptual rhythm," I intend to distinguish the poetic style of biblical poetry from English poetry. English poetry is characterized mainly by meter; Hebrew poetry is not. Meter is found in biblical poetry, but only as one device among many used to achieve a conceptual rhythm. We could define conceptual rhythm as the presentation and explanation of ideas and events through the interplay of lines. Hebrew poetry uses a variety of features, including wordplay and metaphor, to create a rhythm of ideas, not sound. The desired emotional and cognitive effects of this conceptual rhythm are achieved through the use of parallel lines and text units to juxtapose ideas along with various sonic and visual devices that tie together and bring out the meaning of the lines. As a piece of poetry unfolds, it presents the same idea from several different angles presenting a cohesive whole. It circles a topic, achieving a sort of 3D presentation of ideas in contrast with the 2d presentation of prose. Another way to describe poetry is to say that it moves from ambiguity, from initially vague and ambiguous ideas and imagery, to clarity by expanding upon the initial idea or image, looking at it from several different angles.

The three main features of biblical poetry are terseness, literary devices, and parallelism. Terseness describes the intentional minimalism of Hebrew poetry. Hebrew poets keep their words to a minimum: even if the result is ambiguous, they will use three words instead of ten. Like English poetry, biblical poetry also employs vivid imagery, which is usually concrete imagery taken from everyday life (this contrasts with the symbolic imagery of prophecy), and poetic devices such as onomatopoeia, alliteration, assonance,

---

[11] What follows is mainly a description of Hebrew poetry; traditional Greek poetry is distinctly different. However, what poetry is found in the New Testament is heavily influenced by the Hebrew Old Testament and thus bears great similarity to Hebrew poetry.

etc. to communicate. Parallelism describes the use of groups of poetic lines to communicate a single idea or image. For the rest of our discussion of poetry, I want to briefly discuss the way biblical poets use terseness, poetic devices, and parallelism, and then consider a way we can think through poetic texts more closely.

a. *How Poetry Communicates: Terseness and Poetic Devices*

biblical poetry employs many of the same literary features as English: there are metaphors (Hab 1:12), hyperbole (Hab 3:16a-d), onomatopoeia (Hab 2:20), simile (Hab 2:5c-d),[12] alliteration (Hab 3:16e-g), assonance (Hab 1:6b), and acrostics (Ps 119)—among others.[13] Rhyme is not as common as in English poetry, but wordplay and assonance are much more so. Wordplay and assonance are often achieved by using words of the same root (Hab. 1:5) or words spelled similarly (1:6).[14] Words with similar or very different meanings, yet similar spellings, are frequently employed for poetic value. Important to note is also the frequent use of ellipsis, the omission of a necessary word—verb or noun—to be supplied by the parallel lines.[15]

Ellipsis, along with other features, contributes to the terseness of biblical poetry. "Terseness" describes the intentional minimalism of Hebrew poetry. Words are kept to a minimum: even if the result is ambiguous, Hebrew poets will use three words instead of ten.

---

[12] In poetry, a letter following a verse number specifies the line in question.

[13] Though only Habakkuk 3 is written in what I have identified as poetic style, it is the book I am most familiar with and even its prophetic portions serve well to illustrate the devices found in Hebrew poetry. This is because, as we will see under prophetic style, many prophetic texts employ the language pattern of poetry though using a different manner of communication. All of Habakkuk is written in a poetic language pattern, though Habakkuk 3 is explicitly a song and employs a fully poetic style.

[14] Assonance may not be the proper word here, for written Hebrew consists only of consonants and this is primarily what is emphasized in these poetic devices. That being said, I will continue to use assonance to refer to the poetic device of playing off similar sounds, whether consonantal or vocalic.

[15] Wilfred G. E. Watson, "Poetry, Biblical Hebrew," ed. Geoffrey Khan, *Encyclopedia of Hebrew Language and Linguistics* (Leiden; Boston: Brill, 2013), 152; Andrew E. Hill and John H. Walton, *A Survey of the Old Testament*, 2nd ed. (Grand Rapids: Zondervan Publishing House, 2000), 383.

It appears that Hebrew poets do sometimes employ meter in their poems, yet it is only one of many tools used by the Hebrew poet to achieve a conceptual rhythm.[16] When meter is employed, this sonic rhythm is achieved by patterns of syllables, accents, or words. In the first case, a series of sets of lines (a colon) may contain a pattern of syllables that is repeated in each colon or with a rhythmic variation. There may also be a pattern of accents per line or the number of words in each line. Alliteration or assonance also contribute to this sonic rhythm.[17]

Many of the devices used to create a poetic effect in Hebrew are not reproducible in English, yet the genius of Hebrew poetry—including its New Testament counterparts—is its ability to achieve its intended effect even in translation. Because so many devices are used and because the essence of Hebrew poetry is conceptual—focused on making an idea or picture clear—it is easy for the English reader to get the poetic effect of the text. Parallelism, the workhorse of Hebrew poetry, is largely responsible for this, but the use of vivid imagery also helps biblical poetry communicate across languages. Psalm 23, for example, employs to powerful effect the life of a shepherd to communicate God's care; Psalm 84 draws on scenes from the religious life of Israel, from its geography, and its royal court to effectively communicate the blessedness of life with God. The use of vivid, comprehensible imagery to communicate is a hallmark of Hebrew poetry and is one of the ways it can be distinguished from prophetic style, which we will consider below. Instead of drawing on everyday experience, prophetic imagery is otherworldly, it draws on everyday life but uses these experiences in ways that require thought and wisdom—even Divine interpretation—to understand. It is in a sense abstract, for the relationship between the imagery and its intended reference is not immediately discernible, for example, the use of specific materials to indicate different earthly empires in Daniel's vision of a statue (Dan 2). We will consider prophetic style below, but for now we will turn to consider poetic parallelism.

---

[16] Cf. Hill and Walton, *A Survey*, 387; David L. Petersen and Kent Harold Richards, *Interpreting Hebrew Poetry*, Guides to Biblical Scholarship (Minneapolis: Fortress, 1992), 37–39; Watson, "Poetry, Biblical Hebrew," 152.

[17] Hill and Walton, *A Survey*, 383.

The substance of Hebrew poetry, that of which it consists, is series of parallel lines—each set known as a colon. A sort of rhythm is sometimes associated with the number of lines in a colon (*bicolon*, two lines; *tricolon*, three lines), but even here there is no uniformity: using varying numbers of lines is again a tool for achieving poetic rhythm, but not the whole of it.[18] The primary tool used to achieve conceptual rhythm in Hebrew poetry is the parallelism of ideas.

b. *How Poetry Communicates: Lines and Parallelism*

Each series of lines balances in various ways an idea. Usually, lines will parallel each other in their members as well; that is, they may not have the exact correspondence in the number of words but will correspond in word order, absence or presence of nouns, and the use of modifiers.[19] Parallelism employs, as the name suggests, parallel lines—poetic lines related grammatically, phonetically, semantically—to communicate in richer ways than prose. We could describe Hebrew Parallelism as the use of closely related lines for evocation—engaging the affections—and disambiguation. Disambiguation describes the way poets use parallel lines to resolve ambiguity resulting from the terseness and imagery of poetry, the way they use additional lines to bring another perspective and resolve ambiguity.[20]

Thus Hebrew poetry can be considered as analogous to a holograph: it is three dimensional, not two-dimensional language. The poet will present an idea and revisit it in the following lines (sometimes an entire poem looks at the same idea from various perspectives): each line, then, gives a complementary perspective on the ideas the author wishes to communicate, painting a three-dimensional picture. This combination of ambiguity followed by disambiguation produces a sense of elation in us, the readers, as we move from confusion to realization of the meaning. There is a sense of discovery as a poem progresses. The use of multiple perspectives and

---

[18] Petersen and Richards, *Interpreting Hebrew Poetry*, 41.

[19] Hill and Walton, *A Survey*, 383.

[20] The language of ambiguity and disambiguation is borrowed from Adele Berlin's work on Hebrew Poetry. As with the authors cited above, I have not followed her work completely or closely in this section, but I have profited from her analysis. Adele Berlin, *The Dynamics of Biblical Parallelism* (Bloomington: Indiana University Press, 1985).

compact language, as well as liberal use of metaphor, contributes to the rich emotional impact Hebrew poetry has.

Here are several examples from Habakkuk Chapter 3 and Psalm 84:[21]

Example 1 (Hab 3:13):

[13]You come forth for the salvation of your people,
    for salvation with your anointed;

Example 2 (Hab 3:11):

The sun and the moon stand in their exalted abode,
    to make your arrows that fly gleam,
    to brighten your flashing spears.

Example 3 (Ps 84:9):

Behold our shield, O God;
    look on the face of your anointed!

Example 4 (Ps 84:10):

For a day in your courts is better
    than a thousand elsewhere.
I would rather be a doorkeeper in the house of my God
    than dwell in the tents of wickedness.

These examples serve to illustrate some of the various ways in which parallelism is used in the Old Testament. In example one, the second line is used to explain how God is going to save his people; he will do so through his anointed, Chaldea. In example 2, the second and third line (11b & 11c) explain why the heavenly bodies are standing tall in the sky, in order to highlight the weapons God will use to achieve salvation for his people. In example 3, the second line explains what is meant by the first: "Behold our shield" could mean a million different things, yet the second line identifies this shield as the king and "behold" is a call for God to consider and show favour to the king, the protector of God's people (hence, "shield"). In

---

[21] All translations from Habakkuk are my own, as printed in my forthcoming commentary, *Habakkuk: An Exegetical-Theological Commentary*.

example 4, the first colon (the first two lines, 10a-b) uses the second line only to finish the thought of the first. In the second colon (10c-d), the second line is used to make a powerful contrast between the pleasures of even the lowliest position in God's temple and the most luxurious one apart from him.

By understanding a few of the ground rules of Hebrew poetry—that we should expect terseness and parallelism resulting in initial ambiguity that is clarified as we read on—we can better appreciate the beauty of this art and see more clearly the meaning God intends through it.

c. *Study Strategy: Mapping Parallelism*

As with narrative, there is a technique we can use to visually display a poetic text and think through the relationships of its pieces. We could call this *mapping parallelism*; it is similar to the technique we will see below for prose, called arcing. Mapping parallelism forces us to think through the relationships between lines and identify what lines should be read and interpreted together. To begin, we must select the text we will use. Going through the text, break the text into discrete lines of text. There is no clear guide for doing this—it is more of an art than a science. However, English translation or Hebrew bibles will often break the text into lines; studying their divisions can help identify what is poetry and then how lines can be identified. Most often, a line will represent a complete grammatical thought—though the author may ellipse a word or two. The exception is the use of enjambment, where a sentence is continued in the next line (cf. Ps 84:10a-b; Hab 1:8b-c).

If you read Hebrew, another indicator of line divisions is the use of ו (v^e, and) with no clear conjunctive or adverbial function (i.e. it does not clearly mean "and" or "but" or have an adverbial function, "even"). Though it often has a conjunctive meaning, connecting verbal clauses, ו also often indicates line division (e.g. Hab 1:16, 2:5). Your initial division of lines will not be perfect, but this step is necessary as we begin to analyse the text.

Next, take a blank piece of paper or a document and write out each line in a vertical row (some might prefer to write the whole line, others just the verse and line number, e.g. 1a). Having identified lines, we now need to identify colons—groups of lines. Poetry is most often divided into bi-cola (plural of bicolon), groups of two lines, but will also use tricola (groups of three lines) and the occasional tetracolon (a group of four lines). Sometimes translations or commentators will identify a monocolon (an independent line), but in many cases, these are better seen as parts of a tricolon. Begin by identifying lines that most clearly belong together; an example would be two lines where one has a word ellipsed (is missing a word) and the other supplies it. In many cases, lines that share synonymous, antithetical, or closely related words should also be grouped together (e.g. love and beneficence, righteousness and wickedness, joy and blessedness). Enjambment or verbal clauses connected by a ו (v^e, and) are also important clues for identifying groups of lines. Draw an arc or box connecting the cola (groups of lines) you have identified (see the illustration below).

Once you have discovered the most prominent sets of lines, go back through your list and identify whether the remaining lines are most closely related to another ungrouped line or to one of the more evident groups of lines. Again, draw lines connecting the grouped lines together. After doing this several times, every line should be grouped with another line or several others.

Having identified the groups of lines that make up a poetic text, the next step is to identify larger groups of text—groups of bicola, tricola, and tetracola. Most poems, except the largest and smallest, can be divided into two larger groupings, stanzas and strophes. In my terminology, strophe refers to the largest unit of poem, made up of several stanzas, and stanzas to the next largest unit of a poem, made up of groups of bicola, tricola, and tetracola. Sometimes these larger divisions can be identified by thematic unity or the use of keywords, but there are several explicit devices uses by poets to divide their texts at these large levels. One of these is the Hebrew word סֶלָה (*selāh*), used in songs to indicate a musical transition of some sort (cf. Psalm 84, Habakkuk 3). At other times, there will be the repetition of a key word once every several lines, such as the word הוֹי (*hōy*, which can have the sense "woe") (cf. Hab 2:6-20; Ps 84:4, 5, 12) or a repeated set of lines that form a refrain (e.g. Hab 2:8c-d, 17c-d; Ps 42:5, 12, 43:5).

Once a poem is divided into these various groups of lines, identify the basic relationship displayed between the lines. You can do this by describing each group on the same or a separate piece of paper. Alternatively, you could come up with a series of abbreviations such as those used in arcing (see below) to communicate the relationship between lines and groups of lines. I am not providing a list of such relationships because there is an indefinite number of possible relations; in the past, scholars have attempted to group all these relations into three broad categories, but these categories proved too broad to be useful.[22] I will note several possible relations, but this is by no means exhaustive.

Lines could be grouped together in antithesis. That is, one line could give an idea and the next its opposite or a juxtaposing idea (Ps 84:10). One line could be grammatically subordinate or related to another and so complete or expand it (Hab 3:11). Sometimes lines will display logical progression, such as is found in prose (Hab 1:4). Lines can be simply descriptive of the noun or verb in the first line (Hab 1:6). A set of lines can function like a narrative to expound a temporal series of actions (Exod 15:10). Sometimes a whole group of lines clearly communicates the same idea from different perspectives (Exod 15:8). More complex relations can also be found, such as a chiasm (a-b-b'-a' pattern; Hab 2:15-16). It is common in the proverbs for lines to present several distinct yet related ideas, the thing they share in common being the point (e.g. Prov 30:18-19).

Putting all this together, grouping lines, cola, and stanzas with annotation will look something like the example below, which diagrams Habakkuk 2:6e-11b. As will be seen, a lot is left unsaid by such a diagram. For this reason, it is helpful to write out below the diagram or on the back of the diagram an explanation of each relation, asking, for example, what it means for Habakkuk 2:6e-g (labelled a-b below) to be a series interrupted with an exclamation. Generally, these lines give different perspectives on Babylon's ravaging of the nations; from the perspective of the conquered, it is described in terms of both what they take and how God perceives their theft—it is a heavy debt they will not be able to pay.[23]

---

[22] Many scholars have worked to revise this understanding. E.g. James L. Kugel, *The Idea of Biblical Poetry: Parallelism and Its History* (New Haven: Yale University Press, 1981); Berlin, *The Dynamics of Biblical Parallelism*; Robert Alter, *The Art of Biblical Poetry* (New York: Basic Books, 1985); J.P. Fokkelman, *Reading Biblical Poetry: An Introductory Guide*, trans. Ineke Smit, First edition. (Louisville: Westminster John Knox, 2001).

[23] This is my translation, taken from my Habakkuk study guide, *Believe the Unbelievable* (Teleioteti, 2018), and my commentary on Habakkuk (Teleioteti, forthcoming).

Habakkuk 2:6-11

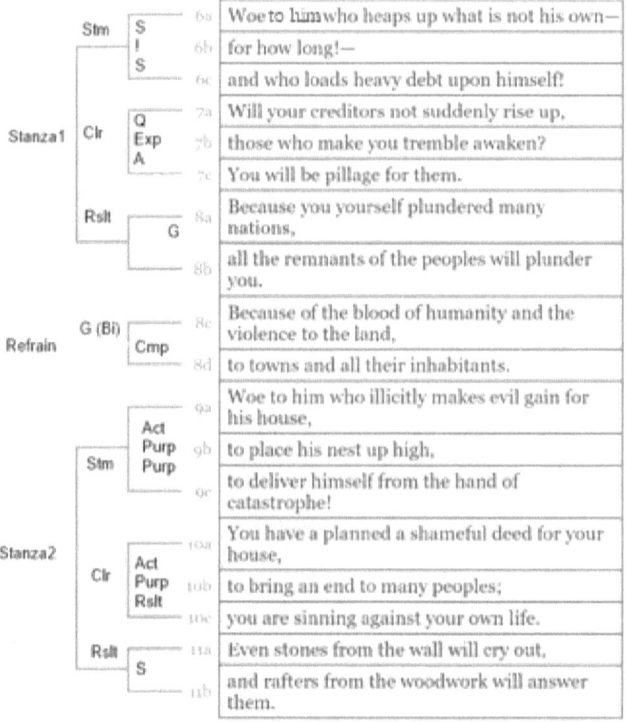

The section of Habakkuk I have selected is two stanzas with a refrain between them. The first stanza consists of two tricola (6a-c, 7a-c) and a bicolon (8a-b). The first three lines present a simple series (S) interrupted by an exclamation (!). Together the tricolon (the three lines as a group) gives a statement (Stm) that will be clarified (Clr) in the next lines. These next three lines present a question (Q), expanded upon in 7b (Exp) and then affirmed or answered in 7c (A). 8a-b gives the result of the first two tricola, with 8a giving the ground (G) for the statement in 8b.

The refrain in 8c-d gives the ground (G) for both Stanza 1 & 2; hence, it is bilateral (Bi). 8d completes the statement in 8c (Cmp).

Stanza 2 has the same structure as Stanza 1, two tricola followed by a bicolon, giving a statement (Stm, 9a-c), its clarification (Clr, 10a-c), and the result (Rslt, 11a-b). Lines 9a-c and 10a-c have a similar pattern. 9a-c gives an action followed by two lines explaining the Chaldeans intent with this act. 10a-b presents an action with its purpose, but 10c gives the result of this action. 11a-b is a series, describing how the peoples whom Chaldea subdued and used to build their "house" (9a) will indict them.

Because of the variety of possible connections lines of poetry may have and because their force is found not in their logic but in the collective picture they paint and their emotive effect, such an analysis is often not very helpful. However, when you are struggling to figure out what the text means or are seeking to translate the passage and want to understand how the units of text are related to one another, such an analysis can be quite useful.

C. Didactic Prose

Poetry and narrative engage our hearts and draw us into the world they present, but neither communicates to our minds quite like didactic prose. When it comes to making an argument or spelling out in careful detail truth or instruction, nothing beats didactic prose. Prose, broadly, forms an opposition with verse or poetry. Without a rhythm scheme or line structure, prose is composed of sentences and paragraphs. Narrative, direct speech, and theological treatises are all examples of prose, broadly conceived. However, we can distinguish within this broader category a non-narrative form of prose. "Didactic" refers specifically to teaching, yet I think it is a fitting term to describe the non-narrative prose of Scripture found in prophetic books, direct speech, and especially the New Testament epistles. When used in this way, "didactic prose" refers to the non-narrative and non-poetic texts of Scripture that are used to communicate truth or description and instruction to God's people.

Didactic prose shares several features that distinguish it from narrative and poetry. Like narrative and unlike poetry, didactic prose uses sentences instead of lines and paragraphs instead of strophes or stanzas. Unlike narrative, didactic prose does not follow a temporal plot: it does not relay events that follow one another in time. Thus, it is not *paratactic*, stringing sentences along in a coordinating fashion (and… and… but… and). Instead, didactic prose is structured logically and rhetorically. Logically, it communicates through *hypotaxis*, using conjunctions (and, but, however, for, etc.) to indicate the logical relationship between clauses and sentences. Rhetorically, didactic prose often follows a standard structure of communication, such as the typical letter form of the epistles or the lawsuit form of the prophetic books. Unlike poetry, didactic prose tends to be very concrete and literal, though it occasionally incorporates strong metaphor and symbolism. For the rest of our discussion of prose, I want to consider how it uses grammar and logic to communicate and the interchange of indicative and imperative found in much didactic prose. To conclude this section, we will briefly consider two tools to help us better analyse didactic prose.

a. *How Prose Communicates: Grammar and Logic*

In poetry, grammar is often sacrificed for the sake of art, and the logic behind a text is often implicit, rarely made explicit. In narrative, relatively few types of clauses are used, and the structure is not driven by logic but by narrative progress, thus "and" and "but" are common but clauses indicating logical result ("therefore"), purpose ("in order that"), and explanation ("for") are relatively rare. What is absent from poetry and narrative forms the backbone of didactic prose. It is in prose that in-depth grammatical study and logical precision become invaluable tools for understanding an author's thought.

In English, translators have endeavoured to simplify complex Greek grammar in a manner that is clear for English readers. Primarily, for the English reader, the grammar needed is knowledge of different clause types, how they are formed, and how they function. A clause is a part of a sentence that contains a complete predication, a verb plus its complement (*I ate food* is a clause; *ate* is the verb and *food* the complement). A clause may be modified in various ways by prepositional phrases ("*for* dinner," "*in* the bedroom," etc.) or adverbs ("quickly," "hesitantly"). Its constituent nouns (in this case, "I" and "food") may be described with various adjectival phrases (large, tall, tasty, wonderful, which was just cooked, etc.). Clauses come in two forms, independent (which stand on their own) and dependent (which require another clause to make sense). Conjunctions are used to connect clauses to one another and are essential to understanding the logic of a prose text. In Greek and Hebrew, these same units of grammar are present but are indicated in different ways. The biblical languages are very good at making clear the relationships between the various parts of a clause and sentence. In both languages, specific verbal forms (infinitives and participles) and prepositions take on a much more significant role in indicating logical connection than they do in English. For the English reader, these connections are often made explicit in translation, but different translations may understand the relationships differently. This is where knowledge of the original languages is very helpful; such knowledge will help you understand the range of possibilities and what makes the best sense in context. In the last part of this section, we will briefly consider two methods for thinking carefully about the grammar of a didactic text and the logic behind it. Before that, we can consider the broader logic of didactic prose texts.

b. *How Prose Communicates: Indicative and Imperative*

None of the books of the Bible are intended to be a bare philosophical or theological treatise. That is, none of them is interested in merely describing or explaining a truth or aspect of the world. On the contrary, they are circumstantial and intended to bring about some sort of response in the reader. To say that they are circumstantial is to say that every biblical text is written to specific people to address specific circumstances. We saw in the first part of the book how we are part of the audience of Scripture, but the method God has used to instruct and guide us is to teach us through instances where he addressed his people in history to guide and correct them. For this reason, no biblical text is an abstract treatise but is intended to bring the truths God has revealed about himself and his world to bear on real-life issues. It does so to draw forth a response, to bring the unbeliever to faith (e.g. John), to challenge the stagnating Christian to persevere (e.g. Hebrew), to correct false teaching (e.g. Galatians, 1 John), or to encourage right behaviour among God's people (e.g. Romans, James).

This means that truth is put in service of exhortation: think rightly about God so that you will respond rightly towards him, his people, and his world. There is, therefore, a common pattern in didactic prose, indicative followed by imperative. Indicative refers to clauses and sentences that make statements, describing something or presenting a truth. Imperative refers to exhortations and commands. Didactic texts in the Bible root their commands in truth, whether it is in God's authority, character, or truth about his ways and his creation (e.g. Matt 5:48; Rom 5:1-5). Therefore, as we read didactic texts, we need to ask the questions, "why is this truth given?"—i.e. what should we do about it—and, "what truth undergirds this command?"

c. *Study Strategy: Arcing and Sentence Diagramming*

To understand both these questions, we need to get a firm grasp on the grammar of a text, how all the pieces come together, and the logic of paragraph or unit of text—how sentences and units of sentences relate to one another. There are several tools to do this, but there are two that I have found most helpful. We do not have space to go to great depth with either of these tools, but there are several great resources to further your understanding of them.

For sentence diagramming, a basic tool for looking carefully at clauses, Thomas R. Schreiner's *Interpreting the Pauline Epistles* is an excellent guide. Additionally, Biblearc.com is a free online platform that facilitates sentence diagramming and offers some instructional videos for doing it and using the program. Basically, to diagram a clause, you identify its specific parts (the verb, nouns, pronouns, adjectival phrases, adverbs, prepositional phrases, etc.) and visually represent the relationships the pieces have with one another. A usual method to do this is to identify the verb and put it in the centre of a line on a piece of paper. To the left of the verb, write out the subject and to the right the object. On the far left of the same line, write out the conjunction where present. Then, write out all adjectives and adverbs or adverbial phrases indented beneath the word they modify (see the example below).

> ## *Review of English Grammar*
>
> For various reasons, many of us do not know English grammar as well as we should. Even at a seminary level, I have found it necessary to review the basics of English grammar in order to facilitate sentence diagramming and arcing in language and exegesis tutorials. Here is an overview of basic grammatical units that are important for using these tools:
>
> **Verb**: the main component of a sentence, describe an action or a state. (is, was, run)
>
> **Adjective**: modifies a noun, specifying it (which man? The *green* man)
>
> **Adverb**: modifies a noun, verb, or adjective, specifying the modified word in various ways (*when, as, too, not*).
>
> **Noun**: describes a person, place, or thing. A pronoun replaces a noun.
>
> **Object**: receives the action of the verb (he threw *the ball*).
>
> **Subject**: performs the verbal action or is predicated (he threw, he was tall). In the passive, is acted upon (*She* was chosen).
>
> **Indirect object**: receives the action of the verb secondarily (he passed *him* the ball).
>
> **Clause**: A clause is complete grammatical unit, containing both a verb (more technically, a predicate: verbless clauses are quite frequent in

> Greek and Hebrew and occur occasionally in English) and its complements (minimally, a subject). "He ran," "She quickly drove to the store," "because the dog ran."
> **Independent clause**: An independent clause is a clause that contains a completed thought, and so could be a sentence by itself (e.g. "He ran").
> **Dependent clause**: A dependent clause is a clause that cannot stand on its own, it needs to be connected to a dependent clause (*because the dog ran*, he caught the car).
> **Proposition**: Especially in the context of arcing, discussed below, a "proposition" refers to a clause, a grammatical unit consisting minimally of a predicate and subject.

Sentence diagramming forces us to slow down and consider carefully how an author has communicated and why he has done so. It forces us to think carefully about what we usually do intuitively. This tool is especially helpful when a sentence is ambiguous.[24] For example, sentence diagramming may force you to ask whether "like a dove" in Matthew 3:16 refers to the manner of the Spirit's descent or the physical manifestation he takes (though I cannot identify a significant difference in meaning). Matthew is not clear either way, and maybe both are intended (though cf. Luke 3:22), but such a question will probably lead you to ponder the significance of the Holy Spirit descending as a *dove*. More significantly, sentence diagramming will force you to think through the connection between the pieces of Revelation 13:8 and the phrase "before the foundation of the world." Theologically, the text cannot mean that Christ was slain before the foundation of the world, yet some have argued it is elliptical and means "Book of the life of the lamb whose slaughter was ordained from before the foundations of the world."[25] Otherwise, it

---

[24] Some exegetes use a related tool, creating a sentence flow, to identify the key themes and terms and the progression of the argument of a passage. I find arcing, discussed below to be a better tool for the latter and marking up a passage on paper or in a Bible best for the former. However, see Gordon D. Fee, *New Testament Exegesis: A Handbook for Students and Pastors*, 3rd ed. (Louisville: Westminster John Knox Press, 2002), 41–48.

[25] E.g. Mounce writes "It is better in this case to follow the order of the Greek syntax and read, 'the Lamb that hath been slain from the foundation of the world.'" However, to anticipate a later chapter, one should take this judgment with a grain of

could be connected to "written," "whose name has not been written from the foundation of the world in the book of life of the lamb who was slain." Whatever the case may be, sentence diagramming will force you to make a decision about what is intended and think through the theological implications of this decision. For Revelation 13:8, a sentence diagram might look like this:

Subject	Verb	Object
name	has been written	
whose	not	
	before the foundation	
	of the world	
	in the book	
	of the life	
	of the Lamb	
	who was slain	

The resources mentioned above will also guide you in the use of our second tool, *arcing*. Schreiner's *Interpreting the Pauline Epistles* has a fantastic chapter on "Tracing the Argument," using arcing to identify the logic of a passage.[26] Biblearc.com, as the name implies, provides a platform for arcing the argument of a text in various modern translations as well as the Greek and Hebrew text. Various free lessons and paid lectures are offered for learning how to arc a text. Arcing is a way of visually diagramming and thinking through the relationships of clauses and paragraphs within a chosen text. My instructions on mapping parallelism in the last section are inspired by arcing, so it is very similar. However, because didactic texts relate clauses logically, we can be much more precise about the possible relationships clauses will have to one another, so most instructions on how to arc a passage

---

salt. Greek syntax is notoriously flexible and there are good reasons why the phrase "from the foundation of the world" may be put at the end of the Greek sentence. Robert H. Mounce, *The Book of Revelation*, NICNT (Grand Rapids: Eerdmans, 1977); G.K. Beale, *The Book of Revelation: A Commentary on the Greek Text*, NIGTC (Grand Rapids; Carlisle: Eerdmans; Paternoster, 1999).

[26] This document on biblicaltraining.org is adapted from Schreiner's chapter, http://nt504.biblicaltraining.org/Flow_and_Tracing.pdf. The full chapter is available through this link https://blog.biblearc.com/blog/tracing-the-argument/.

will provide a list of possible relationships clauses can have to one another. Schreiner writes,

> All propositions relate in either a *coordinate* or *subordinate* way to previous propositions. We can see the relation between propositions in sentences. For instance, coordinate propositions are found in compound sentences. Compound sentences have two or more independent clauses joined together. The sentence 'I listened to the radio, and I washed my car' is a compound sentence. Both of these clauses are independent and could be separate sentences. Also, there is no dependent relationship between the two clauses. Two separate activities were performed: washing the car and listening to the radio. However, these two clauses can easily be rewritten so that one clause is a *subordinate* clause. If I write, I listened to the radio while I washed my car," then the sentence is now a complex sentence (containing at least one subordinate clause) instead of a compound sentence. The clause "while I washed my car" is not an independent clause but a subordinate one.[27]

In brief, this method is exactly like mapping parallelism in the last section. But instead of dividing the text into lines, it is necessary to break the text into its constituent clauses (the main verb with a complement, such as an object or subject, and various modifiers). After identifying the clauses or propositions (in Schreiner's terminology) that make up your passage, lay out the propositions on a vertical or horizontal line (either using the full clause written out or its verse and clause reference [e.g. 1a, 1b, 1c; 2a, 2b, 2c], see the example below). To trace out the argument of the passage, identify the clauses that are most closely related and indicate their relationship by connecting them with an arc. Continue to identify relationships between clauses and groups of clauses and indicate these relationships with further arcs. Do this until you have one arc that encompasses the whole text. Then, using the list of possible relationships clauses could have with one another, identify how each clause and group of clauses is related and mark it with the pertinent symbol. When you have finished, explain in writing each

---

[27] Thomas R. Schreiner, *Interpreting the Pauline Epistles*, 2nd ed. (Grand Rapids: Baker Academic, 2011), 99.

relationship and the reason you have identified it as such. Using biblearc.com and its system of reference, an arc of Romans 5:1-5 might look like this:

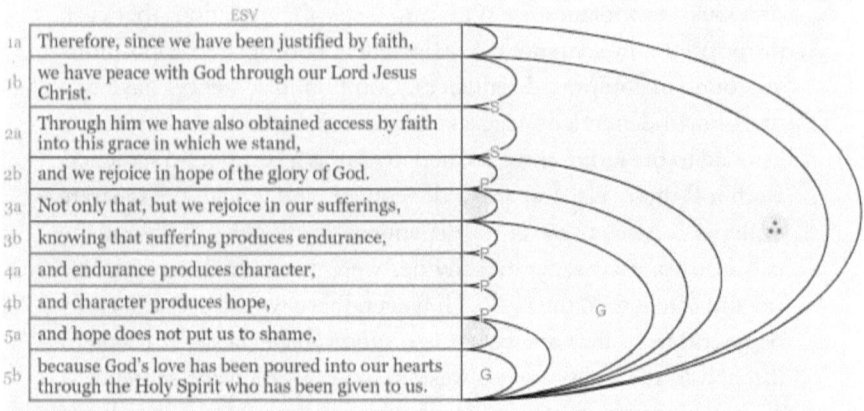

Though I am not convinced that this exhausts all possible relationships that could be identified between clauses, the list Thomas Schreiner provides is quite helpful. He lays out the possible relationships between clauses in the following way (we do not have space to thoroughly explore each relationship, but his chapter, available through the link above, and the website biblearc.com, explains each category):[28]

I. Coordinate Relationships – in a coordinate relationship, each clause presents a different action that is not grammatically dependent on the others

    A. Series (S) – in a series, actions are presented sequentially without logical dependence.

    B. Progression (P) – unlike a series, actions in a progression build upon one another, often they are logically dependent on the previous action though grammatically coordinated (e.g. "I tied my shoes, I opened the door, and I left the building": each action is grammatically coordinate yet there is logical progression).

---

[28] The brief explanations provided are my own. See also, http://www.bradcopp.com/PTH223/propositions.pdf

    C. Alternative (A) – when actions or states are alternatives, they present two or more alternatives, none of which are dependent on the others. For example, "we could go to the store or to the theatre"; "for dinner we could cook steak, eat out, or order Chinese food."
II. Subordinate Relationships – subordinate clauses (or propositions) do not stand alone but relate in some way to the main clause; they provide further specification (time, manner in which the action was performed, motive, etc.) or give more information for background.
    A. Support by Restatement
        1. Action-Manner (Ac/Mn) – an action is given, then the subordinate clause explains the manner in which the action was performed.
        2. Comparison (Cf) – a clause is explained by providing a comparable situation or action.
        3. Negative – Positive (-/+) – two antithetical statements are provided, alternatives that juxtapose sharply (cf. Eph 5:17)
        4. Idea-Explanation (Id/exp) – The idea or statement given in the main clause is explained by a subordinate clause.
        5. Question-Answer (Q/A) – One clause presents a question which is then answered in another.
    B. Support by Distinct Statement
        1. Ground (G) – A clause is a ground when it presents the logical reason for or cause of the main clause.
        2. Inference (∴) - A clause is an inference when it presents the logical result or conclusion to be drawn from the main clause.
        3. Action-Result (Ac/Res) – the main clause presents an action and another clause the result.
        4. Action-Purpose (Ac/Pur) – the main clause presents an action and another clause the reason the action was performed or its goal.
        5. Conditional (If/Th) – One clause presents a condition ("if," the protasis) and another clause the result if that condition is met ("then," the apodosis)

6. Temporal (T) – the subordinate situates the main clause temporally.
7. Locative (L) – the subordinate clause situates the main clause in a location, giving the physical/geographic setting.
8. Bilateral (BL) – a bilateral proposition is a bridge between a preceding proposition or group of propositions and one that follows, closely connected to both. It could perform any of the above functions for the preceding and following propositions (cf. Eph 5:21).

C. Support by Contrary Statement
1. Concessive (Csv) – The supporting clause presents a contrasting situation by which the main clause is to be understood. E.g. *"although the journey was difficult, they sailed all the way home"* (cf. Heb 5:8, 1 Cor 4:15).
2. Situation-Response (Sit/R)[29] – One clause presents a response given to a situation presented in another clause (or series of clauses), e.g. *"'Rabbi, when did you come here?' Jesus answered them, "...."* (John 6:25-26).

Often the relations are indicated by specific conjunctions or verbal types, so knowledge of the underlying Greek or Hebrew text can be very helpful in identifying the specific relationship a clause or group of clauses has/have with one another (the resources above provide some of the most frequent Greek conjunctions used to indicate these relationships). Using these categories, we can explain the arc of Romans 5:1-5 like this:

> **Verses 5:1a-2b**: in these first two verses, Paul draws three ideas from the truth that we have been justified by faith; since we have been justified, we have *peace, grace,* and *hope.* This is a series: they do not explain each other but are three inferences drawn from the truth of justification (argued for in the previous chapters of Romans, as indicated by *therefore*).

---

[29] The explanations are my own, informed by Schreiner's work and others. Schreiner, *Interpreting the Pauline Epistles*, 111–112.

> **Verses 2b-5b:** 3a-5b expand upon the *hope* Christians have because of justification; Paul draws forth the implications of this hope for the Christian life. He does this through a series of progressing coordinate relationships. In 5:1a-2b, the coordinated clauses are a series; they are on the same level, each an inference from the statement in 1a. However, in 2b-3a and 3b-5b, the coordinate clauses are a progression: each clause builds upon the preceding result of hope until it reaches a climax in 5a-b.
>
>> **Verses 2b-3a:** 3a presents an unlikely way that rejoicing expresses itself in the Christian life: rejoicing in the hope of the glory of God means rejoicing even in suffering. It presents a coordinating action—"not only doing this but also"—yet the second action serves to specify and explain the first. So, though grammatically coordinated, it is in a sense subordinate (a specific example of a general idea, rejoicing in hope).
>
> **Verse 3b-5b:** In the following clauses, Paul gives the reason that the Christian can rejoice in suffering; it is because they know that the end of suffering is glory—that hope will not be put to shame. 3b-5a is a progression, giving a step-by-step analysis of how suffering produces as a result worthy of rejoicing.
>
>> **Verse 5a-b:** in the final verse of this text, the progression of hope is fulfilled in glory. The Christian will not be shamed because God's love will ensure they receive the object of their hope (cf. Romans 8). 5b provides the ground for 5a: because God's love has been poured out through the Spirit, the Christian is sure that their hope will be realized.

One could go to a further depth than I did here, identifying the relationships the various prepositional phrases (e.g. "in which we stand," "through our Lord Jesus Christ") have to the clause they modify. But this should suffice to give you an idea of what arcing might look like. "It may appear," writes Thomas Schreiner,

> that tracing the logic in this way is a very laborious way to state what was obvious from the beginning. Even in short texts, however, this method is valuable because it constrains the reader

to slow down and to note the function of every proposition in the text. The reader then begins to observe more closely what is in the text, and then proceeds to ask questions about how the text coheres. In addition, the longer the text, the more such an analysis is necessary. It may be easy to consider the relationship between only two verses, but tracing the entire argument for extended paragraphs or even the entire letter can easily slip from our grasp unless we have some way of holding before our mind the logic of the text.[30]

The point of this chapter is not to teach these methods in detail; there are many books and free resources that do a better job than I could. Instead, I hope only to introduce these techniques and show how they fit into the method I am unpacking in this work.

D. Prophecy

The last type of biblical text we will look at is prophecy. To say a text is prophetic does not refer to a text type in the same way as poetry, narrative, or didactic prose. Those three categories involve the stylistic categories I call in *The Gift of Reading – Part 2* "language pattern" and "manner of communication." *Language pattern* refers to the distinct way these styles of text connect units of thought, e.g. whether through sentences (prose) or lines (poetry) and coordination (narrative prose) or subordination (didactic prose). *Manner of communication* refers to the way the language pattern they use communicates, such as through a story involving a narrator and plot (narrative), logical argumentation and explanation (didactic prose), or conceptual rhythm through the use of imagery in conjunction with poetic devices and parallelism (poetry). What I am calling prophetic texts do not have a distinct language pattern. Instead, prophetic texts can usually be classified as poetry or didactic prose—often blurring the lines between these two. However, because of the distinct way prophetic texts communicate, both as prose and as poetry, it is worth considering it separately. That is, what I am calling prophetic texts have a distinct manner of communication.

---

[30] Ibid., 103.

At times, prophetic texts can be divided into lines and poetic units. In these cases, we can analyse a prophetic text by mapping its parallelism. At other times, prophetic texts can be divided into sentences and paragraphs. In these cases, we can use arcing to identify the relationships between clauses and sentence diagramming to understand what is being said precisely. What makes prophetic texts distinctive is the symbolic imagery that they use.

a. *How Prophecy Communicates: Symbolic Imagery*

As I observed above, poetry often uses concrete metaphors. To be concrete, a metaphor must relate to human experience. These are metaphors that draw on our memories and shared experience to provide their emotional force. Psalm 84, for example, uses common imagery to incite the imagination of those singing it. Lines like verse 3 would resonate with the experience of many Israelites,

> Even the sparrow finds a home,
> > and the swallow a nest for herself,
> > > where she may lay her young,
> > at your altars, O LORD of hosts,
> > > my king and my God.

More familiar to many of us will be the imagery of Psalm 23. Though drawn from a culture different from ours, we can still see the concreteness of its shepherd imagery.

The reader of biblical prophecy, such as is found in the Old Testament prophetic books, in Daniel, and in Revelation, will immediately notice that its imagery is often of a different sort. In Numbers 12:8, God himself identifies prophecy as riddles or ambiguous sayings in contrast with the Law delivered to Moses, which is a clear word. Consider the following examples:

> Even stones from the wall will cry out,
> > and rafters from the woodwork will answer them (Hab 2:11)

> The cup of YHWH's right hand is coming around to you,
> > and disgrace will come upon your glory. (Hab 2:16)

> And though a tenth remain in it,
> > it will be burned again,

> like a terebinth or an oak,
>> whose stump remains
>> when it is felled."
> The holy seed is its stump (Isa 6:13)

> I saw in my vision by night, and behold, the four winds of heaven were stirring up the great sea. ³And four great beasts came up out of the sea, different from one another. ⁴The first was like a lion and had eagles' wings… (Dan 7:2-4)

> Then came one of the seven angels… and spoke to me, saying, "Come, I will show you the Bride, the wife of the Lamb. ¹⁰And he carried me away in the Spirit… and showed me the holy city Jerusalem coming down out of heaven from God, ¹¹having the glory of God, its radiance like a most rare jewel, like a jasper, clear as crystal. (Rev 21:9-11).

Like the imagery of the psalms, prophecy obviously draws on the experience of its readers and hearers. Yet, there is often a greater distance between the experience and the intended meaning of the imagery in prophecy than in poetry. In each of the above examples, the experiential basis for the imagery is recognizable, but the meaning is not so readily apparent. In such cases, we are heavily reliant on the interpretation provided by the author in context or by a heavenly messenger recorded in the text to make sense of the text.

In Habakkuk 2:11, we see from the context that the stones and rafters represent the peoples Babylon has conquered to build their empire. These people groups are crying out to God for vengeance in the very song in which this line is written. In Habakkuk 2:16, we can make sense of "The cup in YHWH's right hand" from the use of this image in the rest of the Bible; it represents the wrath of God. Isaiah 6:13 only makes sense in light of the last line, from which we see that the stump is a sign of hope remaining in a future Davidic king. We only know the meaning of Daniel 7 because an angel interprets it later in the chapter (7:15-18). In Revelation 21, the angel's words introducing the vision present the explanatory key; the holy city is the people of God united with God in their midst. The text goes to a great length to describe the future glory of this people as endowed by God; notice the parallels between the description of the city's appearance and the throne of God earlier in Revelation, where the beauty of jewels is also used to describe the glory of God (Rev 4:3-6). If the imagery of prophecy is generally more symbolic than regular poetry, the imagery of the so-called "apocalyptic" books, Daniel, Revelation, parts of Ezekiel, and Zechariah, are more so. They represent "an intensification of prophecy."[31]

i. Apocalyptic and Prophecy

Some readers may find it problematic that I have identified apocalyptic literature with the prophecy, for in New Testament and Biblical studies, these are not considered the same (indeed, Apocalyptic is considered a genre; prophecy is not always recognized as a distinct genre). I discuss genre in *The Gift of Reading – Part 2* and argue for a better way of understanding it, as a way of grouping similar texts in order to better see their commonalities. In terms of what I have presented so far in this work and my argument in the latter work, grouping apocalyptic texts with prophetic texts makes sense. The particular common ground they share is in their manner of communication. Prophetic texts (as defined above) and apocalyptic texts both take a stance of revelation, revealing something told to them or shown to them by God. The Book of Revelation, for example, is identified as a prophecy revealed by the Lord Jesus Christ (1:1-3). The manner in which these prophetic revelations communicate is similar in both prophetic texts—such as Habakkuk 2, Jeremiah 51, and Ezekiel 32:1-8—and apocalyptic texts, such as Revelation 6 and 19.

However, G.K. Beale is right to identify the latter as intensified; both prophetic texts and apocalyptic texts share a similar symbolic nature, yet the symbolism of the latter texts is of a greater magnitude in both quantity—apocalyptic having more symbolism—and quality—the symbols being more complicated and abstract, disconnected from their intended referent (such as a beast representing the kingdoms of earth, Dan 7:1-8). Yet clear continuity is seen in the way symbols are used to reveal truths about God and his ways, how we are to interpret this symbolic communication (through context and intertextuality), and even in the symbols themselves (cf. Hab 2:6, Rev 16:19). Beale writes of Revelation,

---

[31] Beale, *The Book of Revelation: A Commentary on the Greek Text*, 37.

> Though there are many definitions of apocalyptic (according to either form, thematic content, or function), it is best to understand apocalyptic as an intensification of prophecy. Too much distinction has typically been drawn between the apocalyptic and prophetic genres.... Apocalyptic should not be seen as too different from prophecy, though it contains a heightening and more intense clustering of literary and thematic traits found in prophecy. That this is the case especially in Revelation is borne out by its self-description as a "prophecy" In 1:3, as well as in 22:6-7, 10, where verbatim parallels with 1:1, 3 are found (see also "prophets" in 22:6...). The word "apocalypse" in 1:1 is a direct allusion to Daniel 2, where the word is used of the prophetic revelation communicated form God to the prophet Daniel....[i]

In the Gift of Reading – Part 2, I argue that the common understanding of genre, reflected in Beale's analysis, is flawed, yet the insight that the style of revelation is similar to prophecy, an intensification of it, is very helpful and helps us begin to interpret so-called apocalyptic texts.

---

[i] Beale, The Book of Revelation: A Commentary on the Greek Text, 37.

b. Study Strategy: Intertextuality

Because the imagery in prophecy is often so detached from its experiential basis, we must pay careful attention to the context to determine what the symbolism means. Reading prophecy, for this reason, is often a whole Bible endeavour. To understand the imagery in Revelation, for example, we need to pay careful attention to the book of Daniel and the interpretations provided there. Understanding Jesus's Olivet discourse in Matthew 24 requires a background understanding of the imagery used in Jeremiah and Isaiah for the end of Babylon and the nations, the embodiments of opposition to God (e.g. Isa 34, Jer 51). Symbolism, as found throughout prophetic texts and intensified in so-called apocalyptic texts, uses a symbol, such as an object (Hab 2:16) or number (Rev 20:3), in order to tell us something about the idea, event, or person/thing that is signified by the symbol. The meaning of the symbol is found in the comparison made between the signified and the signifier, the symbol.[32] For example, in Revelation 20:3, the use of "the thousand years" is symbolic of an indefinite but lengthy period of time in which (according to my interpretation of the passage) Christ reigns over the earth before his return. As a symbol, "1,000" is like the period of Christ's reign in the sense that it is lengthy. The number 1,000 is a regular symbol in the Bible for a lengthy period of time (cf. 2 Pet 3:8). The symbol "cup" in Habakkuk and elsewhere in the Bible is a part of a greater image of the wrath of God like an intoxicating drink, overwhelming and destroying its recipient. The comparison lies in the destructive effect that both God's wrath and strong drink have on the one who receives them. Our best tool for figuring out the significance of the symbols used in prophecy is the Bible itself. By turning to other passages where the same symbol is used, we can learn from the context or from a specific interpretation given by God how the symbol ought to be interpreted. Sometimes many comparisons may be drawn between the symbol and the object or idea it is signifying or pointing to.

Prophetic texts in the Bible use rich symbolism to communicate; they bring the subject of the text into relation with something else, the symbol, in order to teach us. The relationship between the subject and the symbol, their similarities or dissimilarities, teaches us what we are to learn about the subject.[33]

---

[32] "There are three crucial parts of a metaphor: the literal subject (tenor), the figurative subject (vehicle), and the resulting point of comparison. The figurative subject always explains the literal subject in some way. The figurative subject is a filter or lens through which the main point (or points) of comparison is (or are) deduced and applied to the literal subject. The point of comparison usually carries both cognitive and emotional elements. If "George is a wolf" is said in a context in which George is understood to be a dangerous criminal, then we understand better through the picture of wolf [sic] that George is someone who hurts people, and this image evokes a feeling of fear." Ibid., 55.

[33] In this way, prophetic symbolism is exactly like abstraction in other fields, as I have unpacked in the first book of this series and will unpack further in the fourth book. Rutherford, *The Gift of Knowing*, 102–105; J. Alexander Rutherford, *The Gift of Seeing: A Biblical Perspective on Ontology*, God's Gifts for the Christian Life Part 1 - The Christian Mind III (Vancouver, BC: Teleioteti, 2021).

FURTHER READING[34]

* Adele Berlin – *Poetics and Interpretation of Biblical Narrative* [B-I]

Jean Louis Ska – *"Our Fathers Have Told Us": Introduction to the Analysis of Hebrew Narratives* [I]

Robert Alter – *The Art of Biblical Narrative* [B-I][35]

* V. Phillips Long - *The Art of Biblical History* [B-I]

Douglas Stuart – *Old Testament Exegesis: A Handbook for Student's and Pastors 4th edition* [I-A]

* Gordon Fee – *New Testament Exegesis: A Handbook for Student's and Pastors 3rd Edition* [I-A]

* Thomas R. Schreiner – *Interpreting the Pauline Epistles* [I-A]

---

[34] I do not recommend any poetry books below because most of them are ultimately not helpful in actually reading Biblical poetry. My approach is a synthesis resulting from a survey of the classic and contemporary approaches to Biblical poetry mediated through my own experience studying Hebrew poetry. The bibliography contains books I have used and found of some help in this regard.

[35] Alter and Berlin are Jewish, so they come to the text with a different theology of Scripture than a Christian would. With Alter this is particularly evident; he is good at observing things in the text, but his interpretations are usually way out in left field.

8

KNOWING BIBLE TRANSLATIONS

⁵Look, all of you, among the nations and behold—
    and be astonished and astounded!
For a deed I am doing in your day;
    you would not believe it though it were told.
– Habakkuk 1:5

⁴¹ "Look, you scoffers,
    be astounded and perish;
for I am doing a work in your days,
    a work that you will not believe, even if one tells it to
    you."
– Acts 13:41

So far in this part of the book, we have considered the act of reading the Bible and the features of the Bible that we need to be aware of, with some consideration of tools we can use to read the various styles of biblical writings. For the rest of part 2, we will consider various tools we have available in our reading of Scripture. We will consider bible translations in this chapter and the biblical languages in the next chapter. In Chapter 10, we will consider the use of various secondary resources to check our interpretation of a text. We will conclude in Chapter 11 with a consideration of how we can evaluate our own interpretation and the interpretations of others.

Whether we like it or not, we are all indebted to and reliant upon Bible translations in our study of the Bible. Even for those who will be reading in the original languages, it is often Bible translations that serve as our first recourse for interpretive help. It is essential, then, that we have a firm understanding of Bible translation in general and the translations we will be using. First, we will consider Bible translation in general, its nature and limitations. Second, we will consider general approaches to Bible translation as exhibited in the major English translations. Finally, I will offer an evaluation of several of the most prominent English translations, considering their value and limitations.

A. <u>Bible Translation</u>

What is a Bible translation? Our answer to this question will have a significant impact on how we translate the Bible or how we interact with Bible translations. For example, if we say that a Bible translation presents the *content* of the original Greek and Hebrew text, we may produce or seek a very free translation that aims at communicating the ideas and truths of a text without attention to the way it communicates them. As an answer to this question, I want to show that a translation is a specific use or interpretation of the original texts and that there are two broad types of translation that are commonly used.

In our discussion above, I suggested that when we speak of the "meaning" of a text, we are thinking of specific ways that text could be used. "You shall not murder" means "it is wrong to murder," "it is wrong to kill another person without God-given authority," etc. We could say that these are all meanings of לֹא תִרְצָח (*lōʾ tirṣāḥ*) (Exod 20:13). It may be helpful to consider a translation as the communication of the meaning of a text from one language to another. Texts may mean countless things, for they apply to innumerable situations. However, there is no one-to-one correspondence between an original language from which we are translating and the receptor language into which we are translating. Therefore, in its attempt to communicate the meaning of a text, a translation by necessity restricts the meanings of a text.

Consider our example above, "You shall not murder" translates more of the text's meaning than "You shall not shoot a person indiscriminately," yet it does not replace the original Hebrew. "You shall not murder" employs the English word "murder," which is similar to but not identical with the Hebrew רצח (*rṣḥ*); it will thus have a similar but not identical range of meanings. For example, the Hebrew command includes what we would call "manslaughter," killing without pre-mediation. It also covers criminal negligence, accidental killing or negligence that results in death. The English translation "you shall not murder" captures one set of meanings indicated by the Hebrew but excludes others. Like application, translation attempts to communicate the meaning of a text to an audience, yet it attempts to do so in a way that is analogous or as close as possible to the original. A translation may attempt to follow the word order and style of the original as much as possible, but even when this is not attempted, a translation will attempt to communicate with the same text type: we translate poetry as poetry, narrative as narrative, etc. Like an application, translation necessarily restricts the meaning of a text to communicate it to an audience, to a specific culture and language, yet it generally attempts to retain as much of the **meaning potential** of the original text as possible and tries to mirror its form to some extent.[1]

This is an important point for us to see. If a translation is by necessity a restriction of meaning, an application, no translation will ever replace the need for the original texts. Even if we could guarantee that every translation would be perfect, there would need to be new translations as language changes and new translations as new ways we need to apply the text become apparent. In theory, then, there can be many legitimate and helpful translations in the same language; they may even complement each other where they differ (they may choose different yet equally legitimate ways of translating a text). Consider, for example, the way Paul uses Habakkuk 1:5 in Acts 13:41. Paul quotes from the Septuagint (LXX), the Greek translation of the Old Testament. It is clearly different from the Hebrew represented in English translations, yet Paul's use of it indicates that it is a valid translation in one way or another. If we consider what Habakkuk 1:5 means in context, we see that it is both a declaration of God's salvific intent (e.g. Hab 3:18) and a revelation of his coming judgment (Hab 1:12). A general translation, one that seeks to convey as best as possible the full meaning potential of a text, will translate the text in such a way that allows for the text to be applied in

---

[1] Meaning potential refers to all the possible applications a text could have. This is natural extension from our discussion in Chapter 5. If meaning refers to the different ways a text may apply, then any text has many meanings, as many as there are possible circumstances to which it could apply. Furthermore, these meanings are only potential, or latent, until they are met with a circumstance to which they apply. Thus, we may rightfully speak of a text's "meaning potential."

both senses. However, a translation that seeks to make a more specific application of the text may narrow it down to either the salvific or the judgmental aspect of the text:

> The LXX ... here correctly (though restrictively) conveys the sense of the Hebrew text. If we judge the LXX here as a word for word translation, it fails. But if we consider it an application [a specific translation], it succeeds and is ideal for Paul's intended application of this text. In Hab 1:5, the Septuagint focuses on the judgment aspect of God's vision, ignoring the salvific side. Paul uses it because he is preaching that same aspect, though elsewhere he preaches Habakkuk with the salvific aspect in view (Rom 1:17).[2]

The Septuagint here is an adequate, even helpful, translation of Habakkuk 1:5, but it is not sufficient to convey all the possible meanings or applications of the Hebrew text. Other translations will be required to communicate all that God intends for his people from this text.

B. TRANSLATION THEORIES

In the history of Bible translation, both general and specific translations have been produced. The Latin Vulgate, Luther's German Bible, and the English King James Version represent *general translations* of the Bible. They attempt to communicate as much of the meaning potential of the original texts as they can. These translations are designed to be used in preaching, teaching, and general reading of the Word of God.

However, at times pastors and teachers have seen fit to produce their own translations of biblical texts. Sometimes errors in the general translations have required it, but at other times, this has been necessary because they have needed to communicate a specific nuance or application of the original text that the broader translations do not communicate. Sometimes these individual translations are *general translations*, trying to present the fullness of the original meaning, but often they are paraphrases or *specific translations*

---

[2] J. Alexander Rutherford, *The Book of Habakkuk: An Exegetical-Theological Commentary on the Hebrew Text*, A Teleioteti Old Testament Commentary 1 (Vancouver, BC: Teleioteti, Forthcoming).

that attempt to narrow the meaning to a specific application.[3] In our day, this is seen especially in paraphrase or loose translations of the Bible, such as *The Message*.

In modern translation theory, general translations are the goal, yet there are two broad approaches taken to produce general translations. On the one hand, there are translations that attempt to achieve formal equivalency. These translations try to convey the form and meaning of the original text; "in its stricter form, this theory of translation espouses reproducing even the syntax and word order of the original."[4] The NASB and ESV—among others—are contemporary attempts to attain different degrees of formal equivalency. On the other hand, some translations seek dynamic or functional equivalency; they are not so concerned with the form of the original text (its shape, size, emphasis) but with its meaning (usually conceived of as singular) and force (its intended effect). Formal equivalence does not attempt to close the historical distance between the ancient biblical texts and the modern culture; it will attempt to retain the impression of ancientness a reader of the original languages will experience. On the other hand, dynamic or functional equivalence is

> the attempt to keep the meaning of the Hebrew or Greek but to put their words and idioms into what would be the normal way of saying the same thing in English…. Such translations keep historical distance on all historical and factual matters but 'update' matters of language, grammar, and style.[5]

All contemporary translations fall somewhere between these two extremes, with wooden literalness on the one hand and loose paraphrase on the other. The formal equivalency and functional equivalency of contemporary translations fall right and left of centre.

---

[3] I have defended the appropriateness of such individual translations elsewhere. https://teleioteti.ca/2017/12/05/a-defence-of-an-authors-translation-part-1/

[4] Leland Ryken, *The Word of God in English: Criteria for Excellence in Bible Translation* (Wheaton: Crossway, 2002), 19.

[5] Gordon D. Fee and Douglas K. Stuart, *How to Read the Bible for All Its Worth*, 3rd ed. (Grand Rapids: Zondervan, 2003), 41.

We will consider how this looks in the following section, how translation theory plays out in specific translations. However, as far as theory goes, I think neither one of these theories is ideal. If our goal is to produce general translations—translations that are readable and useable for daily devotions, teaching, and preaching—then our goal should not be driven by a bare theory of how to translate but be adaptive towards the goal of translation. The goal should be to convey as much of the meaning-potential of the original text as possible to a contemporary audience. The word of God is sufficient for all the Christian life; a general translation should seek to facilitate its function in this way for the reader. This necessitates the balance both formal and functional equivalency are trying to reach. If a translation is too awkward and foreign for the reader of English, they may not understand any of the meaning intended by the text. However, if the text is too loose and specific, the reader may not hear the specific application the Holy Spirit would have for them.

I would endorse, then, a form of what Leland Ryken calls "essential literalness." Ryken defines essential literalness as "a translation that strives to translate the exact words of the original-language text… but not in such a rigid way as to violate the normal rules of language and syntax in the receptor language."[6] Paraphrasing this, I would say that a general translation should seek to retain the maximum possible meaning potential of the original text by retaining its wording and emphasis—its form—, its clarity, and its literary force (beauty, rhythm, technicality, simplicity, etc.) in a translation that conforms to the rules of the receptor language. The goal is to stay as close to the original as possible—lest you lose some of the ways it might apply to the reader—while maintaining its ability to be understood and the more subjective effects reading produces.

These theories of translation are worked out in the many translations with which God has blessed the English-speaking world. No translation adequately communicates the full meaning potential of the original texts, so we need to employ a variety of translations in our study if we are to see all that God has for us. If we are reading in the original languages, the variety of modern translations will help us to grasp better what is being said and help us learn to read and understand the original languages.

---

[6] Ryken, *The Word of God*, 19.

C. Bible Translations

There are dozens of English Bible translations available; I have chosen only to discuss below those that are most commonly used and, in my estimation, the most helpful. It should be observed that there are many unhelpful "translations" out there, those produced by various cults or by individuals without a considered approach to translation and without sufficient knowledge of the original languages. For this reason, it is good to research where a translation comes from if it is not one of the more commonly recognized Bible translations. Some of those produced by individual scholars are quite helpful, but the number of bad translations out there necessitates a comment.

From our discussion so far, it will probably not be a surprise that I recommend the more formal equivalent translations for study while suggesting that translations on the functional equivalence side are valuable for gaining insight into the meaning and application of specific texts. The following translations are given in alphabetical order, not in any way reflecting my estimation of their merit.

a. *ESV*

The English Standard Version is the translation I have chosen to employ throughout this book and other projects. The ESV is generally an attempt at formal equivalence but one which seeks to maintain the literary nature of the original texts at the same time. In the translators own words, "we have sought to be 'as literal as possible' while maintaining clarity of expression and literary excellence.... As an essentially literal translation, then, the ESV seeks to carry over every possible nuance of meaning in the original words of Scripture into our own language."[7] This effort leads them, for example, to maintain cultural and historical difference where it is present in the original text.

Because of its emphasis on both the literary quality of the translation and faithfulness to the original meaning, the ESV is a great study resource. Its strength is in its preservation of the meaning potential of the original text, not only in what it says but also in the effect its literary art conveys, such as the way narrative can draw you in and poetry can evoke various emotions. Textually, the ESV is based on the latest critical editions of the New

---

[7] ESV Preface

Testament and on the Masoretic text of the Old, as much as the translators deemed possible.[8]

b. KJV

The King James Version is old; it has gone through several revisions but is rooted in the early days of the reformation. I include it on this list both because it remains a commonly used translation and has some, though limited, value for contemporary study. In its day, it represented the height of biblical scholarship and literary quality. Though seeking to be literal in many ways, it nevertheless succeeded in communicating the beauty of Hebrew poetry, for example, in a way many modern translations fail to do. Its main value for contemporary study is the way it offers access to a different era of biblical scholarship. Though the translators did not have access to many of the tools we have today—and this is at times evident—they also had a great knowledge of the Bible and translated on the basis of the tools they had access to and their understanding of language. For all the advances we have made in philosophy and the study of language in the modern age, we have not left the historical tradition of these things in the dust. In many ways, the beliefs that have informed modern translations are as influenced by our own culture and its deficiencies as the KJV translators were influenced by theirs. For this reason, the KJV sometimes offers a superior perspective on how to interpret a text (such as is the case in Hab 3:13). However, because of its evident deficiencies, the KJV needs to be used carefully.

There are two major issues presented by the KJV to the modern reader. The first is that its language is outdated. That is, the English language has evolved significantly since the King James Version was produced, even since its latest revisions. This means that words and grammatical structures that were once clear and understandable are no longer so, words have fallen out of our vocabulary, and some words have changed meaning (e.g. Phil 4:6, Rom 13:13, Psalm 37:14). The second issue is the quality of its underlying text. That is, though it is based on most of the same Old Testament texts as we

---

[8] Though I am not too familiar with it, the preface of the Holman Christian Standard Bible expresses a translation theory similar to the ESV. However it does not present itself as part of the KJV tradition, so it is a new translation based on the MT text presented in the BHS and the Greek critical text presented in the NA27. From my limited experience, I find the HCSB closer to the NASB in its final result as far as readability/eloquence is concerned.

use today (MT, LXX, and Vulgate), its New Testament text is based on a single tradition of the Greek text that today is not thought to be highly reliable. Therefore, though the KJV could conceivably have some use in study, it is not better than or to be preferred to contemporary translations.

c. NASB

If you were looking for a very literal translation of the Bible based on the best scholarship of the years prior to its latest update in 1995, the NASB is where you would go. The goal of the NASB was to preserve the legacy of the KJV and its significant American version, the ASV, "by incorporating recent discoveries of Hebrew and Greek sources and by rendering it into more current English."[9] Thus, it sought to remedy the two significant issues that face the contemporary reader of the KJV. It is probably the closest to formal equivalency among the major contemporary Bible translations. Its close adherence to the wording of the original texts makes the NASB an invaluable tool for those beginning their journey with the original languages. It is often easy to identify how the NASB is translating the underlying Hebrew or Greek words without having to use an interlinear Bible. For these reasons, it is a valuable tool for study. I have often found in my own study that it also presents an alternative Evangelical perspective on difficult texts than that which the ESV offers, so it is useful for comparing and contrasting translations.

As compared to the ESV or even the KJV in its own day, the NASB does not do as good of a job—in my opinion—of conveying the rich literary beauty of the original language texts. This is not an insignificant issue, for the artistry of the biblical texts is essential to understanding their message. The skilled use of poetry and narrative in the Bible is intended to lead the reader to the appropriate understanding and response to the text.

d. NET

Compared to the others, the NET is a relative newcomer to the translation scene, a whole new translation (not a revision) published in 2005. The goal of the NET is to produce a translation that is "accurate, readable, and

---

[9] From the Preface of the NASB 1995 update.

elegant."[10] It seeks to preserve the meaning intended by the original authors in an understandable manner and to maintain the literary elegance of the original. Like the NIV, the NET attempts to achieve functional or dynamic equivalency in its printed text. However, it is accompanied by extensive footnotes that explain the literal readings of texts and why they were translated the way they were.

The use of extensive translators' notes makes the NET a tremendous asset to students of the Bible. For those using the original languages, its insight into the difficulties of grammar and text criticism is invaluable. For those who are not using the languages, its explanation of how they got to their translation from the original text can be helpful for resolving or at least identifying the reasons for differences between translations. The NET was produced by Evangelical scholars and so is informed by a broadly Evangelical theology in its translating choices. Though its notes are helpful for getting beyond the problems with dynamic equivalency, it still suffers from a similar problem as the NIV. That is, the text is sufficiently specified for our culture today to remove much of the meaning potential the more literal translations are attempting to preserve. For this reason, the NET is a great study asset, but I would recommend using a translation like the ESV or NASB as the basis for your study and Bible reading.

e. *NIV*

The NIV is the standard translation for the dynamic or functional equivalence approach to translation. It has been produced by a top-notch group of over a hundred scholars representing many different protestant denominations. The NIV has been translated wholly from the original Greek and Hebrew texts, so it is not a revision of a previous English Bible (as the ESV, NASB, and NRSV are). It was first published in 1978 and has seen several revisions since then.[11] The NIV has sought to prioritize "accuracy, clarity and literary quality" with the purpose of creating a multi-purpose Bible translation (a *general translation* in my terminology). The translators that make up the Committee on Bible Translation, which stands behind the NIV, believe that the best way to attain this goal is through the functional equivalence model of translation.

---

[10] From the preface of the first edition of the NET.

[11] The edition I am using is from 2011.

The NIV is based on the latest biblical scholarship and often represents keen insight into the meaning of the biblical texts. For this reason, it is a great study resource, especially for checking your interpretation and seeing if other interpreters are seeing the same thing. However, as I have suggested above, it seems to me that the principles of functional or dynamic equivalency do not retain the meaning potential of the original text to the same extent a more formally equivalent translation is able. The nature of a translation philosophy that seeks to be intelligible and clear throughout while communicating the author's meaning accurately often necessitates moving from the generality I have argued for to specificity, narrowing down possible and potential meanings. By "possible meanings," I mean that such a translation must often choose between mutually exclusive interpretations of a phrase or sentence in cases where an essentially literal translation will do its best to maintain the ambiguity. By potential meaning, I refer to the innumerable applications a text may legitimately have. All translations will narrow this range, but functional equivalency often narrows this range beyond what is necessary for communicating the text in English. Consider a few of these examples:

> For on him God the Father has placed his seal of approval." -- John 6:27 (NIV 2011)

> for on him the Father, God, has set his seal." – John 6:27 (NASB, cf. ESV)

> For it seems to me that God has put us apostles on display at the end of the procession, like those condemned to die in the arena. We have been made a spectacle to the whole universe, to angels as well as to human beings. – 1 Cor 4:9 (NIV 2011)

> For I think that God has exhibited us apostles as last of all, like men sentenced to death, because we have become a spectacle to the world, to angels, and to men. – 1 Cor 4:9 (ESV, cf. NASB)

> to call all the Gentiles to the obedience that comes from faith for his name's sake. – Rom 1:5 (NIV 2011)

> to bring about *the* obedience of faith among all the Gentiles for his name's sake, – Rom 1:5 (NASB, cf. ESV)

I am not suggesting that the NIV is wrong in the interpretation it presents in these passages, only that it is clearly presenting a greater restriction—a further specification—of the text than is necessary to communicate in English. Consider Romans 1:5, to translate "obedience of faith" as the NASB or ESV have communicates roughly the same range of possible meanings as the Greek phrase that stands behind it. The NIV's translation makes the meaning clear, yet the meaning they make clear is only one possible interpretation among several. 1 Corinthians 4:9 adds additional interpretive comments that are thought to be invoked by the word the ESV translates "exhibited," yet this is not what the text says, nor is it certain that the word would carry those connotations. Therefore, the translation is more specific than the text justifies. Similarly, in John, "seal of approval" interprets the significance of the act of sealing.

A particularly significant area where this is evident is the debate over so-called "gender-neutral" terminology. There are many places in the Bible where a term can mean *either* a male or a human in general; accordingly, most Bible translations will translate one or the other (man or human being). However, there are specific words that have a component of meaning that is particularly male and yet are used to refer to both men and women. For example, υἱός (*uios*, son) means a male child yet is used to refer to male and female Christians. Should we, then, translate it "son" or "child"? It may seem common sense to translated "child" because it *refers* to men and women, yet this makes the interpretive judgment that the male component does not affect the meaning of the passages in question. Therefore, if we are to leave open possible and potential meaning, we should translate what the text says (sons), not what we think it means (child). Furthermore, in many cases in the New Testament, the use of the word υἱός meaning "son" is *intentional*, for example, in Romans 8:14. That is, it is the son who inherits from the Father; it may very well be—and probably is the case—that by calling men and women together sons, the biblical authors intend to say that all Christians are inheritors of God's good promises to his children. Furthermore, Doug Moo suggests that "son" in Romans 8:14 makes an explicit connection between our status as Children and Christ's status as God's Son, a connection lost by translating υἱός as "son" in one case and "child" in another.[12] Schreiner also suggests that the use of son echoes the description of Israel as God's son.[13] For whatever reason, Paul chooses to use the more general term τέκνα (*tekna*), children, in latter verses (Rom 8:17); so if we are to honour his intent—whether meaningful or stylistic—we should render the two words with their more formal English equivalents (υἱός as son, τέκνον as child).[14]

f. *NLT*

So far, the translations we have considered are all around the centre of the spectrum, with the NIV on the dynamic side and the ESV on the formal side. The New Living Translation moves us much farther down the line of dynamic equivalency. The NLT translators sought to "render the message of the original texts of Scripture into clear, contemporary English."[15] The goal was to be "faithful to the ancient texts and eminently readable." Where the original text was clear, this meant taking an approach that was more formally equivalent, but where the text was more difficult, they took a more dynamic approach. The resulting translation is quite a bit more dynamic than the NIV. Like the NIV, a strong team of Evangelical scholars stand behind the NLT.

The NLT has much the same strengths as the NIV, though it is harder to use for translating and understanding the original texts. In its weaknesses, it is generally the same, though by taking a more dynamic approach, these weaknesses are magnified. Thus, the NLT is useful for reference in your studies but would not serve well as the basis for study or the primary translation for comparing translations.

g. *NRSV*

With the NRSV, we are back towards the centre. The NRSV follows in the same English Bible tradition as the ESV and NASB but moves towards the

---

[12] Douglas J. Moo, *The Epistle to the Romans*, NICNT (Grand Rapids: Eerdmans, 1996), 499–500.

[13] Thomas R. Schreiner, *Romans*, Baker Exegetical Commentary on the New Testament 6 (Grand Rapids, Mich.: Baker Books, 1998), 423.

[14] Cf. Vern S. Poythress and Wayne A. Grudem, *The Gender-Neutral Bible Controversy: Muting the Masculinity of God's Words* (Nashville: Broadman & Holman Publishers, 2000), 247–250.

[15] From the preface of the 2015 edition.

dynamic side of things. The NRSV fares much the same as the NIV and NLT, though closer to the NIV. It is the least evangelical of the translations, and this is at times evident in its translations. Overall, it makes a helpful reference but not a good basis for your study or reading.

h. *The Message*

The Message is the most dynamic of all the translations we have considered here. It is the product of the late Eugene Peterson, a popular pastor who was extensively trained in the original languages. *The Message* offers the most specified of these general translations; in an effort to communicate to a contemporary audience, it restricts most possible and potential meanings. This makes it unhelpful for primary use in study or for reading the Bible and should not be used in these ways. Furthermore, in dozens of places, the translation adopted is, in fact, unhelpful and does not reflect the original text (e.g. Rom 1:26-27). However, given Peterson's writing abilities, it is probably the most readable and poetic of the translations considered. The main use to be made of *The Message* in Bible study is as a reference, to get an idea how someone has made an application of the text.

FURTHER READING

Gordon Fee – *How to Read the Bible for All Its Worth*, 33-53 (B)
* Leland Ryken – *The Word of God in English* (B-I)
Vern S. Poythress & Wayne A. Grudem – *The Gender-Neutral Bible Controversy* (B-I)

9

KNOWING BIBLICAL LANGUAGES

לֹא־יָמוּשׁ סֵפֶר הַתּוֹרָה הַזֶּה מִפִּיךָ וְהָגִיתָ בּוֹ יוֹמָם וָלַיְלָה לְמַעַן תִּשְׁמֹר
לַעֲשׂוֹת כְּכָל־הַכָּתוּב בּוֹ כִּי־אָז תַּצְלִיחַ אֶת־דְּרָכֶךָ וְאָז תַּשְׂכִּיל׃

The book of this law must not depart from your lips, but you shall meditate on it day and night so that you may be careful to act according to all that is written in it, for then you will succeed in your ways, and then you will have wisdom.[1] – Joshua 1:8

From my time learning Hebrew and Greek and serving as a teacher's assistant for language classes, I have observed two responses students have towards learning the biblical languages. On the one hand, some students rise to the challenge of the languages and begin to delight in reading the Bible in a whole new way. On the other hand, some students find the languages too difficult to manage or do not give the adequate time necessary to really learn them. I think that everyone can learn Hebrew and Greek—it is not so different from learning French, Spanish, German, or Arabic. And if you learn Hebrew, you can learn Aramaic—the third biblical language. However, to learn these languages takes a tremendous commitment of time and a lot of effort, time and effort not all of us are able to give.

For this reason, I have two purposes in this chapter. First, I hope to underscore the importance of the biblical languages, especially the *proper use* of the languages. Second, I want to outline two ways the biblical languages often relate to Bible study, namely word and grammar studies. I hope that this chapter would encourage those of us with the ability, namely the time

---

[1] My translation

and diligence, to learn the languages to do so. For the rest of us, I hope that it has been clear so far in this book—and I hope that it will remain clear throughout this chapter—that the biblical languages are tremendously important, yet not all of us have to learn these languages to reap their benefit. God has gifted the church with many people who are able to competently handle the challenges of language study and translation so that the rest of us may reap the benefit. It is necessary that some of us learn the languages but not all of us. For the reader who will not be undertaking the task of learning the languages, the discussion in this chapter will be best used as a primer for evaluating the claims of secondary resources (e.g. commentaries) you will use in study.

A. The Importance of the Biblical Languages

Not many of us take the biblical languages—Hebrew, Aramaic, and Greek—as seriously as Martin Luther did. Luther was adamant that the very Gospel itself was at stake when it came to studying the biblical languages,

> Let us be sure of this: we will not long preserve the gospel without the languages. The languages are the sheath in which this sword of the Spirit is contained; they are the casket in which this jewel is enshrined; they are the vessel in which this wine is held; they are the larder in which this food is stored.... If through our neglect we let the languages go (which God forbid!), we shall ... lose the gospel.[2]

Was Luther correct in his assessment? Everything we have seen so far, especially the last chapter, suggests that he was indeed correct. And history confirms it. Church history is full of minor (and major) errors made in doctrine and teaching because people did not have access to the languages, errors resulting from either mistaken or unclear translations or sloppy handling of the original language texts. If what I have argued so far is true, namely that translations necessarily restrict the **meaning potential** of the biblical texts and that there is and will be a continued need for new Bible

---

[2] From his letter "To the Councilmen of All Cities in Germany That They Establish and Maintain Christian Schools."

translations, then there is now and will always be a need for Christians who are well trained in the biblical language.

First, it is essential that we have *Christians* trained in the languages. For all sorts of reasons, many people who do not proclaim Jesus Christ as Lord have learned Greek and Hebrew and have positions as biblical scholars. But translating is by no means a neutral endeavour; it involves interpretation. Therefore, we need many men and women committed to Christ who will learn the languages and use them to serve the Church.

Second, if translations by their very nature restrict the meaning potential of a text, then pastors and teachers must—wherever possible—learn the languages. That is, if they are to preach the full counsel of God and be equipped to address every need their congregations have, pastors and teachers need to have at their disposal everything God has given them—access to all the potential applications Scripture has. Though using multiple different Bible translations addresses this issue to some extent, this still does not replace careful interaction with the original text. Thus, wherever possible, present and future leaders of the church should seek to acquire competence in at least biblical Greek and Hebrew.

Third, not only is there a need for languages in the context of local church ministry, but there is also a continual need for translating the Bible into English and other languages. So long as cultures and languages change, we will need revisions of old Bible translations and sometimes entirely new ones. There will always be a need for Christians willing to take up the arduous task of carefully translating the original languages for contemporary audiences.

In addition to these practical necessities that demonstrate the importance of the biblical languages, knowledge of the biblical languages is also important for correcting faulty interpretations of the Bible. Because the original texts are the final standard for meaning, adjudication between competing interpretations of texts must at some point have recourse to the original texts. This may come through means such as dictionaries, commentaries, and computer software, but those using these tools must have sufficient knowledge to do so, and there must be others with the requisite knowledge to produce such resources. Furthermore, as observed above, if we Christians do not produce resources for using the languages well, others who do not share our commitments about Scripture will.[3] Therefore, there is a great need for Christians today to carefully study and become competent in the original languages.

As I have argued throughout this book, all believers are able to read the Bible—whether they have the languages or not. But I think it is has been clear in each chapter that there is a certain measure of clarity that comes from studying the original languages that is not possible without them. My first teacher of Hebrew, Brad Copp, suggested that reading the Bible in the biblical languages was like switching from black and white to colour TV, or standard definition to HD. The content is the same, yet you begin to see things you did not see before. This is true in addition to what we have already seen concerning the way translations limit the meaning potential of a text. For this reason, the biblical languages are not necessary for every individual Christian, yet everyone who learns to read them will profit and the Church as a whole needs Christians who read the languages.

B. The Appropriate use of the Biblical Languages

So what goes into learning and using Greek, Hebrew, and Aramaic? Let's be clear about one thing: it is not simply a matter of learning how to navigate Bible software! Bible software such as Logos and Accordance has made way for those with enough money to access high-quality language resources and to view the original language source behind many contemporary translations. This is in many ways a blessing, yet it also harbours a curse. With easy access comes the temptation of sloppiness and laziness. When it comes to learning and maintaining a language, such habits can be deadly.

There are two routes for learning to use Greek, Hebrew, and Aramaic in Bible study. The first is learning the tools for word and grammar studies. For many of us who do not have the privilege of studying the Bible as a full-time job, this will be our primary option. The second is to learn to read the languages. In my estimation, the latter option is both the hardest and the most beneficial. To learn to read takes dedication and a daily effort to engage

---

[3] In the first book of this series, *The Gift of Knowing*, I show how commitment to Christ is essential to all human knowledge and knowing. This implies the point I am making here, that Christian commitments are essential to studying the Biblical languages. I make this point in different language throughout this book.

with the Greek and Hebrew Bible. For the rest of this chapter, I want to focus on the use of the biblical languages in Bible study for those who have enough of a foundation to engage in such a study (I would recommend the equivalent of an introduction to biblical Languages course or first-year Greek or Hebrew course, the equivalent being *Greek for the Rest of Us* or *The Basics of Biblical Greek* and their Hebrew equivalents). For those without such a foundation, the following guidelines may help you evaluate the discussion in commentaries and other study aids. At the end of the chapter, I will provide resources I have found helpful for learning to read the languages, including free online classes to do so.

The two main uses of the biblical languages other than textual criticism are word studies and grammar studies. Let's first consider some broad rules for study using the biblical languages and then consider word and grammar studies.

a. *Ground Rules for Language Study*

Greek and Hebrew are not simple languages, nor is it a simple matter to move from one language to another. The work of translation is a noble endeavour, and we ought to be deeply grateful for the translators of our Bibles. They have laboured a lifetime to learn the languages and have put great thought into how they might best translate Greek, Hebrew, and Aramaic texts into English. For this reason, we ought to have great humility when we attempt to use the languages for biblical study.

Now, translators are not inerrant; they make mistakes. Sometimes the mistakes they make are their own or result from the resources they have used. Also, the English language changes, so we may not be sure what was intended by a specific translation. Furthermore, studying the original languages may reveal that a specific translation is acceptable but does not present the best interpretation of a text. For these reasons, I think it is appropriate to dig beneath translations and look at the original texts; however, we must do so with great humility. Whatever our background is, we are all standing on the shoulders of giants as we use Greek, Hebrew, and Aramaic language tools. We may conclude that some of them were wrong and that there is a better interpretation available. However, we must come to these conclusions with careful thought and due diligence. So our first rule for language study is humility; if you come to a conclusion that no one else has reached or one that is vastly different from what others are saying, check yourself. You are more likely to make a mistake than those who have spent a lifetime reading the biblical texts.

Along with humility, we also need to remember that as much as translating is an art, it is also a science. That is, there is a certain amount of subjective intuition necessary to produce a beautiful translation, yet languages behave according to certain patterns that need to be observed in translation. I highly recommend D. A. Carson's *Exegetical Fallacies* in this regard.[4] The first two chapters, addressing word study and grammatical fallacies, respectively, provide a necessary corrective to many common mistakes that are made when using the biblical languages in Bible study. His writing is dense, but the book rewards careful study. In addition to familiarizing yourself with Carson's book, it will also be important to gain a working knowledge of the Hebrew and Greek alphabet and some of the differences between English and these languages. For this purpose, two books by Zondervan will be helpful; *Hebrew for the Rest of Us* and *Greek for the Rest of Us*.[5]

b. Word Studies

The way Greek and Hebrew are most commonly used in Bible Study is for word studies. A word study investigates the meaning of the original language term rendered in an English translation. Word studies are helpful when we are looking to see how a term is used throughout the Bible or in a particular set of writings. They are also helpful for identifying the exact meaning of an ambiguous English word used in translation.

Word studies will not reveal any profound insight into theology or the meaning of a text, but they bring precision to our study and help us to better interpret Scripture by Scripture. Regarding clarity, they help us identify what exactly is intended by our English translations. Consider, for example, Joshua 1:8. The seventh word in this verse, הָגָה (*hāgāh*), is translated "meditate."

---

[4] D. A. Carson, *Exegetical Fallacies* (Grand Rapids: Baker Books, 1996).

[5] Lee M. Fields, *Hebrew for the Rest of Us: Using Hebrew Tools without Mastering Biblical Hebrew* (Grand Rapids: Zondervan, 2008); William D. Mounce, *Greek for the Rest of Us: The Essentials of Biblical Greek*, Second Edition. (Grand Rapids: Zondervan, 2013).

This may bring confusion to a reader at first glance, for in modern English meditate has at least two meanings. On the one hand, "meditate" usually means to empty oneself of thought in order to achieve inner peace and clarity, or something of this sort. However, an older meaning of meditate is to think carefully and repeatedly about something. The translators of our Bibles only intend one of these meanings. We have two tools to figure out what is intended. The first is context: words only have meaning from their context, so we must ask how the word is being used. Joshua 1:8 clearly indicates the second meaning, for the first part of the sentence calls Joshua to not let "the book of this Law" depart from his lips. The verse is not about a mystical inner peace (though a different sort of peace will result from meditation on the Word), instead it is about grounding oneself in God's revelation. If we remain unsure or want to be more certain, we can do a word study to see how the Hebrew term is used throughout the rest of the Bible.

If we search for הָגָה in Hebrew Bible, we will see that it is used 25 times. The most recent English language lexicon of Hebrew (lexicon = dictionary) lists five different ways the "Qal" stem of הגה is used.[6] In some texts, it refers to the noise an animal makes (Isa 59:11, Ezek 7:16), in other texts to the moans of mourning (Isa 16:7), to human communication (Isa 50:3, Ps 35:28), in several texts to the act of meditation, and in three texts to plotting or imagining (Ps 2:1, 38:13; Pr 24:2). Our text is clearly an example of "meditating." The contexts in which this word is used, along with the range of meanings (these five different things it could mean) suggest that in our context the word means to think carefully and repeatedly upon something. Our study confirms what we can see from the context of our English translation.

In another situation, we may not need clarity on the basic meaning of a word but how the author is using it. This tends to be the case for words used technically, that is, words that are used frequently with a specific connotation (such as the word αναστασις, *anastasis*, which generally means "the act of rising" but is often used in the New Testament specifically for a resurrection). Now, we must not confuse concepts with terms; though an author may frequently use a specific term (αναστασις) to refer to a concept, such as a

---

[6] Qal is one of several forms a Hebrew verb may take. Many Hebrew verbs will take on a different meaning depending on what stem they are found in.

resurrection from the dead, this does not mean that the term only means "resurrection" or that we can learn all we need to know about a "resurrection" from this term. It can be helpful to study each occurrence of a word, but this only tells us how a word is used, not what a concept such as *justification* or *resurrection* means. To learn about a concept, we need to understand the context in which the term is used and how that concept is treated in other passages, where other words may be used for the same idea.

For example, it would be a fruitful study to identify how the word translated justification, δικαιόω (*dikaioō*), is used in Paul's writing and the New Testament in general. This would help us identify key texts for the doctrine of justification by faith. This would not, however, reveal all the texts involved. Such a word study would confirm that the word means "to be declared righteous," but we would need to dig further to discover what is meant by "righteous." This might lead us to study the whole word group,[7] the nouns δικαιοσύνη (*dikaiosunē*; righteousness) and ἀδικία (*adikia*; unrighteousness); the adjectives δίκαιος (*dikaios*; right, righteous) and ἄδικος (*adikos*; unjust, unrighteous); and the Old Testament words that are related, namely the צדק word group (*ṣdq*; to be righteous). This may lead us to the conclusion that "righteousness" within the Bible is both a legal and covenantal term; that is, the term refers to a right standing within God's covenants. It refers to both a status of not-guilty, so free from covenant curses, and of being in the right, as such a recipient of covenant blessing. Δικαιόω means "to declare someone to be in the right or to be righteous," yet a word study will lead us to explore how the Bible deals with the topic of righteousness. We may then conclude that when Paul uses the word δικαιόω and its relatives, he intends the covenantal idea of righteousness expounded throughout the Old Testament.

---

[7] Word groups are found in all languages but are prominent especially in the study of Hebrew. Words are often formed from the same basic form, or *root*, to form verbs, nouns, adjectives, adverbs, etc. For example, in English, deity, divine, divinity, to deify, and deification are all from the same word group. In languages such as Greek and English, where the language has evolved for a long period of time in many different contexts, it can often be dangerous to assume that words from the same word group will have the same meaning. However, this is sometimes the case in Greek and English and more so in Hebrew.

To do a word study, we first need to identify which Greek or Hebrew word is being translated in our English translation.[8] A generation or so ago, two tools you could use for this purpose would be an English concordance or an interlinear Bible. Web resources and Bible software have essentially made these tools obsolete. There are several free Bible study resources online that will show you what Greek word is being translated with the click of a mouse. On Netbible.org, you can use the NET translation and a Greek parallel text to identify the word in question. To do so, navigate to your passage and open the "Greek" panel on the right side of the interface. Hovering over a word in either the NET or the original language text will automatically highlight the word being translated on the one side and its translation on the other. If you search for your text in your desired translation on BlueletterBible.org (BLB), the "tools" option contains an interlinear that will display a list of every English word in a selected passage and the corresponding Greek word. On BLB, the Greek is given in its lexical form, what they (inaccurately) call a root.[9] Similarly, on Netbible.org, you can click on a word in the Greek text, and a box will appear giving you relevant information about it, including the lexical form, again called a "root." This is the form you will need to search for in the Bible and to look up in a lexicon.

If you are studying a Hebrew word, especially a verb, things get a little more complicated. It is important if you are studying a Hebrew verb to also note what stem it is in. The Hebrew verbal system is quite complicated, but a single verb will have different meanings depending on which stem it is in; thus, a word study cannot be on the verb but only on the verb in a specific stem.[10] The only online resource I am aware of for finding the Hebrew stem

---

[8] You can find diagrams of the following procedures online at https://teleioteti.ca/2019/08/09/word-study-guide/.

[9] In language study, "root" refers to a basic set of letters that are modified to become nouns, verbs, adjectives, etc. For example, the root of δικαιόω and ἀδικία is *δικ. The lexical form, what is necessary for a word study, simply means the form of the word without any morphological changes—it is not changed for gender, number, possession, tense, etc. A lexical form, therefore, is the form of the word you would find in a lexicon: in English, you look for "see" not "saw" in a dictionary.

[10] If you study Hebrew to a greater depth, you will begin to see how the stems relate and benefit from a broader study, but this requires an advanced knowledge of the Hebrew language.

and lexical form is biblehub.com/interlinear/.[11] Select under the heading "Hebrew interlinear" the option "interlinear verses." Navigate to your passage; you will be presented with a slew of information. It will present the Strong's number, transliteration, Hebrew word, translation, and parsing.[12] For Josh 1:8, the word translated "meditate" is described as V-Qal-ConjPerf-2ms. What is relevant for our purposes is the stem, in this case, *Qal*. The most common Hebrew stems that will be given are *Qal, Niphal, Piel, Pual, Hithpael, Hiphil,* and *Hophal*.[13] To find the lexical form, the form you need to search for, select the Strong's number at the top. Most of the information presented on the page that appears is concordance data; I do not recommend using it for a word study.[14] All we need on this page is the "Original Word," by which they mean the lexical form (what BLB and Netbible.org call a root). In this case, it is הָגָה (*hāgāh*). Alternatively, you can download a Logos 8 basic package for free (as of May 2019); this product contains the Lexham English Bible (LEB) and the KJV. If you hover the cursor over a word in either Bible, it will show you the lexical form and parsing. You can also right-click on the word and see this data displayed.

With the lexical form of a Greek or Hebrew word, and the stem of a Hebrew verb, we can then do a word study. The goal of a wordy study is to come to a better understanding of an original language word as it is used in the Bible, and sometimes by a specific author. The next step is to produce a list of every use of your word in the Bible using a search platform. I recommend using Biblearc's "scholar search," though Logos' search is

---

[11] As of 2021, Esv.org offers similar resources based on the ESV translation.

[12] Parsing is a description of the inflections of the word in the text. In English, we may parse "the horses'" as a definite, plural noun. In the discussion below, I presuppose that you will use Bible software or a website for parsing. However, there is a print way to discover the parsing of a Hebrew or Greek word, known as an analytical lexicon.

[13] There are variations of these stems, yet a consideration of these is beyond the scope of this book.

[14] Concordance definitions do not tell you what a word means but how a specific translation has translated it.

good.[15] In Logos, you can use right click on a word and select "morph" under the search options. You will need to deselect every search option but stem for a Hebrew verb. For a Hebrew verb, your search option should look like "Lemma:הגה@va" (a = Qal, other stems will be represented by a different letter). For every other word, Greek or Hebrew, it should be "lemma:" followed by the word.[16] On Biblearc, you cannot choose to select a specific Hebrew verb stem, so only use it for Hebrew noun/adjective searches or Greek word searches. To search on Biblearc, open a scholar search tab. Select the WLC Hebrew text or NA28 Greek text (depending on the language of your search). Select "word" on the bottom left-hand side of the screen and select "Lemma/Strong's" from the box that appears. Either use the provided on-screen keyboard to type out the word you will search for or copy the word into the bar.[17] From the options available, select the word you want to search for. Close the box with "update" and press enter or select the magnifying glass to perform the search. The results for both Biblearc and Logos will be in both English and the original language. On Biblearc you can select the English translation with the box marked by default +ESV under the search bar.

For many words, they will only appear several times, so you will want to consult the entire Bible. For more common words, it is good to search the whole Bible, but it will be more practical to focus on the way an author or even a specific book uses the word. For instance, you may consider how John uses the Greek word κόσμος (kosmos, world or universe): this word often takes on a specific theological connotation in his writings, referring to the whole world conceived of as in opposition to God.

With all the passages displayed, your next step is to write out all the ways the word in question is used. I recommend that you provide the English translation and jot beside it what is meant by that specific English word in its context, e.g. "meditate," to think repeatedly and intently about (Josh 1:8). This will provide you with the range of meanings for your word. Consider

---

[15] Biblearc is actually faster and will display results in NASB and ESV translations. The free Logos package will only show search results in the KJV or LEB.

[16] "Lemma" indicates that you are searching for the lexical form.

[17] Alternatively, you can use the Strong's number provided in the online resources mentioned above.

how other translations have translated the same verse to get a better handle on what the word means. Then consult the standard lexicons for the language in question.[18] See if they provide any further senses of the word that you do not have or if they provide alternative translations or meaning for the word in a specific context. Though these resources are produced by men and women who have laboured hard to understand how different terms in the Bible are used, they are not inerrant and free from error. Though we approach these resources from a posture of humility, "we must remember that these resources are created by fallible human beings who sometimes show their mental frailty or theological biases."[19] Indeed, at every point these resources are dependent on the theological biases of their authors and this at times leads them to conclusions that are contrary to the teaching of Scripture.[20]

The final step is to bring the insights of a word study to bear on the study of your passage. After ascertaining the range of meanings your word could have, you must then ask how it is being used in your specific passage. That is, words have a range of meanings or senses, but authors only intend one of these senses at a time. There are exceptions where an author employs intentional ambiguity that plays on two senses a word may have. Such is probably the case in John 3:3, where "born *again*" probably means "born *again* & *from above*," two possible senses of ἄνωθεν (*anōthen*).[21] However, such cases are exceptions; far more frequently, only one sense will be intended. Therefore, it is important to summarize the results of your word study as it impacts your passage; how is הָגָה (*hāgāh*) being used in Josh 1:8

---

[18] We will consider in the following chapter the standard works in this regard. They are all quite expensive, so having access to an academic library, well-equipped church library, or a language package for Bible software will probably be necessary.

[19] Andreas J. Köstenberger, Benjamin L. Merkle, and Robert L. Plummer, *Going Deeper with New Testament Greek: An Intermediate Study of the Grammar and Syntax of the New Testament* (Nashville: B&H Academic, 2016), 480.

[20] For example, the authors of *Going Deeper* rightly observe that Louw & Nida are wrongly led by their theology to exclude "propitiation" from the senses that the Greek word ἱλασμός (*ilasmos*; propitiation, place of propitiation) can have. Cf. Johannes P. Louw and Eugene A. Nida, eds., *Greek-English Lexicon of the New Testament Based on Semantic Domains*, 2nd ed., vol. 1 (New York, N. Y.: United Bible Society, 1989), 40.12.

[21] Cf. D. A. Carson, *The Gospel According to John*, The Pillar New Testament Commentary (Leicester; Grand Rapids: IVP; Eerdmans, 1991).

or how is δικαιόω (*dikaioō*) being used in Gal 2:16? If your word study is broader—for example, to understand how *Paul* uses δικαιόω—still summarize how he uses it in each passage where it occurs, for it will be used for different purposes and nuances in each case.[22]

c. *Grammar Studies*

In addition to word studies, it may also be useful to study the grammar of a passage in the original languages. Sometimes we need to do a grammar study. Such a study might consider the nature of a verb used, perhaps to explain why my translation of Habakkuk 3:3 has "God *comes in* from Teman" but the ESV has "God *came* from Teman." It may also consider the role of a specific clause, such as the clause introduced by לְמַעַן (*lᵉma'an*, "so that") in Joshua 1:8. A grammar study could also be used to investigate the difference between the translations of the NET, "the faithfulness of Christ," and the ESV, "faith in Christ," in Galatians 2:16. Whereas word studies deal with the meaning or sense of a word, a grammar study deals with the meaning of clauses and phrases or the translation of grammatical details such as verbal tense. Because grammar does not have as close a correspondence between original and receptor languages as words, a grammar study will require a greater understanding of the languages. For this reason, only experienced students of the biblical languages should pursue grammar studies. If you do not have experience with the languages but have a grammatical question, it would be wise to seek the assistance of someone in your church with such experience.

When you have identified a grammatical detail you want to investigate, such as a difference in translations that goes beyond word meaning, you will first need to identify the grammatical construction that is responsible for the difference. If you have your first year of Greek or Hebrew under your belt, the best way to do this is to attempt to translate the passage for yourself and identify where the difficulty lies. Alternatively, you may find a discussion of details of grammar in a commentary or study Bible and use this as your

---

[22] Fee's *New Testament Exegesis*, Stuart's *Old Testament Exegesis*, and Köstenberger's *Going Deeper* go to a bit more depth than I have, but I have intentionally diverged from them on minor points. This accords with the greater argument of this book. Carson's *Exegetical Fallacies* chapter 1 provides greater insight into the technical details behind word studies and will help the exegete avoid common errors.

starting point for a study. Whether you use a secondary resource or your own study of the text, a grammar study begins with identifying the particular grammatical feature involved.

In the cases cited above, the differences in Habakkuk 3:3 will not be resolved by grammar alone, for the verbal form used could indicate either tense depending on the context. In Joshua 1:8, a study of the function of לְמַעַן in different clauses will need to be studied. In Galatians, the general relationship between a head noun and a genitive noun will need to be studied, and particularly those instances where the head noun is verbal noun (where it has a corresponding verb; πίστις [*pistis*], faith, is related to πιστεύω [*pisteuō*], to believe) and the genitive is a personal noun (a pronoun or name). When you study a specific word that has a syntactical function (to indicate different clauses), you can use both grammars and lexicons to do your study. You will want to look up the specific word and identify how it is broadly used. When it comes to conjunctions or prepositions, a lexicon and grammar will tell you what the marker means when used with specific grammatical forms. For example, for לְמַעַן (*lᵉma'an*), *William's Hebrew Syntax* tells us that it could be used with a personal noun to indicate "for the advantage of"; it could be used with an object to indicate cause, "because of"; with an infinitive construct or an imperfect verb, it could indicate purpose, "in order to"; and it could be used for result, often with an infinite construct, "so that."[23] The Dictionary of Classical Hebrew (DCH) only tells us that it could mean "in order that" or "so that" with an infinitive construct or imperfect verb.

In the case of Galatians 3:16, Bible software or a Greek Bible will show that the phrase "the faithfulness of Christ" or "faith in Christ" are translating πιστεώς Χριστοῦ (*pisteōs Christou*). This is a verbal noun, πίστις (faith or faithfulness) with a personal noun Χριστός (Christ) in the Greek genitive case. The NET and the ESV disagree on how the genitive Χριστοῦ should be related to the head noun πιστεως. Looking up the genitive case in a reference grammar like Wallace's *Greek Grammar Beyond the Basics* or in *Going Deeper* will reveal all the different ways that a genitive could function with a noun. Several of these, namely the subjective and objective genitive, only occur when a genitive noun is connected to a verbal head noun, as in

---

[23] Ronald J. Williams and John C. Beckman, *Williams' Hebrew Syntax*, 3rd ed. (Toronto: University of Toronto Press, 2007), 134–135.

this case. Knowing that Christ is a proper name (i.e. a personal noun), we can see if a grammar gives specific details on how a personal genitive is used with a verbal noun. Bible software actually enables us to search for the specific combination of a verbal noun with a personal genitive, yielding the different ways that this construction could be used. As in a word study, such a grammatical study of a phrase, such as πιστεώς Χριστοῦ, or a clause marker, such as לְמַעַן in Joshua 1:8, will yield a range of possible functions a phrase or clausal marker could have.

At this stage, you will have a list of possible functions the specific grammatical combination or clause you are studying could have, much like a word study yields a range of meanings a word could have. The next step is to identify the particular function the grammatical feature you are studying has in context. In Habakkuk 3:3, I have come to the conclusion that the imperfect verbs used throughout the chapter are best translated as English present tense verbs, for they set the reader immanent events before the eyes of. That is, though the events are properly future (describing the coming Chaldean invasion), the song is intended to relate the events immediately as the object of reflection.

In Joshua 1:8, I have followed the ESV in rendering the לְמַעַן clause as a result clause, "so that you may be careful to act according to all that is written in it." Though *William's* does not explicitly say that result clauses are found with imperfect verbs, this is evident from the uses of the combination (consider DCH's list) and is implicit in his statement that result clauses are "often" found with the infinitive construct—not exclusively. Context leads to the conclusion that result is intended, not purpose. However, our study also reveals that there is a more subtle interpretive choice being made in this translation; English forces us to choose whether we think the result is cause-effect, "so that you *will* be careful to act," or an action that is made possible, "so that you *may* be careful to act." The latter seems more likely in light of the passage in general and the biblical teaching about the necessity of human effort in right action (e.g. Phil 2:12-13).

Concerning Galatians 3:16, your study may reveal that both the NET and ESV provide acceptable translations in terms of conventional grammar and the meaning of the terms. The ESV's "faith in Christ" understands Χριστοῦ (*Christou*) to be an objective genitive, providing the object of a verbal noun. The NET's "faithfulness of Christ" understands Χριστοῦ to be a subjective genitive, that Christ is the one who acts with faithfulness. There are examples throughout the New Testament of both objective and subjective genitives, and both are found with personal nouns. In fact, there are more subjective genitives that occur with personal nouns. However, because both combinations are possible, we must turn to context to decide which reading is better. Much has been written on this question, but I am convinced that the traditional Reformed reading—that it is an objective genitive ("faith in Christ")—makes the best sense of the various uses of the phrase. Namely, I would argue that "faithfulness" is never used in the Old or New Testament for covenant obedience or status, as it must be interpreted if it is a subjective genitive, but it is used for loyalty or faithfulness directed towards another party. Among many reasons, this is why I would say that "faith in Christ" is the best translation of this phrase.[24]

In this chapter we have considered the importance of biblical languages and considered two significant ways that the biblical languages are employed in Bible Study. This supplements the discussion of translation and text criticism in previous chapters. Overall, we have seen that the knowledge of the biblical languages is invaluable and essential to the healthy use of Scripture within the Church. However, we have also seen that those who do not have the time or ability to learn Hebrew, Aramaic, and Greek can have confidence in their Bible translations and make some use of the languages in their studies. God has provided us with those gifted in the languages in order that the rest of us can profit and have confidence in our access to God's Word, but those of us who are able must pursue the languages for the benefit of our own study and the rest of the Church. At the end of the day, however much or little we use the languages in our study, a good rule to remember is this: "the pastor's study of the Greek text should be like undergarments—providing support but not publicly visible."[25]

---

[24] So Moo, *The Epistle to the Romans*; Douglas J. Moo, *Galatians*, Baker Exegetical Commentary on the New Testament (Grand Rapids, Mich.: Baker Academic, 2013); Schreiner, *Romans*; Thomas R. Schreiner, "Galatians," ed. Clinton E. Arnold, Zondervan Exegetical Commentary on the New Testament 9 (Grand Rapids, MI: Zondervan, 2010). Though many academic commentaries and journal articles argue the opposite point.

[25] Köstenberger, Merkle, and Plummer, *Going Deeper*, 477.

FURTHER READING

D. A. Carson – *Exegetical Fallacies* (I)
John Piper – *Brothers, We Are Not Professionals* (pgs. 98-105) (B)
Vern Poythress – *In the Beginning Was the Word: A God-Centered Approach* (I-A)
Moises Silva – *Biblical Words and Their Meaning* (I)

Using the Languages

Lee M. Fields – *Hebrew for the Rest of Us* (B)
William D. Mounce – *Greek for the Rest of Us* (B)
Logos Bible Software
Accordance Bible Software
Daniel B. Wallace – *Greek Grammar: Beyond the Basics* (I-A)
Ronald J. Williams & John C. Beckman – *William's Hebrew Syntax* 3rd Edition (I)
Bruce K. Waltke and M. O'Connor – *An Introduction to Biblical Hebrew Syntax* (I-A)

Reading the Languages

Gary D. Pratico and Miles V. Van Pelt – *Basics of Biblical Hebrew* (B)
Andreas J. Köstenberger, Benjamin L. Merkle, and Robert L. Plummer – *Going Deeper with New Testament Greek* (I)
Mile V. Van Pelt – *Basics of Biblical Aramaic* (I)
William D. Mounce – *Basics of Biblical Greek* (B)

Reader's Bibles[26]

German Bible Society - *Biblia Hebraica Stuttgartensia: A Reader's Edition* (I)
German Bible Society - *UBS Greek New Testament: Reader's Edition* (I)

---

[26] A reader's Bible assumes a first-year knowledge of the relevant language. It aids the reader by providing footnotes explaining relatively rare vocabulary (beyond what you would learn in a first-year class) and parsing difficult or rare verbs. Because it facilitates the first-year student getting into the Bible and beginning to read, these may be the most helpful tool for learning to read and for acquiring and retaining vocabulary. See my review of these bibles on Teleioteti.ca, https://teleioteti.ca/2019/05/20/a-review-of-hebrew-and-greek-readers-bibles/.

Richard J. Goodrich and Albert L. Lukaszewski – *A Reader's Greek and Hebrew Bible* – 2nd Edition (I)

Dirk Jongkind, ed. – *The Greek New Testament: Reader's Edition*, Produced at Tyndale House, Cambridge (I)

Web Resources

Biblicaltraining.org

Concordia Seminary - offers video lectures on Hebrew and Greek through iTunes.

10

KNOWING TOOLS FOR READING BETTER

> Now a Jew named Apollos, a native of Alexandria, came to Ephesus. He was an eloquent man, competent in the Scriptures. He had been instructed in the way of the Lord. And being fervent in spirit, he spoke and taught accurately the things concerning Jesus, though he knew only the baptism of John. He began to speak boldly in the synagogue, but when Priscilla and Aquila heard him, they took him aside and explained to him the way of God more accurately. – Acts 18:24-26

With the last chapter, we have concluded our discussion of the practice of exegesis, how we go about studying the Bible. What we have yet to consider are the various resources that will aid us in our study. I have recommended books that are similar to this one, which discuss the theory and practice of exegesis or reading the Bible, but I have yet to talk about the resources that will help us when we look at specific texts. There is a wealth of information available online in this regard; in fact, some print resources traditionally used have been replaced by the various free computer-based resources we have talked about. There remain some tools that you will need to purchase or find access to if you want to wrestle deeply with the biblical text and its interpretation.

A chapter like this could be lengthened without end, but I want to restrict our discussion to several of the resources that I believe will be most helpful for our studies. I want us to consider, first, the tools for understanding specific biblical books and texts; these are broad introductions to the Bible and its books, Bible dictionaries, and commentaries that offer close insight into texts. Then, we will consider some resources for reading the Bible as a whole, several helpful volumes on biblical Theology. Lastly, we will consider the primary tools for using the languages, namely Lexicons and Bible software. My goal in this chapter is to familiarize you with significant resources to be aware of and to introduce broader types of Bible study tools that are available and their purpose.

A. Tools for Understanding Biblical Books and Passages

It is impossible for any of us to attain an exhaustive understanding of the Bible—it is just too big! It would be years of work, starting from scratch, to outline the thought of and explain the broad contours of any individual biblical book. But if we need to know the context of a passage to understand it, we cannot dispense with this step; we cannot avoid our need to come to an understanding of whole books of the Bible. However, we do not have to do this alone. Christians have been studying the Bible since it was first penned, and they have passed on the fruit of their labours for generations to follow. The result of almost 2000 years of study is a body of resources to help us come to an understanding of the Bible. This can be a daunting thought at first, yet 2000 years of study—at its best—has not produced anything that is not already to be found in the text. We, therefore, do not *need* to wrestle with the history of Christian interpretation to understand a biblical text, but we have the blessing of looking to this wealth of insight for wisdom when we are struggling.

On the other hand, every generation faces its own challenges and its needs to confront its own presuppositions, so turning to secondary resources (resources that help us understand the Bible) can provide its own challenge. Sometimes these resources will spend pages expounding an issue that has no relevance to the needs of our churches and society today; other resources will spend pages lost in details that are ultimately useless for understanding the text before us. I will offer some advice in the following chapter for navigating these challenges and have written a companion volume to this book, *The Gift of Reading – Part 2*, that will examine the hermeneutical assumptions, or beliefs about interpreting the Bible, that produce much error—or at least distraction—in Bible study resources.

My advice when using these tools is as follows; the needs of God's people change throughout the ages, but the text stays the same, so insights into the text itself are timeless, but sometimes particular applications are unnecessary for us and our churches. Furthermore, because we are concerned with how the text is speaking to us and to our churches, do not get caught up in academic discussions about source material and ancient situations that are not mentioned in the text (more on this in the following chapter, in the first part of this book, and the companion volume). Lastly, there are many insights that are historically interesting and may very well be true, but they do not help us see the text and its meaning, so do not trouble yourself with them.

a. *Introductions to the Bible*

Generally, an "Introduction" or "Synopsis" provides an overview of the content and academic discussion around a book of the Bible. Usually, an introduction of this sort will deal with either the Old or New Testament, but there are interpretive handbooks or introductions that address a specific body of biblical writing, such as the Pentateuch, Gospels, or Pauline letters. Introductions are good for giving you an overview of a book and providing key interpretive details for making sense of its parts. When it comes to an introduction, not all are of the same quality, nor do all have the same purpose. There are introductions from all over the theological spectrum, including from non-Christians and atheists, and there are more or less popular treatments as well as academic ones.

Generally, there are theological, historical (or "special"), and critical introductions to the Bible. The two former types are often Evangelical, while the latter is not. I do not find much use of critical introductions to the Bible: they tend to focus on purely academic issues, often with an explicitly non-Christian perspective. Of the other two types, both have their place. Theological introductions focus on the major themes, literary forms, and theological contributions of biblical books. Historical introductions are the most common; they focus on the traditional question of Evangelical Historical-Grammatical Exegesis; who is the author? who and where is he writing to? where did he write from? what is the date of the letter? what sources did he employ? and what was his purpose? I have suggested—and will argue at length in *Part 2*—that much of this data is unnecessary for interpreting the Bible. Often these details distract us from what the Bible is actually saying. Nevertheless, these volumes regularly yield helpful insights into the structure of biblical books and their purpose. There are also more general introductions that cover theological, historical, and sometimes even critical perspectives. Here are several biblical introductions I have found useful in my own studies:

i. General

Bill T. Arnold, Bryan E. Beyer – *Encountering the Old Testament*

Walter A. Elwell & Robert W. Yarbrough – *Encountering the New Testament*

ii. Historical

Tremper Longman III & Raymond B. Dillard – *An Introduction to the Old Testament*

D. A. Carson & Douglas J. Moo – *An Introduction to the New Testament*

iii. Theological

J. Ligon Duncan and Richard Belcher – *A Biblical-Theological Introduction to the Old Testament*

J. Ligon Duncan and William B. Barcley – *A Biblical-Theological Introduction to the New Testament*

b. *Bible Dictionaries*

Sometimes there is a particular theme you may want to explore, or you may have a more general question about a concept that appears in your studies. For example, you may want to more about "apostles" beyond just the meaning of the word, which is what a word study reveals. Or you may want to know more about parables, what crucifixion was like beyond what the Bible tells us, what the Bible tells us about the fall of Babylon, or you may want to have an outline of the history of Israel as recounted in the Bible. Such questions can often be answered by looking up articles in a good Bible dictionary.

A Bible dictionary is an example of a tertiary source in academic studies: it does not teach something new or present an interpretation of a primary source. Instead, it offers a summary of the more detailed studies that are available. They are most helpful for finding a bibliography for more in-depth study but will often suffice for our Bible study purposes. There are several single-volume Bible dictionaries that are readily available, but for the most part, they are not very helpful. The Lexham Bible Dictionary that comes with most Logos packages is somewhat helpful, but the most helpful Bible Dictionaries are devoted to specific areas of biblical studies or specific sections of the Bible. The IVP Bible Dictionary set is a particularly helpful resource for Bible questions, but it is expensive and on the academic side of things.

c. *Commentaries*

Commentaries can be the most helpful and most confusing or distracting tools at our disposal. The good use of a commentary can sharpen our exegesis and application, but the bad use can lead us far away from the text. A commentary is concerned with providing an interpretation of a text, so there are as many commentaries as there are interpretations and interpretive approaches to the Bible. Now, there is something to be learned from any commentary, but many of them are written by authors who do not accept a basic Evangelical bibliology as necessary for interpreting it (see part one of this book). So, though there may be value in wrestling through a classic liberal commentary, your time would be best invested in Evangelical commentaries written by authors who are committed to the Bible as it presents itself.

There are many commentaries that fall into this category. As you engage in biblical study, it is a good idea to keep track of good commentary series and good commentators, those that most often answer the questions you are asking. Even the best series has volumes that miss the mark, and many great authors write in otherwise mediocre series, so it is important to pay attention to both series and the authors who write within them.

Commentaries generally come in several different types. First, there are technical, semi-technical, and popular level commentaries. Technical commentaries are concerned with wrestling through the academic questions of biblical studies and focus on the original language texts. Semi-technical commentaries are based on the original languages and offer comments on them but do so in a way that is accessible to those without language training. Popular level commentaries focus on helping the untrained Christian reader understand the Bible.

Second, we can identify three broad categories of commentaries among these. Most technical and semi-technical commentaries offer a verse-by-verse analysis of the text, sometimes accompanied by a unique translation of the text. Most popular commentaries and some semi-technical ones offer a unit-by-unit, or paragraph-by-paragraph, summary of the meaning of the text. Lastly, some commentaries focus on application, with or without verse by verse and unit-by-unit comment. The most helpful commentaries combine all these approaches in one. Whatever approach a commentary takes, it will often begin with a lengthy introduction to the book in question, providing the same type of information as a more general Bible introduction but to a greater depth. The following are some of my suggestions for helpful technical, semi-technical, and popular Bible commentaries. I am focusing on series, but as I observed above, the individual authors of commentaries are more determinative of quality than the series. It should also be noted that there are some single-volume Bible commentaries, but I have not found these of much use in my study.

i. Popular

The two best popular-level Bible commentary series I have found useful are the Tyndale Bible Commentaries and The Bible Speaks Today. The Tyndale Bible Commentaries come from various theological spectrums, though all generally Evangelical, and features some outstanding biblical scholars among its authors. The usefulness of each volume varies, some being so focused on historical matters that they do not really give any insights into the text. But overall, this is a helpful verse-by-verse series that is accessible to the interested reader. The primary use of this volume will be in understanding the specific meanings of words, grammatical constructions, and wrestling with significant text-critical issues. It offers some theological reflection, but not as much as the following series.

The Bible Speaks Today series focuses more on theology and units of thought than the Tyndale commentaries, making it better for understanding the meaning and application of a text than the Tyndale series. This series also features many outstanding biblical scholars and theologians, so it offers many insights.

ii. Semi-Technical

In my estimation, some of the best commentaries available today fall into this general audience, addressing students, pastors, and scholars. These commentaries assume a bit more understanding than popular level commentaries, but if you have made it this far in this book, they should prove to be no problem for you. I particularly recommend many of the volumes in the New International Commentary on the New Testament (NICNT) and Old Testament Series (NICOT), the Zondervan Exegetical Commentaries (ZEC) series, and the Baker Exegetical Commentaries on the New Testament (ECNT). Though it was discontinued before it was finished, many of the volumes in the Wycliffe Exegetical Commentary Series are also great. The Expositor's Bible Commentary is an affordable yet helpful option as well.

Each of these will comment on the original languages, text-critical issues, and interact with the theological implications of the text. The Zondervan Exegetical Commentary has an explicit section devoted to application—addressing the contemporary relevance of the text—but the NICOT and ECNT will also draw explicit attention to the way the text speaks to our contemporary culture.

iii. Technical

As far as Technical commentaries go, I do not have many to recommend. For the New Testament, I have found the New International Greek Testament Commentary (NIGTC) a reliable guide for understanding the technical intricacies of the New Testament. This series also pays attention to the theological implications of the text, so it is quite helpful across the board. I have yet to find an equivalent series for the Old Testament. On a purely linguistic basis, Baylor University's series "Handbooks on the Greek/Hebrew Text" is very helpful. Unfortunately, this series will not deal with the broader meaning and application of the text.

For text criticism, the Biblia Hebraica Quinta series (which is not yet finished) provides a thorough commentary on text-critical issues in each volume, however it is coming from broadly atheistic presuppositions (the editors are from various theological and religious backgrounds). On the New Testament, the United Bible Society's *Textual Commentary on the Greek Text* is helpful, though the UBS committee and author Bruce M. Metzger are not working from the same presuppositions concerning Scripture as I have argued for in this and other books.

B. TOOLS FOR GRASPING THE UNITY OF SCRIPTURE

I argued in the first part of this book that reading the Bible is a whole Bible endeavour; we need to understand the story and content of the whole Bible to understand its parts. I also argued that understanding how the Bible interprets itself is essential to read it well. The commentaries and introductions discussed above will do this to some extent, especially the *Biblical-Theological Introduction to the New Testament* and *to the Old Testament*. However, there will be many times when you may want a more in-depth treatment of the New Testament's use of the Old or of the metanarrative recounted in and unifying themes of Scripture. There are many significant works in this department, but I will draw attention to only a few.

The book I have found most helpful for grasping the big picture of Scripture may be Peter J. Gentry and Stephen J. Wellum's *Kingdom through Covenant*. This is a technical volume that is available in a more popular form as *God's Kingdom through God's Covenants*. The work of Graeme Goldsworthy is also quite insightful, specifically his books *According to Plan* and *The Goldsworthy Trilogy*. Regarding the Old Testament, the book *Dominion and Dynasty* by Stephen G. Dempster is a helpful overview of significant themes in the Old Testament. The series of which it is apart, *New Studies in Biblical Theology*, is very helpful but quite academic. *An Old Testament Theology* by Bruce Waltke is also helpful, especially its discussion of the Old Testament cultus (pattern of religious ritual) established in the Pentateuch. Regarding the New Testament, G.K. Beale and Thomas Schreiner have great New Testament biblical theologies that are worth consulting. Many of their insights have made their way into this and other books I have written, but these volumes will reward careful study.

All the books cited above deal with the use of the New Testament in the Old to some extent. However, for a more detailed study, G.K. Beale's *Handbook on the New Testament Use of the Old Testament: Exegesis and Interpretation*, is particularly valuable. In addition, the *Commentary on the New Testament use of the Old Testament* edited by G.K. Beale and D. A. Carson is a treasure trove of insight.

This area, understanding how the Bible is put together and how the New Testament uses the Old Testament, is an area of particular interest for me as a New Testament believer academically trained in the Old Testament. I have benefited greatly from each of the above works but have struck a slightly different path in the introduction to this book and in my work on Habakkuk, namely my *Believe the Unbelievable: A Study in Habakkuk* and my commentary *The Book of Habakkuk: An Exegetical-Theological Commentary on the Hebrew Text*. I would suggest using the general approach I have offered and using these resources for in depth study on specific themes and issues that I have not had space to unpack in these pages. In the coming years, as the Lord wills, I hope to write another part to this series dealing with the Bible itself. The first volume, a theology of the Bible, and the second, an introduction to the Bible, will take the general approach and argument of the first part of this book and expand them across book-length treatments.

C. Tools for Original Language Study

The last set of tools we will discuss in this chapter are those that aid us in language study. In the previous chapter, I suggested some grammars that will suffice for studying the grammar and syntax of Hebrew for most readers. I also introduced several online resources that will help with basic language study. In this part, I want to outline the significant lexicons (i.e. original language dictionaries) that will be essential for doing word studies or reading the Bible in these languages. I also want to consider the two major bible software programs.[1]

a. *Lexicons*

When doing a word study or translating, the most useful tool may be a good lexicon. The key word here is "good." There are lots of lexicons available, but not all of them are of equal quality. As a rule of thumb, do not use a concordance-based lexicon, such as a *Strong's* lexicon. These do not tell you what a word means; they only give the range of translation glosses given by a particular English translation.[2] What you want is lexicon that will provide you translational glosses (single word or phrase equivalents for the original language word) accompanied by a definition, an explanation of what it means.

---

[1] There are several free Bible programs available. I do not have much experience with these, yet I assume you will get what you paid for. They will usually have open-source resources; these are not the best quality and are usually open source for a reason (usually outdated). It may also be the case that these programs will not have the highest standards of proof checking (a problem found even in purchased Bible software). Other software is community based and has many pirated resources.

[2] A gloss is a single word equivalent for an original language word. For example, "faith" is often offered as the translation of πίστις (*pistis*). A definition will explain what the word actually means and which sense of an English equivalent is relevant.

The major scholarly lexicons for Greek and Hebrew (usually including Aramaic) will provide a combination of gloss and definitions, along with a sample of uses.

When studying Greek, the major lexicons to use are *A Greek-English Lexicon Of the New Testament and Other Early Christian Literature* (BDAG) and *Greek-English Lexicon of the New Testament* by Louw and Nida (L&N or simply Louw and Nida). The latter is organized according to meaning, so it will require an index; the former is the most extensive biblical Greek lexicon and is organized alphabetically. There are two other lexicons to be aware of. Sometimes free software will come with an older Greek lexicon known as Thayer's. It may be of some use, but it is rather outdated and should not be relied upon. You will also find many references to the massive volume produced by Liddell and Scott (LSJ). Liddell and Scott's *A Greek-English Lexicon* covers ancient Greek up to and beyond the New Testament. It is of some help yet is outdated like Thayer's. Furthermore, it provides mostly glosses, not definitions, and is too broad in its scope to be of immediate value for our purposes. That is, LSJ has many uses for scholars and academics but should not be depended on for a basic word study; our focus should be on the language of the New Testament—which is an example of the Koine Greek dialect. Another lexicon to be aware of is the *New International Dictionary of New Testament Theology and Exegesis*, edited by Moises Silva. This is a helpful reference work that presents extensive word studies on key Greek terms.[3]

When studying Hebrew, the major lexicons to use are the *Hebrew and Aramaic Lexicon of the Old Testament* (HALOT) and the *Dictionary of Classical Hebrew* (DCH). These are the scholarly standards, yet the older work known as the Brown, Driver, and Brigg's Lexicon (BDB) is still helpful, though it should be employed in conjunction with the former works. HALOT and DCH are both organized alphabetically; BDB is organized instead by root words, so the beginning student of Hebrew will need to use an index or software version to find a word. HALOT contains an Aramaic dictionary, but DCH does not. HALOT has been the scholarly standard for

---

[3] The older *Theological Dictionary of the New Testament* should be avoided unless you have familiarized yourself with word studies and have digested Carson's *Exegetical Fallacies*. This volume comes from a broadly liberal theological background and is riddled with lexical fallacies.

many years; the price of DCH hinders it from overtaking HALOT in this regard. All three of these lexicons come from a critical background of Hebrew scholarship, so discernment is necessary when using each of them. They will often point to emendations of the text that should not be followed without a text-critical basis, for which you will need to consult the BHS or BHQ apparatus—both of which also offer emendations of the text.[4] DCH is also a dictionary for all classic Hebrew literature, including the Dead Sea Scrolls and the Hebrew inscriptions. When using DCH, look for the way the language is used by the biblical authors more than its use among the extra-biblical sources.[5] I should also mention that DCH and HALOT both have concise abridgments available: Holladay's short Hebrew lexicon is based on HALOT, and the *Concise Dictionary of Classical Hebrew* is based on DCH. These are helpful tools and are far cheaper, yet they do not contain the extensive treatment of biblical usage found in the larger works.

When using any lexicon, use discernment. The authors are governed by philosophical presuppositions concerning language and by theological presuppositions in their work. Always compare what you read in a lexicon with what you find in a text. Especially in word studies, use the lexicons to supplement and check your work but do not rely on them alone. I have mentioned some of the presuppositions behind the major lexicons in this and previous sections, but take the time to read the prefaces of these lexicons to learn about their methodology and research the authors a bit: this will give you an idea of where the lexicon is coming from and potentially why it comes to different conclusions than another.

b. *Bible Software*

---

[4] An emendation refers to an intentional correction of the consonantal text of the Hebrew Bible, usually done in an effort to "make sense" of the text.

[5] In a paper on Job 30, I present several reasons against accepting these scholarly emendations and also why the Hebrew language of the Bible should be given priority over extra-Biblical Hebrew and Semitic texts. Some of this has made its way into *The Gift of Reading – Part 2*. Cf. J. Alexander Rutherford, "Lament of the Afflicted: A Translation of Job 30" (Teleioteti, 2017), accessed January 8, 2018, https://teleioteti.ca/2017/12/15/the-lament-of-the-afflicted-a-translation-of-job-30/.

The last resources we will consider in this chapter are paid Bible software, specifically Accordance and Logos. Both have pros and cons; you cannot really go wrong with either. Both programs contain an extensive suite of language study tools; this is probably what they are most useful for. Until recently, Accordance and the now discontinued Bible Works were the scholarly standards, yet Logos is growing in its reputation for quality. In my experience, both programs contain more errors than the print edition of study resources, so beware of the potential for such errors. Both Logos and Accordance provide competitive pricing for language study resources, such as grammar and lexicons, when compared to the print editions. You will not save a ton of money if you want to get the best lexicons, for example, yet the digital format makes their use far more practical. Accordance continues to have a strong scholarly reputation and contains powerful language study resources, yet it is less intuitive than Logos.

Both programs have a large selection of resources for purchase; Logos is, from my experience, more feature-driven than Accordance. That is, with Logos, there is a new edition with a new study feature available every year or so. The presence of so many features means that Logos has a steep learning curve if you want to make use of its full potential.

In my opinion, Logos' feature-driven focus is one of its greatest weaknesses. Every few years, Logos releases a new edition of its software, featuring several new books and features. To access these new features, you usually are required to spend another $100 to $200 dollars for the minimum base package required to use these features. This means that in addition to whatever package you originally bought (mine cost me about $1200) you are required to spend an additional $100-200 every few years to take advantage of the new features Logos continually releases. This can quickly make Logos an expensive option. Another thing to note with Logos is that the volume of resources given does not necessarily reflect their value (I am not sure how Accordance fairs in this regard). A basic package may give you several hundred resources, yet many of them are not high quality or are open source. That is, they may not be very helpful, and if they are helpful, they may be accessible for free elsewhere. For this reason, when weighing a package to buy, see if it contains the resources you need and will use and consider if it is worth it just for those resources; you may never use the rest.

Another consideration to make before investing in an expensive Bible software program is the stability of the medium. That is, computers have only emerged in the last 50 or so years and have seen a tremendous amount of change since they first appeared. What was cutting edge in the 90s appears ridiculous today. If computers as we know them today go the way of the floppy disk, it is legitimate to ask if the software we invest in now will remain usable in 10 or 20 years. Also, if either company goes out of business, there is the danger that their product will no longer be supported as technology develops. For this reason, investing several hundred dollars now in Bible software may entail greater costs in the long run.

That said, both Accordance and Logos can make Bible study quicker and easier. They are not essential for studying the Bible but are a great resource to make life a little easier.

FURTHER READING

G. K. Beale – *Handbook on the New Testament use of the Old Testament: Exegesis and Interpretation* (I)

D. A. Carson – *New Testament Commentary Survey* (B)

Gordon D. Fee & Douglas Stuart – *How to Read the Bible for All its Worth* (B)

Gordon D. Fee – *New Testament Exegesis, 3rd Edition* (I)

Tremper Longman III – *Old Testament Commentary Survey* (B)

Thomas R. Schreiner – *Interpreting the Pauline Epistles* (B – I)

Douglas Stuart – *Old Testament Exegesis, 4th Edition* (I)

EVALUATING EXEGESIS AND APPLICATION

> Do your best to present yourself to God as one approved, a worker who has no need to be ashamed, rightly handling the word of truth. – 2 Timothy 2:15

If we are to read the Bible and respond as God would have us, we need ears to hear. We need to be attentive and know how to discern his voice, how to interpret the Word he gives us. In these last six chapters, we have considered the practical side of studying the Bible, how we may pay close attention to hear it well. In chapter 5, we looked at the purpose of reading the Bible—what we are aiming for in our reading—and how we recognize that we have achieved this goal. Essentially, we listen to God's word so we may know him and submit to him. To do this, we need to understand what the text means and how we are to respond to it. We looked at three different criteria by which we can identify if an application is justified or not. To conclude this second part of the book, I want to revisit these three criteria. In our labour to understand the Bible, we encounter varying interpretations of biblical texts. For this reason, we need to have an idea of how to evaluate the interpretations of the commentaries and resources we use and to check our own interpretations at the end of our study. Applying what we have already seen, I want to suggest three ways we can check whether an interpretation is justified or not: we can ask if it is a justified use of the text through the criteria of validity, appropriateness, and fittingness; we can ask if it is justified by asking if it can be argued from the text in its biblical context; and we can ask if it involves a misuse of extra-biblical background material.

A. Is It Valid, Appropriate, and Fitting?

Everything we have considered so far in this section has given us tools to evaluate the interpretations of other readers. Pursuing some of the resources I suggested, such as D.A. Carson's *Exegetical Fallacies*, will equip us further to identify methodological mistakes we and others might make. In addition, the criteria of *validity*, *appropriateness*, and *fittingness* provide a good way to analyse other interpretations. We ask, does the interpretation correspond to the words and grammar of the text (validity)? Does it fit the tone or intent of the text, not twisting the purpose of a text (appropriateness)? Does the interpretation fit with the referents of the text, identifying not only the appropriate historical entity involved but also the audience to which statements and commands are directed (fittingness)?

Regarding fittingness, we must be diligent in asking if the appropriate audience has been understood, especially when reading the Old Testaments and narrative texts—in which characters speak to audiences that do not always include the reader. In addition to these questions, I think the most important question to ask of ourselves and the work of others is, "If they listened well, would other interpreters hear what I think the text is saying?"

B. Can It Be Argued from the Text?

If the text of Scripture is the standard by which our interpretations are considered right or wrong, then it is a standard available to each reader. Assuming they have the same presuppositions concerning the nature of Scripture and its Author—that we are reading within the same worldview—would another interpreter see what I am seeing? Asking this question will often reveal to us where we have entered speculation. We should be able to explain from the text before us, including reference to the rest of Scripture, why our interpretation of Scripture is correct. If we base our interpretation on the meaning of a word, we should be able to appeal to other places in Scripture that show how it means that—whether by example (other uses) or analogy (uses of related words or the same grammatical construction). So, ask yourself if you could show someone else what you think the text means. Not being able to do so does not necessarily mean your interpretation is wrong, but it should force us to evaluate why we think it means this.

When it comes to commentaries and related resources, they have the burden to show us that what they say is what the text means. Sometimes the meaning of the text is obvious to both you and the resource you are reading, so you find their application of the text convincing. However, if they claim it says something that you do not see in the text, look for the reasons they provide. Why do they think it says this? If they do not point you back to the text, if they do not show you how the text means what they say it does, there is no reason to accept their interpretation.

The area where this disconnect appears most often, where the interpretation does not seem evident from the text, is in appeals to extra-biblical material.[1]

C. Does It Illegitimately Appeal to Extra-Biblical Data?

This is ultimately an application of the last question we asked: if a valid interpretation is one that can be argued from the text as read in the biblical context, then extra-biblical data (i.e. archaeological data, extra-biblical Greek and Hebrew texts, historical records, etc.) can only serve a supporting role. Ultimately, such data can help us illustrate the text in our preaching, it can reveal things in the text that we did not notice before, and it can give supporting evidence for an interpretation of the text. That historical data can serve no greater role than this is implicit throughout the argument of this book. However, because appeals to extra-biblical data play a central role in both Evangelical and non-Christian approaches to biblical exegesis, I will address this issue to a greater extent in *The Gift of Reading – Part 2*. To conclude this chapter and so the second part of this book, I want to argue very briefly for this point and then explain what I see as the three legitimate uses of extra-biblical data.

I think my point about extra-biblical data can be made by thinking about the implications of rejecting it. I am claiming that "when a historical parallel is used to explain a text, the evidence necessary to establish a link between a piece of extra-biblical data and the text needs to be sufficient to make the

---

[1] What follows is adapted from my article, The Problem of Extra-Biblical Data. https://teleioteti.ca/2018/08/15/the-problem-of-extra-biblical-data/. I expand upon this in *The Gift of Reading – Part 2*, in which I consider alternate approaches to reading the Bible.

point independently."[2] That is, to legitimately use extra-biblical data, you must first show that it is relevant to the text you are interpreting. You can only do this if the text already says what you want to say with your extra-biblical data. Rejecting this claim leads to some destructive conclusions.

First, a rejection of this claim accepts that extra-biblical data can make the text mean something it does not say. Among conservative Evangelicals, this is called *eisegesis*, reading a meaning into the text that is not there in the first place. This also implicitly rejects the clarity of Scripture and sufficiency, as argued for in the first part of this book.

Second, the most significant implication of this is that extra-biblical data is necessary to interpret the biblical text. This would not have been a problem for some of the original readers of the texts, yet we cannot guarantee that every reader would have had access to all the necessary data. Furthermore, we cannot guarantee that 1st century Christians had the necessary data to interpret the Old Testament, the first parts of which were written over 1400 years before them. Lastly, much of the data used in scholarly literature to explain the biblical text is from recent archaeological discoveries, discoveries that were not available to the majority of the church over the last 2000 years. If this data is *necessary* for reading the Scriptures, and it was not available to the Christians for whom the Bible was intended to guide, then Scripture would be unable to function in its God-ordained manner until this data was recovered. I think this is a theologically untenable position.

Third, if an appeal to extra-biblical data produces meaning that is not discernible from a biblical text read within the biblical context, then such an appeal is an instance of a fallacy sometimes called "illegitimate totality transfer." That is, all words have a range of meaning; they do not mean only one thing but can mean many things depending on the context. However, as we discussed earlier in Chapter 9, words mean only one thing from this range of meanings when they are used. It is, therefore, a fallacy to bring this whole range of meanings into a context. Similarly, phrases and ideas could have many different functions, but they have a specific function in their context. We cannot, then, read into a text all the possible functions or connotations a phrase, idea, or word has in another context; we must ask how the author is using it here (the criteria of validity). This should suffice for our purposes to

---

[2] ibid.

show why extra-biblical data cannot be used to say more than the text says. If this is the case, we must ask what use can be made of extra-biblical data.

As I mentioned above, I see three general uses of such data that are legitimate. First, it can be used to illustrate our application of a text. I suspect that this is how most people intend to use extra-biblical data. Sometimes the meaning of a text is not fully appreciated, sometimes it is not felt by an audience, until it is brought to life through an illustration or story. Sometimes contemporary events and life experiences, or a little imagination, do the trick. However, using illustrations from the practices and history of the biblical peoples can make a point powerfully. For example, we can use Ancient Near Eastern accounts of sieges to illustrate just what Jeremiah and Habakkuk have in mind when they talk about piling mounds of dirt to take a city. This is helpful. However, we must always make clear that we are using this data to illustrate, not to create meaning. If we do not make this clear, we risk teaching those who hear us that the Bible is a text reserved for the experts with the knowledge of and access to extra-biblical archaeology and data.

Second, extra-biblical data can be used to illuminate the text. Sometimes studying extra-biblical accounts or language helps us see things that were before our eyes the whole time. By way of example, archaeological evidence has helped scholars re-examine the meaning of 1 Samuel 13:21 (compare the KJV and ESV) and conclude that the Hebrew word פִּים (*pîm*) is a monetary unit, not a "file."[3] However, there is nothing in the context to suggest פִּים is intended to indicate that the Hebrews were being ripped off by the Philistines, an argument made by some commentators. This may very well be the case, but nothing the author says indicates that he meant this.[4]

Third, extra-biblical data can be used to confirm our interpretations. Sometimes we are in a position where we need to argue for one interpretation over another. The final decision and most decisive argument must come from Scripture. However, there is no reason why we cannot make the argument from Scripture and then confirm it by appealing to extra-biblical data that is consistent with our interpretation and not the other.

---

[3] The KJV's "file" is actually their attempt to explain the phrase "the charge was a pim" (my translation).

[4] It could be argued that by using the word "פִּים" he intends this, however this is a circle.

Hopefully these questions will be of some help in discerning the validity of our own interpretations and the interpretations of others. However, as much as skill and reason is a key aspect of reading our Bibles, it is not the only aspect. No matter how clear our vision and attuned our ears, if our hearts are made of stone, we will not hear God's voice. For this reason, we must now consider the role of the heart in biblical interpretation.

—Part 3—

We Need Hearts to Understand

12

BEGINNING WITH FAITH IN GOD

> And he said, "Go, and say to this people:
>   'Keep on hearing, but do not understand;
>   keep on seeing, but do not perceive.'
> Make the heart of this people dull,
>   and their ears heavy,
>   and blind their eyes;
> lest they see with their eyes,
>   and hear with their ears,
>   and understand with their hearts,
>   and turn and be healed."
> – Isaiah 6:9-10, cf. Matthew 13:10-17

It is a common misunderstanding that the preaching of God's Word and the reading of God's Word has one function, to bring us to faith and lead us in obedience to God (Matt 28:18-20, Rom 1:5). As we have seen, the Bible does do this. It is a covenant document given to lead his people to faith, to give them the knowledge of him, and to lead them in obedience. However, it also has another function.

When God charged Isaiah to preach, it was not to bring salvation; instead, it was to bring judgment. The preaching of God's will would only harden the hearers in their rebellion against him. Instead of turning from their wicked ways, they would double down and sin all the more. This was not only true of Isaiah's ministry. Jesus himself identified the purpose of his parables as hardening the hearts of those who heard them. Jesus speaks in parables because those who heard him already had hard hearts; the preaching of the Word would only seal their judgment (Matt 13:10-17, cf. John 12:36-43). There is, therefore, great danger in coming to the Bible in the wrong way. It may be the means God uses to open our eyes to his glory shining in the face of Jesus Christ (2 Cor 4:6), or it may be the tool he uses to cement our hearts fast in sin. The preaching of the word magnifies the content of the heart; in soil that is tilled and ready, the sowing of the Word yields an abundant crop. In the soil that is shallow and hard, the sowing of the Word leaves the ground worse off than before (Matt 13:1-9, 18-23). Thus, the heart matters when we read the Bible; a right state of heart is essential if we are to read the word rightly. If we are going to read the Bible as God has intended for us to do, then we need to approach it in the right way, with the right heart. We could summarize the biblical posture towards God's Word in this way: beginning with faith in God, we submit ourselves before him to learn with humility. We can divide this into three segments. In this chapter, we will look at "beginning with faith in God," in the next "we submit ourselves before him, and in Chapter 14 "to learn with humility."

We need a right heart to read the Word. Though it is ultimately God through the Spirit that prepares our hearts to receive his word (cf. John 6:44-45), our responsibility is to approach the Word, first, with faith.

Our confession of faith is the result of a changed heart produced by God, of God's Word landing on tilled soil. Our faith lived out is the product of the Spirit at work in us as we labour to persevere in the faith and obey the Lord (Phil 2:12-13). Coming to the Word in faith, believing in God and trusting him for all that he has accomplished in Jesus Christ, is thus the necessary condition of reading the Bible. Without faith, humble dependence on the Lord, we will not read the Word rightly and may find ourselves under the judgment of God.

How does this work, you may be thinking? If our interpretation of Scripture is rooted in the text before our eyes, how is it that the lack of or presence of faith could change the result of our interpretation? In light of what we saw in Chapter 1, I think there are three clear ways a lack of faith blinds us. Without faith, we will not adopt the Bible's own methods for reading it, we will not read the Bible according to what it says about itself, and we will not arrive at the right conclusions because we cannot obey God while in rebellion against him.

We have seen a bit in this book, and I have argued at length in Volume 1 of this series, that no use of our minds (including reading) is a morally neutral act. We approach every task—especially reading and learning—with assumptions about the way the world is, assumptions that determine how we interact with it. To read the Bible rightly—indeed, to do anything rightly—we need a Christian worldview: we need to accept what God says about the creation and act in accord with this. However, if we do not have faith in God, we will not submit to him and learn his ways. This is the fundamental error Paul identifies with the Pagan rejection of the Gospel, "we preach Christ crucified, a stumbling block to Jews and folly to Gentiles, but to those who are called, both Jews and Greeks, Christ is the power of God and the wisdom of God" (1 Cor 1:23-24). He goes on in 1 Corinthians 2, "The natural person does not accept the things of the Spirit of God, for they are folly to him, and he is not able to understand them because they are spiritually discerned" (14). Only by adopting God's perspective on the world, which we do through faith, will we see God's ways as "wisdom" and not "folly." Not only are Christian presuppositions necessary, presuppositions which only come through faith resulting from a changed heart, but we also need to read the Bible as the Bible.

What I mean is this; if we read the Bible as a historical document, as the rants of erring men—i.e. as a fallible document—we will not read it rightly. With these beliefs we may care enough to read the Bible, but we will pick and choose what seems right to us in the Bible.[1] No longer will it be our absolute authority and guide for life in obedience to God; it will only be another sourcebook for us to piece together our own way of life. If we read the Bible primarily as a historical document, we may or may not credit it with authority, depending on the significance of the history it represents, but we will certainly read it according to the canons of modern historical science. Instead of asking what the Bible says about itself and how to read it, we will assume that we should read it like we would any other historical document. This would be to miss its own claims to self-sufficiency, to clarity, and its claims that it is written specifically for the New Covenant people of God throughout the age between Christ's first and second comings. Without faith, we will not approach the Bible as the Word of God, as an authoritative covenant document, as self-attesting, self-sufficient, clear, inerrant, etc. So, without

---

[1] This is evident in the works of classic Liberal scholarship in the 19-20th centuries and in some recent bestsellers, such as Jordan Peterson's *12 Rules for Life*.

faith, we will not approach the Bible with the essential presuppositions to understand it.

Finally, apart from faith, a reader of the Bible has no reason to read it rightly and a great reason to misinterpret it. As Christians, we have every reason to seek to understand what the Bible is saying. We believe that it is the Word of our good God who cares for us, so we know we need to hear what he says. Furthermore, it is the word of our sovereign Lord, our king; we are therefore obligated to obey him and need to know what he is asking of us. It is a serious matter to disobey one who has authority over us, to disobey the ruler of the universe, so it is necessary for us as covenant servants to seek the proper understanding of our Lord's will. We also know that God is present with us, that he knows what we are reading and how we are applying it, so we cannot get away with twisting and distorting his words. To honour him, to love him, to obey him, to serve him, to enjoy him, we need to hear what he is saying.

An unbeliever, on the other hand, has no such reasons. He does not want to obey God, to love him, to serve him, or to enjoy him. Indeed, by suppressing the truth of God in unrighteousness, every unbeliever demonstrates that their fundamental desire is to be their own God and escape the rule of their creator (Rom 1:18-25). This means that they have every reason to avoid a right interpretation of Scripture. They do not want to hear what God desires of them, let alone obey it. Instead, if they give any value to Scripture, it must be as a document that serves their rebellious purposes. So the Bible becomes a record of human insight, man's path, not God's. Or it becomes the fictional accounts of a despicable being that humanity once worshipped. Maybe it is a revelation from a god, but this god is bound by human reason, so every objectionable piece of Scripture must be lopped off. Many unbelievers have learned from reading the Bible and have said true things about it, but these factors will always influence their interpretation.

"Without faith," writes the author of Hebrews, "it is impossible to please him, for whoever would draw near to God must believe that he exists and that he rewards those who seek him" (Heb 11:6). The author of Hebrews has in mind the life of the patriarchs, yet this holds true for all humanity. If someone is said to please God and this requires that they had faith, then it follows that if anyone does not have faith, they cannot please God. Surely reading the Bible, obeying God by listening to his voice and submitting to him to understand it correctly, is pleasing to God. Surely it is pleasing to God to take careful time to discern his voice. Without faith there is no pleasing God, and thus there is no right reading of Scripture. *Beginning with faith in God*, we submit ourselves before him to learn with humility.

13

WE SUBMIT OURSELVES BEFORE HIM

> "Seek the LORD while he may be found;
>   call upon him while he is near;
> let the wicked forsake his way,
>   and the unrighteous man his thoughts;
> let him return to the LORD, that he may have compassion on him,
>   and to our God, for he will abundantly pardon.
> For my thoughts are not your thoughts,
>   neither are your ways my ways, declares the LORD.
> For as the heavens are higher than the earth,
>   so are my ways higher than your ways
>   and my thoughts than your thoughts. – Isaiah 55:6-9

Beginning with faith sets the tone for our reading of Scripture. We start with the assumptions of the Christian Bible, that God exists, that he has spoken, and that he rewards those who seek him—that obedience is worth it. Faith is the foundation, but it takes a specific expression as we live out the Christian life. In Romans 10, Paul describes the fundamental acts taken to become a Christian, to enjoy God's salvation, as "[believing] in your heart that God raised [Jesus] from the dead" and "[confessing] with your mouth that Jesus is Lord" (Rom 10:9). Faith in God's existence and salvific acts manifests in the confession of submission to Jesus Christ as Lord, the covenant king over all creation. A true confession of Jesus as Lord will manifest in a life of submission to this Lord. Similarly, as we read Scripture, a foundation of faith in the God of the Bible will manifest in a way of reading that submits to this God. Beginning with faith in God, *we submit ourselves before him* to learn with humility.

Among many implications, that the God who authored Scripture is our Lord means that we must trust his judgment over our judgment—concerning right and wrong, true and false—and that we must respond to the commands and rebukes of Scripture. Obedience is not optional for a Christian. To be a Christian is to be someone who follows Christ, and to follow Jesus who is Lord is to submit to and obey Jesus as he has revealed himself.

This obedience is not only manifest in dos and don'ts but also in demands upon our reason and moral sensibilities. Scripture calls us to believe in things other worldviews reject and to accept behaviour that other faiths repudiate. Scripture tells us that God created the heavens and the earth and made them good; thus, to deny the reality of matter or its goodness, or to suggest that it is eternal, is not an option for the Christian. The Bible teaches that God created humanity specially, that he created them from two original humans, and that they are distinct from the animals and other aspects of creation. Indeed, the Bible teaches that God created humanity as the pinnacle of his creation. Therefore, any worldview that rejects these claims—such as the evolutionary explanation of speciation and the creation of man—cannot be held consistently by a Christian.[1] If the Bible teaches that the creation of humanity, and so the rest of creation, is a relatively recent occurrence, then it would be inconsistent for a Christian to hold to contrary claims of a far more distant emergence of humanity and the creation. Philosophically, a Christian cannot believe that there are standards of right and wrong or true and false by which God and man are both judged, for this would mean that these standards are independent of and higher than God and that man and God are on equal footing. In each of these cases, if God our Lord—and the Creator and Sovereign who knows something about his creation—tells us something is true or false, we are obligated to obediently accept his Word.[2]

This also applies to our moral sensibilities. We have no right, as covenant servants, to stand in a position of judgment over God and believe that something he declares to be just and good is unrighteous and evil. Now, I am not saying that there are no difficult cases where it is hard to see *why*

---

[1] See the Crossway volume, James Porter Moreland et al., eds., *Theistic Evolution: A Scientific, Philosophical, and Theological Critique* (Wheaton: Crossway, 2017).

[2] On this point and how it is the salvation of reason, see my book *The Gift of Knowing: A Biblical Perspective on Knowing and Truth* (Vancouver; Teleioteti, 2019).

something is just and good, yet we are obligated nevertheless to accept that they are. This, in fact, gives us great freedom. We can trust that God is good, true, and right even when we do not exactly see how. Our hope is that when we see God in glory, our struggles with Hell, with the conquest of Canaan, with the imprecatory Psalms, etc., will fade away as we behold face to face the one true and good God. For now, we know that God himself is the standard of what is right and wrong, so we are in no position to pass judgment upon him and his Word. Indeed,

> who are you, O man, to answer back to God? Will what is molded say to its molder, "Why have you made me like this?" Has the potter no right over the clay, to make out of the same lump one vessel for honorable use and another for dishonorable use? (Rom 9:20-21)

There are answers to some if not all our most difficult questions, yet even with the right answer, we may not like the truth. However, in such circumstances, and in every case where a biblical teaching troubles us, we are confronted with a question, will we trust God or ourselves? Fundamentally, do we believe that God is wiser and better than we are? For if he is, we can trust him even with the most difficult of issues. Isaiah recounts God's compassion and thoughts towards man as being of a fundamentally different nature than man's—they are above and beyond ours (Isa 55:6-9). This means that our thought must be accommodated to his, our sensibility and reason subjected to his ultimate reason and moral standards.[3]

To submit ourselves before God as we read Scripture is fundamental to receiving his Word and rightly understanding it. None of us enjoys submitting to someone above us, so we are naturally inclined to twist and ignore difficult things. We simplify or simply ignore difficult teachings for the sake of our reason and sensibilities. Yet Scripture declares such actions sin, to put ourselves in place of God, to exchange the Creator and his standard for ourselves—the creature. If we are going to read Scripture rightly and truly know God, then we must do so with a posture of submission, to

---

[3] I explore this to a much greater depth in the first volume of this series, *The Gift of Knowing: A Biblical Perspective on Knowing and Truth* (Teleioteti, 2019).

accept the teaching of Scripture no matter where it may lead us. Beginning with faith in God, *we submit ourselves before him* to learn with Humility.

14

TO LEARN WITH HUMILITY

> Now a Jew named Apollos, a native of Alexandria, came to Ephesus. He was an eloquent man, competent in the Scriptures. He had been instructed in the way of the Lord. And being fervent in spirit, he spoke and taught accurately the things concerning Jesus, though he knew only the baptism of John. He began to speak boldly in the synagogue, but when Priscilla and Aquila heard him, they took him aside and explained to him the way of God more accurately. – Acts 18:24-26

Our posture towards God as we read Scripture is one of faith and submission, of trust acted out in humility. We accept his Word even when it offends and troubles us. He is God; we are not. This is essential to reading God's word but not the whole story. The end of our submission is that we might learn from God, implying that we do not have all that we need to know already. We approach Scripture because there is something we need to learn; we do not have sufficient wisdom or all truth. Indeed, we approach Scripture believing some things to be true that are actually false. This necessitates the last heart posture we will consider. Beginning with faith in God, we submit ourselves before him *to learn with humility.*

Faith is ultimately a confession of our inadequacy and evidence of humility. By believing in Christ Jesus for salvation, we admit that we are inadequate. We admit that we have fallen short of God's standard and earned only a curse, that we are not deserving of favour or blessing. We admit that we have not and cannot earn God's favour and that we need him to live an obedient life conforming to his purposes. This same humility is an essential aspect of reading the Bible well.

First, humility is manifest in the confession that we need God to understand his word. We need God to act in our heart so that we do submit when we are challenged. As we discussed in Chapter 5, we need God's Spirit to quicken our sluggish senses and intellects and to soften our stubborn hearts in order that we might perceive and receive God's Word. To learn with humility means that we approach Scripture with Philippians 2:12-13 on our minds, "work out your own salvation with fear and trembling, for it is God who works in you, both to will and to work for his good pleasure."

Second, humility manifests in the way we consider ourselves. None of us has mastered God's word; none of us has exhausted all that it has to say or accurately interpreted every part. Part of the problem is that we are sinful, yet being sinful does not mean that we sin and err in everything we do. We get things right sometimes, even often! Given infinite time and the truth that the Bible is clear, it is possible that someone could rightly understand every part of Scripture. However, none of us has infinite time. For this reason, we need to be humble about our inadequacies; we need to acknowledge that we do not have it all together, that we do not have every answer. We must, therefore, approach Scripture as those who have much yet to learn. We must approach commentaries and secondary resources as those who have much left to learn. And we must approach others in conversation with the self-awareness that we still have much to learn—no matter our experience or education. This leads to the final way we need to see humility manifest in our reading.

Third, humility manifests in the way we conduct ourselves with others in the reading of Scripture. I hope it has been clear throughout this book that the Bible does not present Bible study as a private effort. Bible study is done for the people of God by the people of God in the presence of the people of God. We need one another if we are going to read the Bible well. This is necessary because we all have blind spots, areas in our life that require the insight of others. This is necessary because we all have errors that only others will correct—this is especially true of errors shrouded in pride. Finally, this is necessary because none of us has exhaustive understanding of Scripture or all the ways it could apply. We need the input of others to see how the Bible applies to our lives and the lives of others and that we might come to a right understanding of Scripture. We must enter into discussion with others and must approach the resources others produce with the humility to learn from them, to listen well and receive correction where necessary. Like Apollos in Acts 18, there are instances where we need brothers and sisters to come alongside of us and explain "to [us] the way of God more accurately" (Acts 18:26). If we do not have this posture as we come to Scripture, we will not hear all that God has for us to hear.

This is not to say that there will not be times when we will have to batten down the hatches and fight for our convictions. We will be confronted often in our study by positions with which we rightly disagree. We will need courage and perseverance to hold fast the truth against opposition. However, I suspect that we are more susceptible to the temptation of holding to our own ideas without regard for the insights of others, to the temptation of pride rather than humility. So this is what I have chosen to emphasize.

Reading the Bible is not just knowing what the Bible is and having the skills to figure out difficulties. Reading the Bible engages our minds and affections, our intellect and the posture of our heart. We must come to the Bible prepared to work hard, to think well, and to submit ourselves to God. Our heart must be oriented towards God with faith, reading to submit to him in order to learn with humility.

CONCLUSION

> This Book of the Law shall not depart from your mouth, but you shall meditate on it day and night, so that you may be careful to do according to all that is written in it. For then you will make your way prosperous, and then you will have good success. – Joshua 1:8 (ESV)

We began this book with a question, the most pressing question of our day; "Can I understand the Bible?" I have argued that our answer as Christians should be a resounding YES. I have argued that we can and must understand the Bible, yet doing so will not be easy. It means devoting ourselves to the lifelong study of God's Word, meditating on it and read it continually. I identified three things that are necessary to reading Scripture as God has intended us to read it: we need eyes to see, ears to hear, and hearts to understand.

In Part 1 we considered the eyes or worldview we need to see Scripture. We considered the nature of the Bible (ch. 1), the story and theology taught in Scripture (chs. 2-3), and the two people groups that Scripture is addressed to—the Old and New Covenant people of God (ch. 4). This gave us a foundation by which we could approach Scripture; it offered us a glimpse at the whole teaching of Scripture so that we may interpret its parts.

In Part 2 we considered how we might listen well or have ears to hear God's Word. This proved to be the lengthiest part of our project, extending over about 130 pages and seven chapters. In chapters 5 & 6, we looked at our goal as we read Scripture—namely, justified application—and a method by which we could reach this goal. In the following chapters, we considered various tools and skills that help us look carefully at Scripture. In the final chapter of Part 2, we considered how we could evaluate our interpretations and those of others to determine if they are justified.

In Part 3, by far the shortest of the books three parts, we considered the function of the heart in reading Scripture. I hope it is clear that the size of this section by no means reflects its importance. A right heart is the *sine qua non* of good Bible reading—the condition without which reading will not happen. I capture the role of the human heart with this sentence: beginning with faith in God, we submit ourselves before him to learn with humility. Each of this section's three chapters took one part of this phrase and unpacked what I intend. The foundation of our reading is faith, a right heart produced by God and a resulting belief in and dependence upon God. This posture of faith produces submission in our hearts and minds; as we read Scripture, faith should lead us to accept God's Word over man's and his judgments over our own. This posture of faith also produces a posture of humility towards our own understanding and towards that of our peers. With humility, we approach Scripture ready to always learn and be rebuked; with humility, we approach our peers ready to learn from them and be strengthened in our understanding and faith.

We have been on a long journey. It is my hope that those readers who came to this book convinced they could not understand God's word will now see how God in his mercy has enabled us to read his Scripture and know him through it. For those who were already convinced of this point, it is my prayer that the approach of this book has strengthened your reading skills, challenged your assumptions about the nature of hermeneutics, and strengthened your confidence in the sufficiency and clarity of God's word. For all of us, I hope we have seen our deep need for God and his people if we are to read Scripture well. Ultimately, it is my prayer that we have seen how reading itself is a gift from God. Christians will gladly proclaim that Scripture is God's gift, but how often do we confess that our very ability to read it is a gift from our heavenly Father? That we live among people who are able to teach us about the whole of Scripture is God's gift that we might understand its parts. That the manuscripts and knowledge of the biblical languages have been preserved over 2000 years is God's gift so that we might ever return to the sources of our faith and grow in our knowledge of him. The fact that Scripture is comprehensive in its scope and clear in its teaching is God's gift so that we may truly know him and obey him in this life. From beginning to end, reading the Bible is a gift enabled by our gracious Father.

It is his gift so that we might be fully equipped to know his will and obey him, that we might know him more clearly and enjoy the fullness of life he has promised us through Jesus Christ (2 Tim 3:16-17; 2 Pet 1:3-4). The charge of this book is that which Joshua received; we must meditate on the Word of God day and night "so that [we] may be careful to do according to all that is written in it." This same charge is picked up at the end of the second section of the Hebrew Bible, Malachi 4, and in the first verses of the final section, in Psalm 1. It is with this, the words of our God in Psalm 1, that we will conclude:

> Blessed is the man
> > who walks not in the counsel of the wicked,
> nor stands in the way of sinners,
> > nor sits in the seat of scoffers;
> but his delight is in the law of the LORD,
> > and on his law he meditates day and night.
>
> He is like a tree
> > planted by streams of water
> that yields its fruit in its season,
> > and its leaf does not wither.
> In all that he does, he prospers.
> The wicked are not so,
> > but are like chaff that the wind drives away.
>
> Therefore the wicked will not stand in the judgment,
> > nor sinners in the congregation of the righteous;
> for the LORD knows the way of the righteous,
> > but the way of the wicked will perish. (Psalm 1:1-6)

WORKS CITED

Alter, Robert. *The Art of Biblical Narrative*. New York: Basic Books, 1981.

Arnold, Bill T, and Bryan Beyer. *Encountering the Old Testament: A Christian Survey*. Grand Rapids: Baker Academic, 2008.

Beale, G. K. *Handbook on the New Testament Use of the Old Testament: Exegesis and Interpretation*. Grand Rapids: Baker Academic, 2012.

Beale, G. K., and D. A. Carson, eds. *Commentary on the New Testament Use of the Old Testament*. Grand Rapids: Baker Academic, 2007.

Beale, G.K. *The Book of Revelation: A Commentary on the Greek Text*. NIGTC. Grand Rapids; Carlisle: Eerdmans; Paternoster, 1999.

Beckwith, Roger T. *The Old Testament Canon of the New Testament Church and Its Background in Early Judaism*. Grand Rapids: Eerdmans, 1986.

Berlin, Adele. *Poetics and Interpretation of Biblical Narrative*. Winona Lake, Ind.: Eisenbrauns, 2005.

Black, David Alan, ed. *Rethinking New Testament Textual Criticism*. Grand Rapids: Baker Academic, 2002.

Brown, Francis, S. R Driver, Charles A Briggs, James Strong, and Wilhelm Gesenius. *The Brown-Driver-Briggs Hebrew and English Lexicon*. Peabody, Mass.: Hendrickson Publishers, 1996.

Carson, D. A. *Exegetical Fallacies*. Grand Rapids: Baker Books, 1996.

———. *New Testament Commentary Survey*. 7th Ed. Grand Rapids: Baker Academic, 2013.

———. *The Gospel According to John*. The Pillar New Testament Commentary. Leicester; Grand Rapids: IVP; Eerdmans, 1991.

———. *The King James Version Debate: A Plea for Realism*. Grand Rapids: Baker Book House, 1979.

Carson, D. A., and Douglas J. Moo. *An Introduction to the New Testament*. Second Edition. Grand Rapids: Zondervan, 2005.

Clines, David J. A., ed. *The Dictionary of Classical Hebrew*. Vol. I–VIII. Sheffield: Sheffield Academic Press; Sheffield Phoenix Press, 1993.

Danker, Frederick W. *A Greek-English Lexicon of the New Testament and Other Early Christian Literature*. 3rd ed. Chicago: University of Chicago Press, 2000.

Dempster, Stephen G. *Dominion and Dynasty: A Biblical Theology of the Hebrew Bible*. New Studies in Biblical Theology 15. Leicester: Downers Grove: Apollos; InterVarsity, 2003.

Dunbar, David G. "The Biblical Canon." In *Hermeneutics, Authority, and Canon*, edited by D. A. Carson and John D. Woodbridge. Grand Rapids: Academie Books, 1986.

Elliger, Karl, Wilhelm Rudolph, Adrian Schenker, Donald R. Vance, George Athas, and Yael Avrahami, eds. *Biblia Hebraica Stuttgartensia: a Reader's Edition*. 5., rev. Ed. Stuttgart: Dt. Bibelges, 2014.

Elwell, Walter A., and Robert W. Yarbrough. *Encountering the New Testament: A Historical and Theological Survey*. 2nd ed. Encountering biblical studies. Grand Rapids: Baker Academic, 2005.

Fee, Gordon D. *New Testament Exegesis: A Handbook for Students and Pastors*. 3rd ed. Louisville: Westminster John Knox Press, 2002.

Fee, Gordon D., and Douglas K. Stuart. *How to Read the Bible for All Its Worth*. 3rd ed. Grand Rapids: Zondervan, 2003.

Fields, Lee M. *Hebrew for the Rest of Us: Using Hebrew Tools without Mastering Biblical Hebrew*. Grand Rapids: Zondervan, 2008.

Fokkelman, J.P. *Reading Biblical Poetry: An Introductory Guide*. Translated by Ineke Smit. First edition. Louisville: Westminster John Knox, 2001.

Frame, John M. *Systematic Theology: An Introduction to Christian Belief*. Phillipsburg: P&R Publishing, 2013.

———. *The Doctrine of God*. A Theology of Lordship. Phillipsburg: P&R Publishing, 2002.

———. *The Doctrine of the Christian Life*. A Theology of Lordship 4. Phillipsburg: P&R Publishing, 2008.

———. *The Doctrine of the Knowledge of God*. A Theology of Lordship. Phillipsburg: P&R Publishing, 1987.

———. *The Doctrine of the Word of God*. A Theology of Lordship. Phillipsburg: P&R Publishing, 2010.

Gentry, Peter John, and Stephen J Wellum. *God's Kingdom through God's Covenants: A Concise Biblical Theology*, 2015. Accessed May 29, 2019. https://www.overdrive.com/search?q=0D8CDAE2-3760-4135-B741-B0C9022B879C.

Gentry, Peter John, and Stephen J. Wellum. *Kingdom through Covenant: A Biblical-Theological Understanding of the Covenants*. Wheaton: Crossway, 2012.

Gilbert, Greg. *What Is the Gospel?* Wheaton, IL: Crossway, 2010.

Goldsworthy, Graeme. *According to Plan: The Unfolding Revelation of God in the Bible*. Leicester: Inter-Varsity Press, 1991.

———. *Christ-Centered Biblical Theology: Hermeneutical Foundations and Principles*. Downers Grove: IVP Academic, 2012.

———. *The Goldsworthy Trilogy*. Milton Keynes: Paternoster, 2012.

Goodrich, Richard J, and Albert L Lukaszewski. *A Reader's Greek New Testament*. Grand Rapids, Mich.: Zondervan, 2007.

Goodrich, Richard J, Albert L Lukaszewski, A. Philip Brown, and Bryan W Smith. *A Reader's Hebrew and Greek Bible.* Grand Rapids: Zondervan, 2010.

Grudem, Wayne. *Systematic Theology: An Introduction to Biblical Doctrine.* Leicester; Grand Rapids: Inter-Varsity Press; Zondervan, 1994.

Grudem, Wayne A., and Jeff Purswell. *Bible Doctrine: Essential Teachings of the Christian Faith.* Grand Rapids: Zondervan, 1999.

Hill, Andrew E., and John H. Walton. *A Survey of the Old Testament.* 2nd ed. Grand Rapids: Zondervan Publishing House, 2000.

Jongkind, Dirk. *An Introduction to the Greek New Testament, Produced at Tyndale House, Cambridge.* Wheaton: Crossway, 2019.

Jongkind, Dirk, Peter J Williams, Peter M Head, and Patrick James. *The Greek New Testament, Produced at Tyndale House Cambridge.* Crossway, 2017.

Kline, Meredith G. *The Structure of Biblical Authority.* Rev. ed. Grand Rapids: Eerdmans, 1975.

Koehler, Ludwig, Walter Baumgartner, M. E. J. Richardson, and Johann Jakob Stamm. *The Hebrew and Aramaic Lexicon of the Old Testament.* Electronic ed. Leiden; New York: Brill, 1999.

Köstenberger, Andreas J., Benjamin L. Merkle, and Robert L. Plummer. *Going Deeper with New Testament Greek: An Intermediate Study of the Grammar and Syntax of the New Testament.* Nashville: B&H Academic, 2016.

Kruger, Michael J., ed. *A Biblical-Theological Introduction to the New Testament: The Gospel Realized.* Wheaton: Crossway, 2016.

———. *Canon Revisited: Establishing the Origins and Authority of the New Testament Books.* Wheaton, Ill: Crossway, 2012.

———. *The Question of Canon: Challenging the Status Quo in the New Testament Debate.* Downers Grove: InterVarsity Press, 2013.

Kugel, James L. *The Idea of Biblical Poetry: Parallelism and Its History.* New Haven: Yale University Press, 1981.

Liddell, Henry George, Robert Scott, Henry Stuart Jones, and Roderick McKenzie. *A Greek-English Lexicon.* Oxford: Clarendon, 1996.

Long, V. Philips. *The Art of Biblical History.* Foundations of Contemporary Interpretation v. 5. Grand Rapids: Zondervan, 1994.

Longman, Tremper. *Old Testament Commentary Survey.* 5th Ed. Grand Rapids: Baker Academic, 2013.

Longman, Tremper, and Raymond B. Dillard. *An Introduction to the Old Testament.* 2nd ed. Grand Rapids: Zondervan, 2006.

Louw, Johannes P., and Eugene A. Nida, eds. *Greek-English Lexicon of the New Testament Basd on Semantic Domains.* 2nd ed. Vol. 1. 2 vols. New York, N. Y.: United Bible Society, 1989.

Moo, Douglas J. *Galatians.* Baker Exegetical Commentary on the New Testament. Grand Rapids, Mich.: Baker Academic, 2013.

———. *The Epistle to the Romans.* NICNT. Grand Rapids: Eerdmans, 1996.

Moreland, James Porter, Stephen C. Meyer, Christopher Shaw, Ann K. Gauger, and Wayne Grudem, eds. *Theistic Evolution: A Scientific, Philosophical, and Theological Critique.* Wheaton: Crossway, 2017.

Mounce, Robert H. *The Book of Revelation.* NICNT. Grand Rapids: Eerdmans, 1977.

Mounce, William D. *Basics of Biblical Greek Grammar.* 3rd ed. Grand Rapids: Zondervan, 2009.

———. *Greek for the Rest of Us: The Essentials of Biblical Greek.* Second Edition. Grand Rapids: Zondervan, 2013.

Packer, J. I. *Knowing God.* 20th anniversary ed. Downers Grove: InterVarsity Press, 1993.

Petersen, David L., and Kent Harold Richards. *Interpreting Hebrew Poetry.* Guides to Biblical Scholarship. Minneapolis: Fortress, 1992.

Piper, John. *A Peculiar Glory: How the Christian Scriptures Reveal Their Complete Truthfulness*. Wheaton: Crossway, 2016.

———. *Brothers, We Are Not Professionals*. Updated & Expanded. Nashville: B&H Publishing Group, 2013.

———. *Reading the Bible Supernaturally: Seeing and Savoring the Glory of God in Scripture*, 2017.

Poythress, Vern S., and Wayne A. Grudem. *The Gender-Neutral Bible Controversy: Muting the Masculinity of God's Words*. Nashville: Broadman & Holman Publishers, 2000.

Poythress, Vern Sheridan. *In the Beginning Was the Word: Language: A God-Centered Approach*. Wheaton: Crossway Books, 2009.

Pratico, Gary Davis, and Miles V Van Pelt. *Basics of Biblical Hebrew Grammar*. Grand Rapids: Zondervan, 2007.

Rutherford, J. Alexander. *Believe the Unbelievable: A Study in Habakkuk*. Teleioteti Study Guides 1. Vancouver, BC: Teleioteti, 2018.

———. "Biblical Themes That Define Us (1): Two Kingdoms." *Teleioteti*, November 1, 2017. Accessed May 30, 2019. https://teleioteti.ca/2017/11/01/biblical-themes-that-define-us-two-kingdoms/.

———. "Christians and the World: The Ethics of a City on a Hill." *Teleioteti*, November 29, 2017. Accessed May 30, 2019. https://teleioteti.ca/2017/11/29/christians-and-the-world-the-ethics-of-a-city-on-a-hill/.

———. *God's Kingdom through his Priest-King: An Analysis of the Book of Samuel in Light of the Davidic Covenant*. A Teleioteti Technical Study 1. Vancouver: Teleioteti, 2019.

———. "Is There a Cultural Mandate for Christians?" *Teleioteti*, January 31, 2018. Accessed May 30, 2019. https://teleioteti.ca/2018/01/31/2306/.

———. "Lament of the Afflicted: A Translation of Job 30." Teleioteti, 2017. Accessed January 8, 2018.

https://teleioteti.ca/2017/12/15/the-lament-of-the-afflicted-a-translation-of-job-30/.

———. *The Book of Habakkuk: An Exegetical-Theological Commentary on the Hebrew Text*. A Teleioteti Old Testament Commentary 1. Vancouver, BC: Teleioteti, Forthcoming.

———. *The Gift of Knowing: A Biblical Perspective on Knowing and Truth*. God's Gifts for the Christian Life Part 1 - The Christian Mind I. Vancouver: Teleioteti, 2019.

———. *The Gift of Reading - Part 2: A Biblical Perspective on Hermeneutics*. God's Gifts for the Christian Life Part 1 - The Christian Mind II. Vancouver: Teleioteti, 2019.

———. *The Gift of Seeing: A Biblical (Meta)Metaphysic*. God's Gifts for the Christian Life Part 1 - The Christian Mind III. Vancouver, BC: Teleioteti, n.d.

Ryken, Leland. *The Word of God in English: Criteria for Excellence in Bible Translation*. Wheaton: Crossway, 2002.

Schreiner, Thomas R. "Galatians." edited by Clinton E. Arnold. Zondervan Exegetical Commentary on the New Testament 9. Grand Rapids, MI: Zondervan, 2010.

———. *Interpreting the Pauline Epistles*. 2nd ed. Mich: Baker Academic, 2011.

———. *Romans*. Baker Exegetical Commentary on the New Testament 6. Grand Rapids, Mich.: Baker Books, 1998.

Silva, Moisés. *Biblical Words and Their Meaning: An Introduction to Lexical Semantics*. Rev. and Expanded ed. Grand Rapids: Zondervan, 1994.

———, ed. *New International Dictionary of New Testament Theology and Exegesis*. 2nd Ed. Grand Rapids: Zondervan, 2014.

Ska, Jean Louis. *"Our Fathers Have Told Us": Introduction to the Analysis of Hebrew Narratives*. Subsidia Biblica 13. Roma: Editrice Pontificio Instituto Biblico, 1990.

Sproul, R. C. *The Character of God: Discovering the God Who Is.* Ventura, Calif: Regal, 2005.

Sproul, R. C. *The Holiness of God.* Carol Stream, Ill.: Tyndale House Publishers, 2006.

Van Pelt, Miles. *A Biblical-Theological Introduction to the Old Testament: The Gospel Promised.* Edited by Miles Van Pelt. Wheaton: Crossway, 2016.

Van Pelt, Miles V. *Basics of Biblical Aramaic: Complete Grammar, Lexicon, and Annotated Text.* Grand Rapids: Zondervan, 2011.

Wallace, Daniel B. *Greek Grammar Beyond the Basics: An Exegetical Syntax of the New Testament With Scripture, Subject, and Greek Word Indexes.* Grand Rapids: Zondervan, 1996.

Waltke, Bruce K., and Michael Patrick O'Connor. *An Introduction to Hebrew Syntax.* Winona Lake, Ind.: Eisenbrauns, 1990.

Waltke, Bruce K., and Charles Yu. *An Old Testament Theology: An Exegetical, Canonical, and Thematic Approach.* 1st ed. Grand Rapids: Zondervan, 2007.

Watson, Wilfred G. E. "Poetry, Biblical Hebrew." Edited by Geoffrey Khan. *Encyclopedia of Hebrew Language and Linguistics.* Leiden; Boston: Brill, 2013.

Williams, Ronald J., and John C. Beckman. *Williams' Hebrew Syntax.* 3rd ed. Toronto: University of Toronto Press, 2007.

Würthwein, Ernst, and Alexander A. Fischer. *The Text of the Old Testament: An Introduction to the Biblia Hebraica.* 3rd ed. Grand Rapids: Eerdmans, 2014.

Greek New Testament: The Text of UBS 5, Reader's Edition, 2015.

New International Dictionary of Old Testament Theology & Exegesis. Grand Rapids, Michigan: Zondervan, 2007.

The Greek New Testament, Produced at Tyndale House, Cambridge, Reader's Edition. Wheaton: Crossway Books, 2018.

ABOUT TELEIOTETI

Teleioteti (Τελειοτητι, te-ley-o-tey-tee)—meaning "unto maturity"—is dedicated to faithful, thoughtful ministry. We create resources for Christian discipleship, resources that address theological and pastoral concerns from a Biblical worldview. Our purpose is to see Christ's Church mature in its understanding of God and his Word. We do this through the production of Gospel-centred materials that connect the Bible with the heads, hearts, and minds of Christians. We hope to enable Christians from all walks of life to better understand and glorify God through service in his Church.

To achieve this purpose, Teleioteti publishes books researched with academic rigour yet based upon biblical presuppositions. That is, we are neither academic nor lazy. We use methods, or epistemology, informed by the Bible along with the hard work usually associated with professional research and study. We produce resources directed towards all Christians, but most of our resources are directed towards students, pastors, and theologically inclined lay Christians.

To learn more about us and what we are doing, please visit us at https://teleioteti.ca or contact us at info@teleioteti.ca. If you have found this resource helpful, prayerfully consider supporting us by giving a review on the web (e.g. Amazon, Goodreads, etc.), praying with and for us, or giving financially so that we can produce more resources like this one. For more information on how you can support us, visit us at https://teleioteti.ca/about/partner/ or at our page on Patreon, https://www.patreon.com/teleioteti.

OTHER BOOKS BY J. ALEXANDER RUTHERFORD

God's Kingdom through his Priest-King: An Analysis of the Book of Samuel in Light of the Davidic Covenant (Teleioteti, 2019)

Though many studies have probed the significance of the Davidic Covenant (2 Sam 7:1-17) within the biblical canon, few have endeavoured to explore its significance within the narrative of Samuel. This thesis argues that by weaving references to God's promises made to David (collectively known as the Davidic Covenant) throughout his narrative, the author of Samuel reveals God's will to strip away all human pretension by bringing his promises to fulfilment through the lowly David, whose ascension to kingship and endurance therein is owing all to God. In this way, the author fulfils his purpose to demonstrate God's sovereign working in history to establish his kingdom on earth through his chosen priest-king, a descendant of David, in fulfilment of the promises he made beforehand. Engaging in a literary close-reading of the text of Samuel, the author shows how the narrative of Samuel is shaped towards this end.

> In the present environment of high interest in the Book of Samuel, this contribution by James Rutherford is most welcome. Rutherford is well versed in current scholarship on Samuel, but his work moves well beyond this scholarship to contribute fresh insights, not least in respect of the priestly character of King David. And concerning its structure, Rutherford argues that the Book of Samuel as a whole is arranged and narrated so as to draw attention to the centrality of the Davidic Covenant of 2 Samuel 7. Having myself studied 1 and 2 Samuel for decades now, I was nevertheless benefitted at numerous points from Rutherford's creative interpretive suggestions. His is a work well conceived, well written, and worthy of a serious read.
>
> - V. Philips Long, PhD Cambridge
>   Professor of Old Testament, Regent College

This thesis argues that by weaving references to God's promises made to King David throughout his narrative, the author of Samuel reveals God's will to strip away all human pretension by bringing his promises to fulfilment through a lowly man whose ascension to kingship and endurance therein is entirely owing to God. In this way, the Samuel author fulfils his purpose of demonstrating God's sovereign working in history to establish his kingdom on earth through his chosen priest-king, a descendant of David. The thesis represents an excellent piece of work that does a great job of bringing together into one coherent argument, focused on the Davidic covenant, much of the best recent narrative-critical research on 1-2 Samuel, and from this point of view represents a distinctive contribution to the field of Samuel studies.

- Iain Provan, PhD Cambridge
  Marshall Sheppard Professor of Biblical Studies, Regent College

The Gift of Knowing: A Biblical Perspective on Knowing and Truth – God's Gift's for the Christian Life Vol. 1 (Teleioteti, 2019)

Where do we turn amidst the chaos of this world? Where do we go when the very concept of truth is cast in doubt? Our culture says we should turn inward—look to ourselves. However, the Bible teaches that we need to turn to God if we are to have any hope of living in and knowing his creation. Placing our current crisis in the context of the history of philosophy, the Gift of Knowing shows how God has provided us the Bible as the only foundation for knowing and living in his created world. It is argued that the Bible is sufficient to give us confidence that there is truth and that we can know it. In fact, it is necessary if we are to know truth.

Believe the Unbelievable: A Study in Habakkuk (Teleioteti, 2018)

What do we do when God's actions or words contradict our understanding, contradict what we have believed? The book of Habakkuk answers this question in the face of the Babylonian invasions of Judah. Habakkuk is a book of discipleship, a book written to bring its reader to a deeper faith in Yahweh in the presence of his unthinkable deeds.

Using study questions addressing the text, theology, and application of Habakkuk and explanatory comments on difficult themes, *Believe the Unbelievable* seeks to realize this purpose for the contemporary reader.

Endorsements

James Rutherford is a capable and creative thinker, well equipped to tackle tough projects, such as the book of Habakkuk. In this study guide, Rutherford has produced a very useful resource for individual or group study. He combines theological acumen and well-honed linguistic and literary skills to discover and then to present, in highly understandable fashion, the riches of this not so "minor" Minor Prophet.

- V. Philips Long, PhD Cambridge
  Professor of Old Testament, Regent College

My good friend, James Rutherford, has given the church a gift. He has taken his love for God's Word and focused it on an Old Testament book that most Christians know very little about. The result is a study in Habakkuk that brings together deep insight and real relevance. Habakkuk is a voice among the biblical chorus that believers need to hear today. Thank you, James, for helping us to hear it clearly and faithfully.

- Fredrick Eaton
  Pastor, Christ City Church, Kitsilano

www.ingramcontent.com/pod-product-compliance
Lightning Source LLC
Chambersburg PA
CBHW020523080526
44583CB00013B/712